THE UNITED STATES SOLDIER
BETWEEN TWO WARS

THE UNITED STATES SOLDIER BETWEEN TWO WARS:

Army Life and Reforms, 1865–1898

JACK D. FONER

HUMANITIES PRESS

New York 1970

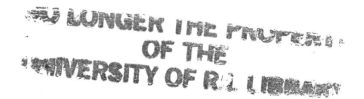

SBN 391–00006–3
LC #78–116447

Printed in the United States of America

TABLE OF CONTENTS

ACKNOWLEDGMENTS

I wish to acknowledge my indebtedness to many persons for the generous assistance rendered in this work. I am particularly indebted to Professor Allan Nevins, under whom I began this study a number of years ago. My thanks are due also to Professor James P. Shenton of Columbia University. His comments were of immeasurable assistance at every stage of my work. I also wish to express my sincere appreciation to Professor Stuart Bruchey of Columbia University who read the entire manuscript and made many most helpful suggestions.

In the preparation of this study I found the source material in the General Oliver O. Howard Papers at the Bowdoin College Library, Brunswick, Maine, an invaluable aid. Special thanks are due Mr. Richard Harwell, Librarian, and Mr. Robert L. Volz, Special Collections Librarian, and Mrs. Mary Hughes, Librarian Assistant, who facilitated my examination of this rich collection of manuscript papers and letters.

I am grateful to the Vermont Historical Society for permission to use the Redfield Proctor Collection, and to Mr. Don Rickey, Jr., for permission to examine his paper, "The Negro Regulars in the American Army: An Indian Wars Combat Record." I am also appreciative of the aid given me by Mr. Gary D. Ryan and Mr. Elmer O. Parker of the Old Military Records Division, National Archives, Washington, D.C.

I wish to express my sincere thanks for the courtesies extended to me by the staffs of the newspaper and manuscript departments of the following institutions: Columbia University Library, the Library of Congress, Illinois State Historical Society, Johns Hopkins University Library, Kansas State Historical Society, Massachusetts Historical Society, Minnesota Historical Society, Montana Historical Society, Nebraska State Historical Society, New Hampshire Historical Society, New York Historical Society, New York Public Library, North Dakota State Historical Society, Ohio State Historical Society, Schomburg Collection of the New York Public Library, State Historical Society of Missouri, University of South Dakota Library, University of Utah Library, Washington State Historical Society, West Virginia Historical Society, Wyoming State Historical Society, and Yale University Library.

For cooperation in obtaining essential materials, gratitude is expressed to Mrs. Claire Appel and the Long Beach Public Library, Long Beach, New York.

I am indebted, also, to Eric Foner and Henry Foner, both of whom gave generously of their time and talents. I wish to thank Mrs. Shirley Lerman for typing the manuscript.

I dedicate this work to my wife, Liza, whose patience and encouragement have been unlimited.

INTRODUCTION

The period following the Civil War was marked by a steady reduction in the size of the Army. From a fairly substantial authorized strength of slightly more than 57,000 officers and men in 1866, its strength was steadily reduced during subsequent years until it reached a low point of 25,000 enlisted men in 1874.[1] Despite urgent recommendations from its leading officers, this figure remained substantially unchanged right up to the declaration of war against Spain in 1898.[2]

It was not only the size of the Army that suffered from Congressional economy moves. Funds were not forthcoming to provide adequate expense for even the reduced number of authorized troops. Each year, the Army Appropriation Act was passed only after bitter debate.[3]

The Congressional reluctance to appropriate Army funds was a reflection of the renewal of popular hostility toward the Army during the postwar years.[4] Contributing to this antipathy was the role that the Army was called upon to play in a number of controversial areas of American life and society—Southern reconstruction, culminating in the disputed election of 1876; the fighting against the Indians, which aroused some opposition in religious and pacifist circles; and finally, the giant railroad strikes of 1877 and 1894, where the use of federal troops provoked bitter resentment in the ranks of labor and its sympathizers.[5] These elements fused with the demand for economy in the public service that arose throughout the nation.[6]

The annual struggle for military appropriations reached a climax on March 4, 1877, when the Congressional session actually ended without appropriating any funds at all for the Army. It took a special session of Congress called by President Rutherford B. Hayes to pass an appropriations bill on November 21, 1877, and even this only after a heated debate.[7]

The continually recurring difficulty experienced by the Army in obtaining its annual appropriation was aggravated by the fact that the organization, disposition and use of troops during this period made it a very expensive institution to maintain properly. The post-Civil War Army was organized for administration purposes on a territorial basis.

1

The country was divided into military departments, each comprising several states or territories. These departments, subdivided into districts, were grouped into three divisions—the Atlantic, the Missouri and the Pacific. Each division and department had its own headquarters, with commanding officer and staff, and constituted the chain of command between the troops in the field and the War Department.[8]

The troops serving in a department were scattered through many posts. These were set up along the lines of travel and communication, to furnish protection to miners, to railroad construction crews, to the inhabitants on Indian reservations, and to the settlers of frontier communities. Each post was commanded by the senior officer present there, though it frequently included companies from several different regiments. In 1869, there were 255 such posts in the Army. Although many bore the imposing title of "fort," they consisted for the most part of temporary structures, usually built by the labor of the troops, for the purpose of housing them.[9] During the 1880's the rapid extension of the railroads and the increase of western settlement led to the abandonment of many of these posts. In 1892, there were only ninety-six posts and thirty-three of these were located east of the Mississippi.[10]

The two basic components of the Army were the line and the staff. The line of the Army—its fighting force—consisted of forty regiments, including twenty-five of infantry, ten cavalry, and five artillery. An infantry regiment consisted of one battalion of ten companies. The commanding officer was a colonel assisted by a lieutenant colonel and a major. Each cavalry regiment was made up of three squadrons of four troops each, or twelve troops to the regiment, and was commanded by a colonel, a lieutenant colonel, and three majors. An artillery regiment consisted of twelve batteries, of which two were equipped as light batteries for field service. After the Civil War, Negro troops were enlisted into the Regular Army for the first time and were confined to four regiments—two of infantry and two of cavalry.[11]

In the years after the Civil War, the term "staff" referred primarily to those agencies charged with administering the Army through the purchase and distribution of supplies, the payment of the troops, and the performance of other administrative duties. To carry out these functions, the staff was divided into ten corps or departments, each with a bureau chief and a number of subordinate officers, and all serving under the immediate supervision of the Secretary of War. The departments and corps were the Adjutant General's Department, the Inspector General's Department, the Judge Advocate General's Department (earlier known as the Bureau of Military Justice), the Subsistence Department, the Medical Department, the Ordnance Department, the Pay Department, the Engineer Corps, the Signal Corps and the Quartermaster Department. The functions of all of them, except the last-named, are clearly indicated by their titles. The Quartermaster Department, however, performed a great variety of duties, including providing transportation, furnishing animals, purchasing supplies and equipment for the troops, and constructing and maintaining enlisted men's barracks, officers' quarters and all other garrison buildings.[12]

The Army was governed by both written and unwritten law. The sources of the former were the Articles of War, enacted by Congress, other statutes relating to the military service, the Army Regulations, and general and special orders and decisions promulgated by the War Department and by department post and other commanders. These were supplemented by the so-called "customs of service," which constituted the unwritten part of the military law and were recognized as having the force of law.[13] Thus, while the law made no provision for who was to administer oaths to witnesses in court-martial proceedings, it was accepted custom for such oaths to be administered by the judge advocates.[14]

On April 10, 1806, the Articles of War, originally adopted in 1776 and revised ten years later, were again altered to conform to "the more liberal spirit of the times."[15] In the years following, laws supplementing the legal code were enacted from time to time as the circumstances required. During the Civil War, a considerable amount of legislation relating to the Army was enacted. Some of these laws expired with the war, others had no time limit affixed. By the end of the war, there was such a patchwork of crisscrossing laws that it was generally agreed that it was advisable to "remodel the whole system."[16]

On June 27, 1866, Congress authorized the President to appoint three commissioners with legal experience to revise, simplify, arrange and consolidate all statutes of the United States. As a result of the work of this commission, a set of Revised Statutes was issued covering all the laws of Congress passed up to and including December 1, 1873. These were approved on June 22, 1874. Section 1342 contained the 128 Articles of War. Since the authority of the commissioners was limited to codifying existing law, the new code was, for the most part, the code of

1806. Nearly all of the 101 articles of the old code survived with either minor changes or no changes at all.[17]

An examination of some of the provisions of the new code reveals how outmoded they were. For example, one regulation prohibited Army courts from sitting after three o'clock in the afternoon—simply because the British Parliament had imposed such a limitation in the eighteenth century, when three o'clock was the dinner hour for British officers.[18] Other relics of the past included the practice of calling the person on trial "prisoner" instead of "accused," and the requirement that witnesses remain standing while giving their testimony.[19] The ancient law of the curfew bell—"a remnant of Norman tyranny and oppression—"[20] found its parallel in the provision for the punishment of any soldier who failed to retire to his tent or quarters at the beating of retreat. One officer declared:

> In our Articles of War, the rock upon which our present system rests, there are anachronisms which should not have survived the first Mutiny Act. They are absurdities in our time, and when they are considered at all, it is only for the sake of jest and derision. But whatever touches the discipline of soldiers ought to be too serious a matter for jest or derision.[21]

With respect to the administration of justice, the Articles were poorly arranged and classified, failed to define offenses adequately, and contained no gradations of crimes and punishment.[22] Thus there was no real distinction drawn between desertion and the lesser offense of absence without leave. Instead, Article 32 provided that a soldier who absented himself without leave should be punished as a court-martial might direct, while Article 34 stipulated that any soldier found one mile from camp, without leave in writing from his commanding officer, was subject to a court-martial on suspicion of desertion. Under these ambiguous regulations, a man who missed the 11 o'clock bed check, or was otherwise absent without specific authority, ran the risk of being charged with desertion. General Samuel B. Holabird was convinced that there were many instances of unintentional desertion caused by the lack of a fixed limit for an absence without leave. "It should be assumed," he went on, "that very clear proof and a fixed period of time are necessary elements in so great a military crime."[23]

Most military prosecutions under the code of 1874 were conducted under the "omnibus article"—Article 62—which stated that all crimes, offenses and neglects to the prejudice of good order and military discipline were to be tried by a military court according to the nature and degree of the offense.[24] One critic insisted that this article was invented as a dragnet to catch any small fish that might possibly escape the meshes of the law as laid down in the preceding articles. Another termed it "The Devil's Article," and a third referred to it as a catchall regulation which, "like charity, covers a multitude of sins."[25]

Article 66 stated that soldiers charged with crimes were to be confined until they were either tried by a court-martial or released by proper authority. This confinement was not viewed as punishment but rather as a necessary precautionary measure, but the word "crimes" was interpreted to embrace every trifling offense for which a soldier might be tried.[26]

Various amendments to the code were made after 1874, but no new code was adopted until August 29, 1916.[27] In 1889 Adjutant General J. C. Kelton declared:

> The necessity for a revision of the whole military code has long since been presented and several times attempted, but without any results whatever in bringing it in full harmony with modern military sentiments and conditions struggling to find expression and existence in the Army and with the humane laws and enlightened condition of the country.[28]

For years after the war, the Army was also handicapped by the lack of well-defined regulations—a set of rules governing its affairs and setting forth the details of military duty and the strictures of discipline. The Regulations of 1861 had been partially revised in 1863. Thereafter they were supplemented by numerous general and special orders and modified by various legislative acts. By the end of the Civil War, there was a generally recognized need for a thorough revision of the entire body of regulations.[29] In 1867, the *Army and Navy Journal* spoke of the "woeful confusion of the present Regulations for the Army, their inadequacy to the wants of the time, and their unfitness for the Army of the future."[30]

Repeated efforts were made to bring about the promulgation of a new set of Army Regulations, but without success.[31] In 1874, Inspector-General R. B. Marcy wrote that the old Army regulations had been so altered and amended by laws and orders, that it often required "considerable study and research to determine their actual signification." The supply of regulations, he went on, was now exhausted, with only a few tattered copies on hand, and unless something was done soon, it would truly be said that the Army had no regulations. In the same year, General Sherman echoed: "No officer can find out the Law and Regulation without examining laws and orders as voluminous as a Civil Code and Commentaries."[32]

During the years following, there were three new editions issued of the existing Army Regulations—in 1881, 1889 and 1895—but by the onset of the Spanish-American War these Regulations had still not undergone the thorough overhauling that many officers felt they needed.[33]

The problem which attracted the greatest amount of public attention to the Army, and which proved most vexing to the military authorities who sought to solve it, was the large number of desertions which occurred each year. Of the "three d's" of the service—discharge, death and desertion, the last constituted the greatest drain on military manpower.[34] This was by no means a new phenomenon. During the gold fever of the 1850's commanding officers in the West sometimes found themselves with only a handful of soldiers in their companies.[35]

The return of peace did nothing to improve this condition. It was reported in August, 1866 that the number of desertions was increasing daily. A year later, the *Army and Navy Journal* described the desertion rate as "absolutely enormous." From an Army whose enlisted strength was 54,138, 14,068 men deserted in that year.[36] In August, 1870, an Army paymaster, returning from a trip to the frontier posts, reported that wherever he had gone to pay the troops, large numbers were missing.[37] By 1871, desertions had reached the total of 8,800—almost one-third of the Army's enlisted strength.[38] A correspondent of the New York *Tribune* felt sure that if Congress had taken into account the spirit of desertion that prevailed in the Army, it would have spared itself the troubled of reducing it. "These fellows," he went on, "have been and are constantly reducing themselves."[39]

Desertions during 1871 reached the highest percentage of the period between the Civil and Spanish-American Wars. After that year, desertions declined, reaching 1,678 in 1878. They then began to rise again, peaking at 3,072 in 1884, and then falling off again. Another rise began in 1887, with desertions reaching 2,835 in 1889. In the next ten years, however, desertions were substantially lower, dropping below 2,000 between 1891 and 1897.[40] Some officers insisted that the bare desertion statistics themselves did not reveal "the extent of the toll" on the Army. They argued that the most accurate index of the problem was to compare desertions with the annual enlistment figures. These figures for the 1880's show that the loss of men resulting from desertion averaged about 40 percent of the gain from recruiting.[41]

The problem of desertion struck at the very root of Army morale and efficiency. It not only removed the deserters from the ranks, but it tended to demoralize those who remained, since the burden of extra work fell upon them.[42] It also resulted in a considerable annual loss to the national treasury. Many of the desertions occurred before the men had rendered any appreciable service. In fact, Secretary of War Redfield Proctor estimated that three-quarters of the desertions occurred during the first year of enlistment. Therefore the expense of transporting, clothing, equipping, feeding and training them was largely wasted. To this outlay had to be added the cost of replacements.[43] It is no wonder that the New York *Sun,* always an advocate of reduced military budgets, complained that the scandal of desertion was undermining the financial stability of the nation. "To us," said the *Sun,* "it seems desirable either to disband the Army altogether, or so govern it that desertion shall diminish to the average rate tolerated in other armies."[44]

What caused so many desertions? There was no lack of answers from sources in and out of the service. Some attributed the problem to the underlying restlessness of the American people. Others felt the deserters had enlisted for the sole purpose of obtaining free transportation from the East to the West, where, upon arrival, they took off for the mines, the railroads, or other fields of operation.[45] "I will venture to say," wrote one officer, "that in a detachment of 100 recruits, at least one-fourth of them enlist for that purpose."[46]

Still others blamed the inferior calibre of men resulting from the Army's haphazard recruiting system. These critics claimed that recruiting officers were more concerned with making a good showing than with attracting and enlisting good soldier material. And since recruiting offices were invariably located in the back alleys of the larger cities, it was considered inevitable that the Army should become a dumping ground for all sorts of misfits.[47] "No squad of recruits enlisted in New York," said Colonel W. B. Hazen, Sixth Infantry, "leaves the city without containing faces familiar to the old city detectives. . . . We enlist men . . . without knowing their names, residences or anything whatever about them. Is it strange that a third of our Army deserts each year?" Major H. B. Burnham, Judge Advocate, Department of the Missouri, also blamed the problem on the character of the men who deserted. "It is manifest," he wrote in 1883, "that if honest or good men only could be enlisted, there would be little or no desertions."[48]

Many officers sought an explanation for desertion in the grievances expressed by enlisted men about Army life. And since almost every aspect of military life was criticized at one time or another, the reasons advanced for desertion included the whole range of conditions—poor housing, improper clothing, bad diet, the necessity of performing labor of a non-military character, the monotony of routine duties, frontier isolation, etc.[49] General O. O. Howard said in 1888 that the system of selling a portion of the soldiers' rations to raise money to purchase items not provided by the government was a major cause of desertion.[50] The Division Inspector of the Pacific, after investigating the problem of desertions, reported to General John M. Schofield that the low bread ration, at posts where gardens could not be cultivated, was "one principal cause."[51] And General Schofield himself, two years later, said he was convinced that the poor housing, the limited clothing allowance for recruits, the inferior meat, and the absence of vegetables at some posts, were "causes of great discontent and probably desertion."[52]

In 1889, Adjutant-General J. C. Kelton made a comprehensive statistical study of the desertion problem, compiling figures for each of the twenty-five regiments of the Army, covering the entire decade of the 1880's.[53] Kelton found that the desertion rate did not vary directly with physical conditions from post to post. The percentage of desertions was about the same for the ten coldest and the ten warmest posts, for the most and least healthful posts, and for posts west and east of the Mississippi. He concluded:

> Leaving out of consideration a certain class of men found in the Army as well as out of it . . . the conviction is forced upon me that the cause of desertion is almost wholly one of administration. . . . This is obvious to anyone who, knowing the Army, critically examines the statistics presented. He will discover at once that a discipline of a kind in which the interests of the soldier are little considered, or too abrupt and rigid for the Army of the United States, and desertion go together.[54]

No single reason can be assigned for the large number of desertions from the Army. The specific causes were probably almost as numerous as the desertions themselves. However, certain patterns do emerge from an analysis of desertion statistics (see Appendix, Tables 1 and 2). Even a most cursory examination of the statistics reveals that economic conditions played a major role in the rise and fall in the number of desertions (see Appendix, Chart 1). Desertions fell off sharply in the mid-1870's, in the aftermath of the Panic of 1873. They declined again during the economic difficulties of the mid-1880's, then rose, only to fall to new lows in the depression years of 1894-97.[55] One officer observed in 1895: "If desertion has varied in accordance with one standard, that standard has been the labor market."[56] During depression years there was a marked increase both in the number of men seeking to enter the Army, and in the quality of prospective recruits. The *Army and Navy Journal* wrote on October 25, 1873:

> One result of the financial difficulties which have interfered with the operations of our traders and manufacturers, is seen in the character of the men now offering themselves for enlistment in the Army. Our recruiting officers never had a better choice of material.

Twenty years later, during the depression of 1893, so many men sought to enlist in the Army that for a time, recruiting had to be stopped.[57]

The influence of economic factors on the desertion rate was further demonstrated by other statistics. It was estimated by Adjutant-General Kelton that 64 percent of desertions each year took place in the months of April, May and June. This was explained by the fact that many men joined the Army when they could not find work, and left as soon as they could improve their condition; and labor was usually in greater demand in the spring months than in the winter.[58] General O. O. Howard observed in 1885:

> Excellent young men every day solicit the privilege of enlisting, but they do it in a strait for work. A workman in Omaha has had from $1 to $1.50 wages, but in winter he is often discharged and not able to get work again till spring, so when a young man finds himself without means and without bread he enlists. Good offers in spring and summer tempt him to desert.[59]

It is interesting to note, too, that the rate of desertion of Negro troops was very low, which may well be attributable to the fact that their economic opportunities outside the service were severely limited in prosperity as well as depression.[60] Commenting on the difference between the desertion rates of colored and white troops, Secretary of War Redfield Proctor wrote that the Negroes' "previous condition in civil life largely explains it." "To the colored man the service offers a career," he went on, "to the white man too often only a refuge."[61]

Sometimes, special circumstances, not associated with external economic factors, caused a sharp rise in desertions. This was the case in 1871, when, as noted above, the percentage of desertions reached the highest level of the period. In July, 1870, Congress had reduced the pay of enlisted soldiers from $16 to $13 per month, effective June 30, 1871. The high desertion rate of fiscal year 1871 was attributed by leading officers to the decision of many soldiers to leave the Army before the pay reduction went into effect.[62]

The years 1865-1898 witnessed two distinct movements for reform of the Army, the first in the early 1880's and again in the late '80's and early '90's. These reforms coincided with the movement for civil service reform, and they attracted a great deal of public attention. They accomplished improvements in diet, clothing, and housing, some advance in the legal system, and in the method of promotion from the ranks. These reforms had a dual motive—to lower the desertion rate and to attract better men into the ranks. Secretary of War Proctor wrote in 1889: "The pith of the whole question is to make the service worth seeking, and then enough good men will seek it and be glad to stay in it."[63]

It is difficult to determine precisely how effective the various reforms were in reducing desertions. The modest reforms of the early 1880's did not seem to affect the desertion rate. Desertions did decline from 1883 to 1888, but this was also a period of economic recession, and it is difficult to estimate whether hard times or better conditions of Army life were responsible for the decrease. The most marked effect of reforms on desertions occurred in the late 1880's and early 1890's. Since economic conditions were relatively good, a rising desertion rate was to be expected. Instead, desertions fell off markedly from 1889 to 1892. In his annual report for 1891, Adjutant-General Kelton interpreted the desertion figures as a sign of increasing contentment in the Army. "This gratifying condition," he went on, "is due largely to the beneficent and wise legislation of Congress. . . ."[64]

It thus becomes evident that the factors involved in desertion and which furnished a background for the Army reform movements were both numerous and interrelated. It is the purpose of the following chapters to examine these factors in detail. Chapter I will discuss the material conditions of life in the service. Since these aspects of the soldier's life have been studied in a number of works during the past few years, they will be discussed in somewhat lesser detail than other subjects.[65] Less attention has been paid to the Army's legal system, to the opportunities for advancement, and to the relations between the officers and men, and accordingly, these subjects will be given more extended treatment. This dissertation will also present the first detailed examination of the Army reform movements during this period. Particular attention will be given to the relative strength of the support for and opposition to these movements in the service, their effect upon the conditions of the enlisted men, and the public reaction to them. Finally, I shall devote some considerable attention to a significant segment of Army life—the position of the Negro soldier, including the system of segregation and the controversy surrounding it.

CHAPTER I

THE LIFE OF THE ENLISTED SOLDIER

The post-Civil War Army depended for its strength upon voluntary enlistments for a five-year period. These enlistments took place at regular garrisons or at recruiting stations located in large cities. Each station was under the command of an officer, assisted by two or three enlisted men.

The law permitted original enlistments to men between the ages of sixteen and thirty-five. The consent of a parent or guardian was required for those under the age of twenty-one. The recruit was required to make a written declaration that he had "neither wife nor child," and married men could only be enlisted with special permission from the Adjutant General's office. However, a soldier could marry after he enlisted if he received the permission of his company commander. In addition to these statutory requirements, the recruit had to pass a medical examination. The ability to read and write did not become a prerequisite for enlistment until the 1890's.[1]

Having passed this brief examination, the recruit was sworn in and sent to one of three depots—one for cavalry at Jefferson Barracks, near St. Louis, and two for infantry and artillery at David's Island, New York Harbor and Columbus, Ohio. There the men were clothed, quartered and fed until they were sent to join a unit. The pressing demand for recruits to fill up existing commands precluded the possibility of providing anything more than the most rudimentary training to the recruits at the depots.[2]

Once they arrived at their posts, the recruits were quickly initiated into the rigors of military life in field and garrison. On the northern plains, snow often came in October and remained until the end of May. Some of the winters were unusually severe. During the winter of 1874-75, Montana, Wyoming, the Dakotas and parts of Kansas were swept by raging blizzards that brought up to fifteen inches of snow. "The winter

13

here, take it all together, has been a 'terror,' " wrote a correspondent from Fort Totten, Dakota in May, 1875.[3]

In Dakota and Montana, the summers were short and intensely hot. Along with the heat and drought came "the myriads of gnats, flies, the swarms of grasshoppers and mosquitoes" which, as one victim complained, consumed "what little the winter leaves of one's anatomy." All this was aggravated by the extreme and sudden changes in temperature which caused considerable discomfort and produced a large amount of respiratory disease.[4]

On the southwest plains, the soldier was exposed to long hot summers, lack of water, barren and parched soil, and an abundance of snakes, scorpions, tarantulas and centipedes. "This is the place," wrote one soldier from Fort Grant, Arizona, "where everything that grows pricks and everything that breathes bites."[5]

Under such conditions of weather and terrain, the soldier had to work hard both in field and garrison. Many soldiers who had served during the Civil War testified that their hardships during that conflict were as nothing compared with the privations they subsequently endured campaigning on the frontier. The *Army and Navy Journal* called upon its readers to "contrast mid-winter service in Montana, Dakota and Idaho, or mid-summer campaigning in Texas, New Mexico and Arizona, with anything known in the armies of the rebellion . . . and it would be found that the latter was a mere picnic of pleasure compared to the former."[6]

The soldier's life in garrison was also hard and demanding. In addition to his normal military tasks, he had to perform a variety of fatigue duties which came under the heading of company and post police details, and upon which the health and safety of the garrison depended. Because of the limited strength of the garrisons, guard duty at many posts had to be repeated several times during the week, a factor considered by some Army surgeons as the one "most concerned in aging men."[7]

The soldier was also called upon to perform a considerable amount of manual labor. For a long time, the troops were practically colonizers, clearing the way for the settlers who came later. Moreover, the appropriation provided for the construction and repair of posts was usually inadequate and did not permit the hiring of a sufficient number of civilian laborers. In 1885, General O. O. Howard noted that "the commanding officer of Coeur d'Alene was required to build a post whose cost could not possibly be less than $150,000 and was permitted only $25,000 to do it with," and that the work of the troops therefore "became a positive necessity."[8]

Whatever the cause, for years after the war, enlisted men could be seen working with axe, with hammer, with pick and shovel, cutting and hauling lumber, burning lime, constructing and repairing buildings, digging and grading roads, stringing telegraph lines and doing scores of other details. There were men in the Army whose main service experience consisted of shoveling and hauling as day laborers.[9] General D. B. Sackett, Inspector General of the Army, reported in 1883 that "military instruction continues to be seriously interfered with by the almost constant employment at fatigue and mechanical labor." And a soldier wrote to the New York *Herald* from Camp Rucklen: "Drill has been suspended because there are cellers to dig, bridges to be built, mason and carpenter work to be done; all because the government cannot or will not afford to employ men who are ready and willing to do that work."[10]

The pay that the soldier received for the performance of these varied duties was hardly considered attractive enough to bring men into the service. By the end of the Civil War, the enlisted man's monthly pay was sixteen dollars, having been temporarily increased to that figure from thirteen dollars in 1864. However, in the act of July 15, 1870, Congress decreed that the soldier's pay would revert to the lower figure on June 30, 1871.[11]

This announcement of a prospective pay cut had a serious effect upon Army morale. "Half of this Army will desert if the pay is reduced," one soldier warned.[12] This prediction, while exaggerated, was basically accurate, since the desertion figures for the year following the enactment of the law reached what Paymaster-General Benjamin Alvord called "the extraordinary figure" of 8,800. This trend continued for the following year after the pay reduction was actually put into effect, when the desertion figure was 8,313.[13]

Disgruntled soldiers informed their officers that, since the government had broken its contract with them, they felt that they were no longer bound by any obligation to remain in the service. "Feeling their cause just," wrote one officer, "they leave in squads, well armed, and prepared to fight for what they believe their right."[14] In his annual report for 1871, General E. O. C. Ord, commanding the Department of California, warned: "I am satisfied that this reduction of pay has lost, and may yet lose to the Government many excellent soldiers, by preventing reenlistments, and by increasing desertions."[15]

On April 9, 1872, Senator Henry Wilson of Massachusetts introduced a new pay bill in Congress. After pointing out that the reduction in pay had created "great dissatisfaction in the Army" and had led to "a great number of desertions," he stated that the object of the measure was "to make it the interest of the soldiers to stay in the Army and serve their time out."[16] As adopted by Congress in May, 1872, the new law left the basic pay for all ranks unchanged, but provided for annual increases of one dollar per month after the second year of service, and for a bonus after each enlistment. The act also contained a provision under which the government paid a soldier 4 percent annual interest on that portion of his monthly pay that he did not draw. Both the annual increases and the amounts on deposit and drawing interest were held until discharge and were subject to forfeiture by desertion.[17]

It is difficult to determine the effect of the new pay law on the morale of the soldiers. While it is true that desertions dropped during the years following its enactment, reaching a low of 1,832 for the fiscal year ending June 30, 1876, the fact is that the most dramatic reduction occurred in the period following the Panic of 1873, when jobs were hard to get and Army enlistments increased.[18]

Even though it was characterized as "the best pay bill" ever passed for the Army, the law did not eliminate the soldier's discontent in the matter of pay. The basic monthly pay schedule of thirteen dollars remained unaltered until after the Spanish-American War, and when economic conditions in the country improved, this was hardly enough to attract citizens into the service.[19] In the years immediately following the Civil War, there was the additional problem of the irregularity and infrequency of pay. While the law required that arrears at no time should exceed two months—unless circumstances made it unavoidable—at distant posts, three, four and even six months might go by without payments.[20] A soldier at one such post, writing in 1873, compared the visits of paymasters to those of angels, and said that when they did arrive, soldiers were as much surprised to see them as they would be "were the airy visitants of the blue ethereal suddenly to flap their heavenly wings and alight among us."[21]

Beginning in 1866, soldiers detailed for more than ten consecutive days in the quartermaster, commissary, or some other department, were entitled to additional pay according to the work performed. Men who were employed as mechanics received an extra thirty-five cents a day, while the laborers were paid twenty cents a day. In 1884 this sum was raised to fifty cents per day for mechanics, artisans, school teachers, and thirty-five cents per day for clerks, teamsters, laborers and others.[22] However, soldiers complained that this extra-duty pay was not always forthcoming, because the men would be detailed to such duties for ten days or less at a time, thereby depriving them of the additional allowance. In 1870, the New York *Sun* insisted that this practice was an abuse which "imperiously demands reform." Two decades later, Adjutant-General J. C. Kelton observed that while "this irregular method" was resorted to less frequently than in the past, it remained "a cause of irritation and discontent."[23]

Until the resumption of specie payments in 1879, the government's controversial monetary policy also worked a hardship on the men. The soldiers were paid in paper "greenbacks," but on the frontier and the Pacific coast, all business was transacted on a coin basis, in silver or gold. Before he could purchase anything, the soldier had to take his paper greenbacks to a broker and convert them into coin, often at a considerable loss. Paper money was commonly discounted at rates of 15, 20 and even 40 percent—"a material difference in an unfortunate soldier's pay."[24] "Amongst several grievances which call for redress," wrote one soldier from Fort Vancouver, Washington, in 1873, "that of currency payments to troops on this coast is one if not the greatest of them all."[25]

For many years after the Civil War, the problem of adequate housing for the troops continued to vex the Army. Since military posts were constructed to meet the demands of the moment, little attention was paid to those features which might make them more habitable for the men. The commanding officers responsible for the choice of sites and the construction of the posts were, as a rule, neither architects nor engineers. As a result, such items as ventilation, sewage, sanitary conveniences and even ordinary comforts were largely ignored.[26]

Since troops were usually stationed at great distances from railway facilities, the buildings had to be constructed from whatever materials were available locally. As they were subjected to the ravages of weather and time, the defects in materials and construction soon become obvious. The foundations, supports and floors warped and rotted, and large cracks developed in the roofs and walls, providing ready access to rats, insects, dust, rain and snow. Under these conditions, the men were easy prey to colds and other illnesses.[27]

The squad room, in which companies of thirty, forty and sometimes nearly a hundred men lived, lacked any comforts or conveniences other than beds, a chair or two and a small number of candles.[28] Reading and writing were almost out of the question, for the few bits of scattered candles served only "to render darkness visible." One officer wrote that if the General of the Army wanted to understand the reasons for discontent among enlisted men, "he has only to look into our dungeon barracks with the men huddled around the flickering flame of one or two candles. How many evenings would he or any officer spend in such a hole?"[29]

Until the early 1870's, soldiers slept in pairs in bunks constructed of rough wood and mounted in two or even three tiers. Their bedding consisted of a blanket and a bed sack filled with straw and hay. This system of making men sleep together was regularly attacked as destructive of both the health and comfort of the troops. One enlisted man pleaded that "provision be made for the men to sleep singly and alone and not keep up the present barbarous and unhealthy system of having the men sleep in couples summer and winter."[30]

Although Army officials had long agitated for single, iron bedsteads to replace the objectionable double bunks, it was not until 1875 that the change was put into effect. However, the new bunks were extremely narrow, had no side slats and were packed close together because of the overcrowded condition of the barracks.[31] Moreover, the quarters were so infested with roaches and bedbugs that, as one soldier said, "to get any sleep in them, the men in warm weather, have to lie outdoors." At several posts, commanders were forced to appeal to the War Department for insect exterminators, only to receive the reply that the government could not "afford to pay the expense of a bed bug war."[32]

For many years, there were no plumbing facilities at all inside the barracks. Water was usually drawn by bucket or in wagons from the nearby creeks and deposited in barrels in the rear of the barracks. The supply was neither ample nor pure. Writing to General O. O. Howard from Fort Bridger, Wyoming, in 1883, Colonel J. H. Taylor observed:

> There is one thing absolutely necessary here—I mean a proper system of water supply—all water for the use of the post is taken by bucket from the stream. When you reflect that during the winter months water is only obtained by cutting through ice—which is reformed in a few hours—you will readily realize the hardship of watering the animals and furnishing the command. . . . As it is now, there is no means of fighting fire except by bucket brigade, and there is not even a water wagon at the post. . . . There is absolute

necessity for an engine with which to furnish water for daily consumption and safety.[33]

Kitchen slops were emptied into crude sewers close to the barracks, which soon became clogged with grease, scraps and other garbage, producing foul odors and attracting flies in swarms. The privies were erected over sinks dug in the earth, and were moved from time to time until the backyards "became literally honey-combed with deposits of filth."[34]

Although regulations required a weekly bath for each man, for years there was hardly a barracks in the United States with adequate washing facilities. One officer wrote in 1881: "The regulations say the men must be made to bathe frequently; the doctors say it should be done; the men want to do it; the company officers wish them to do so; the Quartermasters' Department says it is important; yet we have no bathrooms."[35]

Living conditions in the coastal fortifications were not too different from those at frontier posts. There, men often had to live in casemate quarters that had been intended for wartime use only. They were dark, poorly ventilated, and so damp and moldy that even in the heat of midsummer, it was frequently necessary for the men to light fires in order to live in them. They had neither bathrooms nor lavatories, the troops being forced to rely on wells and cisterns near their quarters.[36] One Army medical officer, reporting on a survey of army posts, explained that he had made no inspection of the barracks or of the casemate quarters of the men at Governor's Island, saying that he might "as well make an examination of a pigsty. They disregard every modern notion of hygiene."[37]

At every post there was a collection of overcrowded sheds and shanties where the married enlisted men lived with their families. Their only uniformity lay in the fact that they were all equally unfit for occupancy. "The location and sanitation of the quarters occupied by many of these people," declared Colonel R. P. Hughes, "are such that their children must necessarily absorb the seeds of disease and physical weakness in the very atmosphere they breathe."[38]

From 1865 to 1872, the uniform issued to the soldier was usually a Civil War leftover. The men complained that requisitioning officers took whatever clothing the quartermaster had on hand and passed it out without any attention to proper fit. Since it was difficult for the men to wear the uniform as issued, it became customary for the soldiers to have their clothing altered by the company tailor. This alteration was done at the soldier's expense and the cost was deducted from his pay.[39] One officer estimated that it cost the enlisted men of the Army about $200,000 a year to alter their uniforms, which he felt was an exceedingly heavy tax "for the privilege of finishing the work of the clothing department."[40]

In 1872, the Army announced that the new uniform would be made according to revised sizes and patterns and would not require any alterations.[41] However, soldiers continued to complain about the fit of the coats, trousers and blouses. In 1881, an officer said he had never seen a human being in the Army of such dimensions that the regulation uniform would fit. He was confident that if a company of troops were to parade in front of the Capitol building with every member wearing each article of clothing just as he had received it from the government, Congress "might be shamed into giving relief."[42]

When used in the field and in fatigue work, the articles of the uniform quickly wore out. The standard woolen uniform was the same for all locations and seasons. It did not provide enough warmth for cold weather and was much too warm in the heat.[43] In 1886, First Lieutenant and Assistant Surgeon Leonard Wood, in a report to the commanding general of the Department of Arizona, pleaded for "a lighter and cooler uniform" for the men stationed along the southern borders.[44]

The regulation shoe came in for special criticism. The leather was stiff and unyielding, and the soles were fastened by brass screws which not only were very uncomfortable, but acted as conductors of heat and cold.[45] "The shoe furnished the enlisted soldier," wrote Colonel Richard I. Dodge, Eleventh Infantry, in 1887, "is a disgrace to the civilization of the age. . . . Many a man is discharged from the service a cripple for life, from having been forced to wear the things called shoes now furnished by the Government."[46]

The soldier's food ration was uniform throughout the Army, regardless of duty or locality. The principal staples were beef, salt pork, bread, coffee and beans.[47] The common complaint of the men was that they were served too little beef and too much salt pork. The latter was extremely unpopular, while the quality of the beef suffered from the fact that the Subsistence Department was required by law to accept the lowest bid for it.[48]

Fresh vegetables, milk, butter, cheese, eggs and other items that would give variety to a mess were totally absent from the legal ration. Regulations provided for the establishment of post gardens, with a separate patch of land allotted to each company to provide it with vegetables. These vegetable gardens helped supplement the bill of fare at posts where climate, water and soil made such cultivation possible.[49] In 1878, Major Brisbin, in a letter to General Sherman, gave an account of the produce of his post gardens at Fort Ellis, Montana, which enabled his men to enjoy a sufficient and varied diet.[50] However, at posts located in areas which suffered from poor soil or lack of water, the efforts to cultivate gardens usually proved unsuccessful.[51]

Aside from the quality and variety of the food, there was the additional problem of its preparation. Instead of providing for trained cooks, the army regulations required that the privates of a company be detailed as cooks in rotation, with each soldier serving for a period of ten days. This procedure had been instituted in order to prepare the men for the demands of field service, where they might find themselves dependent upon their own resources. The men assigned were totally inexperienced, and the meals reflected it. It is no wonder that soldiers commented grimly that the cooks destroyed more men than the Indians.[52]

One aspect of the Army mess system that produced a considerable amount of controversy was the authorization for the establishment of post, regimental and company funds. These funds were to be made up of the proceeds derived, for the most part, from the sale of a portion of the soldiers' rations. Thus, while Army Regulations prescribed a daily ration of eighteen ounces of *either* flour or bread, by issuing it in the form of flour, about one-third of it could be saved and sold.[53]

The funds themselves were used to provide the men with either supplemental foods or a variety of recreational, educational and other facilities that were not furnished by the government. The post fund, for example, was used for the expenses of the post bake-house, garden, library, reading room, gymnasium and school. The regimental fund could be used only for the maintenance of the regimental band. Both of these funds were administered by councils of officers under the direction of their respective commanding officers.[54]

The establishment of these funds was based on two assumptions: first, that the soldier's ration was sufficient to permit a portion of it to be diverted to other uses; and secondly, that the provision of additional facilities constituted a legitimate diversion of the soldier's ration.[55]

Both of these assumptions were widely and seriously questioned. Not only did the critics maintain that the ration was too meager to allow for any reduction, but they also insisted that it was the responsibility of the government to provide the facilities and services for which these funds were being used. Music and books were worthwhile, these critics said, but a soldier ought not to be forced to improve his mind at the expense of his stomach.[56] "The United States government," a soldier commented, "ought to be well able to afford to do something for the education of the enlisted man without making him pay for the same." Another soldier expressed his sentiments in verse:

> Lives there a soldier boy so dead,
> Who never to himself has said,
> For savings I don't care a red,
> My stomach much outranks my head,
> Give me before I go to bed
> My flour rations all in bread.[57]

Of all three funds, the company fund was the one around which the greatest amount of controversy raged. Under Army regulations, "the savings arising from an economical use of the rations of the company, excepting the saving of flour, will constitute the company fund, which will be kept in the hands of the captain . . . and disbursed by him exclusively for the benefit of the enlisted men of the company . . . (1) for improvement of the soldiers' table fare and for their comfort in quarters; (2) for garden seeds and utensils; (3) amusement."[58]

The same arguments that were used *pro* and *con* concerning the post and regimental funds were also raised with respect to the company fund. Its defenders maintained that it was absurd to feed the men continually on fat pork and soup when vegetables and dairy products could be purchased from the savings of the ration.[59]

But critics of the fund argued that the regular ration was not large enough to be diverted—in fact, they said, the exact opposite was true—and that company mess furniture, stoves and cooking utensils, no less than vegetables and dairy products, should be furnished by the government. Colonel Robert E. Johnston, First Infantry, expressed this viewpoint when he said in 1876:

> I should give companies a suitable mess outfit, such as knives, forks, spoons and plates. The soldiers now have to purchase these articles. . . . We have to take it out of the rations. The ration is as small as a soldier ought to have, especially considering the work of a soldier on the frontier.[60]

The soldiers also complained that the company fund system left too much to the discretion of the company commander, both as to the amount of food to be saved and the purposes for which the fund was to be expended. Company commanders were accused of trying to enhance their reputations for efficient management by accumulating savings and building up large company funds at the expense of the men's stomachs.[61] "In nearly every company where the savings are not expended about as fast as they accrue, and very judiciously, the soldiers complain of hunger," said Captain Thomas Wilhelm.[62]

Even more serious were the charges made both in the service journals and the daily press that the company funds were appropriated by the officers and diverted to uses "which contributed more to their delectation than to that of the men from whose rations they came."[63] Officers were accused of using the funds to purchase books and newspapers, to beautify their grounds, to pay for baggage in excess of their allowance, and to decorate their homes and offices with cushioned chairs, fancy desks and carpets.[64] So often were such complaints heard that a correspondent, writing to the *Army and Navy Journal,* commented bitterly that if one were to judge by these communications, "honesty among officers was the exception and not the rule."[65]

The soldier was entitled to free medical care, and each army post was provided with a surgeon who was charged with safeguarding the physical well-being of the personnel. Prior to 1872, no specific appropriation was made for hospitals, and they were mostly improvised out of old barracks or rude huts. Beginning with the Act of June 6, 1872, an appropriation of $100,000 was made annually for the construction and repair of hospitals.[66] But while this was an improvement, complaints continued to be heard about the lack of adequate hospital accommodations. As late as 1889, the state of the enlisted men's hospital at West Point caused the Board of Visitors, appointed to examine the Military Academy that year, to observe that no humane person would permit a horse to live in such a room, and that to place a sick man in this alleged hospital "would appear like an attempt to insure his death."[67]

Although the Civil War had demonstrated that a trained hospital corps was indispensable for the proper care of the sick and wounded, it was not until 1874 that the first step was taken to provide for such a body of men. In that year, the Secretary of War was authorized to appoint a number of hospital stewards who were to be permanently attached to the medical corps. With few exceptions, they served in the hospitals as pharmacists and supervisors. The actual care of the men was usually provided by detailing men on extra duty from the companies serving at the post.[68] One officer lamented the incompetence of too many of the attendants, asserting that they constituted a "terrible peril" to the sick.[69]

The sole provision made for the care of the soldier's teeth was the inclusion of a "handsome tooth-extracting case" in each post surgeon's supply. By general custom, the hospital stewards extracted the teeth. Teeth were constantly being removed which, with proper treatment, could have served their owners usefully for many years, and men had to suffer pain and discomfort which they could have easily been spared by a little dental care.[70] One medical officer, writing in 1873, noted that the British government had long since recognized the importance of extending to its army "the benefits of modern dentistry," and went on to say: "Our national pride, if not our national sense of justice, ought not to allow us to be behind (too far) in any act of humanity, however small."[71]

One of the greatest burdens borne by men stationed in the sparsely settled Western districts after the war was the loneliness and unbearable tedium of garrison life. The soldiers felt isolated from home, parents and friends. They frequently went without mail for long periods of time. They were cut off from participation in any social life, other than that found in the barracks room. One soldier, writing from Fort Townsend, Washington, in 1884, said that no one could imagine what a lonesome and monotonous place it was. It was inconceivable to many officers that men could be induced to enlist for a five-year period on the frontier.[72]

Little was done by the government to encourage organized recreation for the men in the service. Posts were rarely furnished with even the simplest kinds of gymnastic or athletic equipment. In the absence of necessary facilities, soldiers had to rely on their ingenuity and determination or on those interested officers.[73]

Amateur theatricals were popular during the winter months. One officer said that it was wonderful to discover the amount of talent that existed among "the boys in blue." From Camp Halleck, Nevada, came praise for the Variety Troupe that made its debut in June, 1871, "astonishing all and doing themselves much credit." The hope was expressed that "the irksome and monotonous duty" which attended a soldier's life on the frontier would now be somewhat enlivened by their frequent appearance.[74]

At the close of the Civil War, Congress took the first step toward providing for the education of the enlisted men, but there was actually little opportunity afforded for soldiers to overcome the handicap of illiteracy. The Act of July 28, 1866, fixing the peacetime strength of the Army, had authorized the establishment of schools at all posts, garrisons and permanent camps, and had empowered the Secretary of War to detail the officers and enlisted men necessary to carry out this program. The same act had also sanctioned the appointment of a chaplain for each regiment of colored troops and included among his duties the instruction of the enlisted men in the "common English branches of education." In September of the same year, the War Department issued a general order requiring the Quartermaster Department to erect chapels, reading rooms and schoolrooms where suitable space was available for these purposes.[75]

However, since the operation of a school, except at posts where Negro troops were stationed and whose chaplains were required to maintain an educational program, was an optional service provided for by the individual post, and since no specific appropriations accompanied the law, the program immediately ran into serious obstacles. Rooms in which classes could be conducted were rarely available, and very little was done to carry out the regulations intended to meet this need. Many officers regarded the educational program with either indifference or outright hostility. Others considered the entire plan impracticable, since officers had neither the time nor inclination to act as elementary school teachers, while few enlisted men were competent to teach.[76] A West Point graduate wrote indignantly from a post where several commissioned officers had been selected for this duty: "To call upon an officer to teach an enlisted man his ABC's (and there are numerous instances at this post of such blissful ignorance), I say is beneath the dignity of an officer which he is bound to possess or cultivate."[77]

In those instances where the education program was wholeheartedly applied, the results were gratifying. One officer told of men becoming "quite proficient in algebra, geometry, grammar, military tactics and other useful studies" in the course of eighteen months at a post school. The chaplain at Fort Clark, Texas, reported that from his personal knowledge of the progress made at that post, he was convinced there should be a school at every military post. "The colored soldiers," he went on, "even under all the disadvantages of the present system of education, are known to the present writer to have made great improvement."[78]

For the most part, however, schools were conducted in a perfunctory manner, mostly to accumulate data for the annual report. At many of the posts there were no schools at all. "Now, during my ten years' service," wrote one non-commissioned officer in 1874, "I have been as much as three consecutive years at one post—a large post at that—and I have not seen any sign of that benefactor of the human race, the school master." [79]

In December, 1877, Secretary of War Robert McCrary convened a board of three prominent officers to review the entire question of education for the enlisted men. After a full inquiry, the board issued a report in which it expressed its conviction that too much money was needed to carry out an effective educational program under the existing statute. It therefore recommended the use of available means in the form of post funds for procuring books, as well as a more liberal application of the Quartermaster Department's appropriations for the erection of school rooms. The board also urged that the system of voluntary education be retained, but that commanding officers should actively encourage the men to attend the post schools.

Pursuant to these recommendations, a general order was issued in May 1878, instructing all officers to cooperate in the encouragement of study and the promotion of learning among the enlisted men.[80] But the matter was not permited to rest there. Quartermaster funds were made available for educational purposes, and by the end of 1881, fifty-two chapels, school and reading rooms had been built at the various military posts at a total cost of about $60,000. The soldiers, it was reported, derived much satisfaction from assembling after retreat to read periodicals and newspapers from the cities and learn what was going on in the outside world.[81]

In 1881, Chaplain George G. Mullins, who had long been indefatigable in his efforts in behalf of the enlisted men, was placed in charge of education in the Army. Writing on this subject in the *United Service* magazine, he declared:

> We must recognize that a keen sense of the importance of universal education is now the very soul-power of modern civilization. That all the people should be educated is becoming a dominant conviction, confined to no particular class, but influencing all thoughtful men.[82]

But serious obstacles still hindered the attempt to carry forward this educational program. Since attendance at school was strictly voluntary, those who needed it most very often failed to take advantage of the opportunity. "At this post," wrote one soldier from Fort Shaw, Montana, in 1882, "there are only eight men out of four companies and the band who attend regularly, or who take any interest in it." [83] It was noted that at a number of posts, many of the men who had to acknowledge receipt of their pay with a mark instead of a signature were not even enrolled at the schools. At small posts, the men's time was so fully occupied that they actually had no time for school even if they wished to attend. For this reason, post schools were conducted in the evening, usually after a day of hard work—hardly a time when soldiers were inclined to attend school.[84]

Frequent assignments to guard duty also seriously interfered with regular school attendance. In some departments, the numerous calls for troops for field service practically closed the schools during the greater part of the year. At a number of posts on the frontier, a continued lack of suitable rooms or buildings prevented classes from being conducted.[85]

The main barrier to the establishment of post schools was the lack of competent teachers. There were many posts at which it was impossible to find a man to do a job for which he received only an additional thirty-five cents a day in extra-duty pay, while still being subjected to all other duties in garrison and field. Even at that, early in 1883, some schools had to be discontinued because of a lack of money for this *per diem* allowance.

Of the limited number of teachers secured, fully one-half were found, upon trial, to be unfit for their work. Too often, a teacher would be detailed as such in order to compensate him for other work performed for which no pay could otherwise be obtained. At several posts, the enlisted men contributed one dollar for themselves and one dollar for each of their children to hire civilian teachers.[86] "I need a school badly for the enlisted men and children," wrote one officer, "and I should delight to establish a good school, but we have no teachers and no lights." And the *Army and Navy Journal* observed: "The Army has its schools. Has it its school-masters? If the school system is to be of practical good, competent school-masters must be provided."[87]

Even though schools for the enlisted men did not flourish as widely as had been hoped, some progress was made in the field of elementary education in the Army. By 1883, there were 3,729 students in attendance, of whom somewhat fewer than half were enlisted men, the rest being

children of officers and soldiers and civilians. "The night school for enlisted men has just closed for the season," came a report for Fort Niobrara, Nebraska, in 1886. "It has been a great success, having an
enrolled membership of fifty-four, mostly colored troops. Many men who
did not know their letters at the beginning of the season now read and
write with considerable facility, and the pride with which they 'sign the
pay roll' is pleasant to witness." [88] Officers who had an opportunity to
observe these schools spoke enthusiastically of their benefits to the
service. In one garrison, the school was held responsible for reducing the
average daily number of men under arrest by one-half. The school men,
who constituted a large percentage of this garrison, were never found in
the guardhouse or before a court-martial and the best marksmen at the
post were also among the most eager students in the school. The post
school was also hailed as "a hated and powerful opponent to the dram-
shop and the gambling den." [89]

In the absence of adequate facilities for recreation and diversion at a
frontier post, the post trader's store became the gathering place of men
hungry for some social exchange. His establishment was a virtual store-
house of shoelaces, needles, thread, tobacco, and a hundred other
articles that the soldiers could not get elsewhere. Post traders had the
exclusive right to trade upon the military reservation to which they were
appointed, and no other civilian was permitted to compete with them.
Prices charged for the goods sold were fixed by the post council of administration, the same body charged with administering the post fund.
Until President Hayes' order abolishing the sale of whiskey went into effect in March, 1881, hard liquor was legally sold by post traders, both
by the drink and by the bottle.[90]

The men complained that the post traders overcharged for articles of
poor quality—particularly for liquor on which by far the greatest profit
was made, and which they described as "a vile compound of chemi-
cals."[91]

With the military post so largely dependent upon them for its needs, it
is hardly surprising that in time, the post traders became a strongly en-
trenched and powerful body of men.[92] "Applications are pouring in thick
and fast for the post trader's store," came a report from Fort Riley. "It
is not at all surprising, either. The store is nothing less than a young gold
mine."[93]

After the war, provision was made for the President to appoint a
chaplain for each of the four regiments of Negro troops and thirty other

chaplains to serve at the various army posts. But in 1874, the Military Post Library Association reported that there were three hundred military stations with only thirty chaplains.[94] In the same year an Army captain noted: "At these isolated posts men have no religious instruction, or chaplain, and never see a religious teacher from one year's end to another." Another officer observed that it was almost "an utter impossibility for officers or soldiers to attend divine service," because the army regulations required that inspections and reviews be held on Sundays.[95]

The government made little effort to furnish bibles, hymn books and religious reading matter for the enlisted men, but the chaplains were allowed to solicit this literature from civilian sources. Such organizations as the U.S. Army Aid Association of New York City, the Young Men's Christian Association and the Military Post Library Association sent both religious and secular books, papers and magazines to army garrisons in the West. Libraries were furnished by the latter organization for $50 and sent to any post with the name of the donor. It also sought to stimulate the soldiers to form reading clubs, debating societies and temperance lodges.[96] One soldier wrote in 1870 about the work of the temperance lodge at his post:

> When I joined the troop in July, 1868, it was what is generally called "a hard crowd." A sober man, until money and sutler's credit was exhausted, was a *rare avis*. Scenes of drunken dissipation, now the exception, were the rule. . . . But now, the guard reports . . . show but one solitary name of a member of our troop confined for drunkenness during the past 12 months. This, I claim, has been caused by the success of our lodge of Good Templars.

Two years later, a sergeant who had been in the service for more than twenty-six years said that he had never seen anything done to advance "the moral, social and intellectual standing of the soldier, that could in any way compare with what was done by the Military Post Library Association." And in 1876, the New York *Tribune* referred to it as "a most admirable association."[97]

In spite of these efforts, the soldier who was not engaged in the performance of duty had few wholesome activities—mental or physical—to absorb him. Under these circumstances, even the best men sank into a dull apathy and became weary, discontented and demoralized. Many men who would have become good soldiers became disgusted with the service and sought an avenue of escape from the discomforts and monotony of their lives.[98] "If an enlisted man frequents saloons and liquor stores," wrote one soldier, "he does so in most cases more for the sake of company to relieve his mind from the oppressive, dull routine in the garrison." Another soldier insisted that the government should not be surprised that the men were tempted to leave without authority and seek, in the brightly-lighted saloons, a cheerfulness and relaxation that it denied them. And the *Army and Navy Journal* commented:

> When off duty and at leisure, the soldier needs to refresh his spirit after toil; he seeks diversion, pastime, sport. The Government also makes it incumbent on courts-martial to punish the misdemeanors resulting from drink, and its usual concomitants, but does little or nothing to encourage athletic sports as a means of recreation for the men . . . .[99]

The vast distances involved, coupled with the lack of sufficient funds for transportation, made it impracticable for a regular rotation program to be established. As a result, troops were retained in one locality for as long as ten, fifteen or twenty years, even at the most undesirable stations. This policy, aside from its effects upon the health of the men, was anything but beneficial to their morale and discipline, since it meant that soldiers could not look forward to transfer to regions of greater comfort.[100] "By all means let us have a change," came a cry from Arizona in 1882, "to some department where . . . building of roads, new posts, and living in mud hovels . . . with the thermometer at 150 degrees in the shade a fourth of the time, and in comparative isolation, are unheard of, or, at least, are among the things of the past."[101]

CHAPTER II

THE ENLISTED SOLDIER AND THE ARMY'S
LEGAL SYSTEM

A highly controversial feature of the post-Civil War Army—and one that drew the heaviest fire from critics both within and outside the service—was the administration of military justice.[1] The Army court-martial system was not only considered unnecessarily cumbersome, but it was also condemned as being completely out of step with the democratic social and political life of the country. One observer felt that it provided a tribunal "inconsistent with the spirit of our institutions, and unsuitable to our soldiers, who never cease to be citizens."[2] Others held that it was little more than a system to enable commanding officers to dispense punishment legally, rather than to provide justice.[3]

Except for a few unimportant cases, punishment could only be legally inflicted upon a soldier by sentence of a military court. A soldier could be tried by any of three kinds of courts-martial, depending upon the nature of the offense. The most serious cases required the convening of a general court-martial. After 1874, these could only be appointed by general officers commanding separate divisions or departments. In 1884, this authority was extended to colonels commanding separate departments. A general court-martial was to be made up of thirteen members, unless the demands of the service prevented that number of officers from assembling. In no event, however, could there be fewer than five members.

Trials of enlisted men for minor offenses were handled by regimental or, in the vast majority of cases, by garrison courts-martial of three members appointed by the commanders of the regiments or posts. The maximum sentence that could be imposed by these minor courts was one month's hard labor or forfeiture of pay for a similar period. If the accused believed that a member of the court was prejudiced against him, he was permitted a challenge, but the cause had to be stated to the court, which then determined the validity of the challenge.[4]

While the presiding officer of a court-martial was generally responsible for its conduct, officers authorized to designate a general court could also appoint a separate trial judge-advocate. In the minor courts, however, it was a custom of the service for the junior members to perform the duties of such a court officer. In 1879, the War Department ruled that a separate judge-advocate must thereafter be appointed for a minor court-martial as well as for a general court.

Unlike the members of the court, the judge-advocate was not challengeable. He was not considered a member, but an assistant assigned to prosecute in the name of the government, and to record the proceedings of the court. By Act of March 3, 1863, the judge-advocate was authorized to appoint a stenographer to record the proceedings and testimony. However, such employment was authorized only in important cases or when the other duties of the judge-advocate did not permit him to take down testimony in the ordinary manner.[5] One officer observed that the written record of the judge-advocate of the court was "as meager and brief as it can possibly be made." Another complained that in the conduct of its military courts, the government lagged behind even the most remote backwoods civil courts, practically all of which employed official stenographers to assist the court.[6]

Any officer could prefer charges against an enlisted man and order him confined under guard for an alleged crime or offense. At the same time, he had to deliver a signed statement of the offense with which the accused was charged. All prisoners against whom no written charges had been made were to be released by the officer of the day at guard-mount, unless orders to the contrary were received from the commanding officer.[7] It was up to the accused soldier's commanding officer to determine whether there was sufficient evidence to support the arrest. He could either dismiss the charge or institute court-martial proceedings. There was no legal requirement for a preliminary examination into the basis for the charge, although in some instances department commanders required that this be done. However, even when such an investigation was undertaken, it was usually neither thorough nor effective.[8]

If the commanding officer decided that the offense warranted trial, he formally prepared the charges. These consisted of two parts—the charge proper and the specification. The former defined and designated the alleged offense, while the latter set forth the facts constituting the offense. In general court-martial cases, the post commander forwarded the charges to the department commander with a recommendation for trial.

They were then referred to the department judge-advocate for his opinion. The territorial extent of the military departments and the difficulty of communication led to serious delays in acting upon charges forwarded from the various posts.[9]

In April, 1868, Brevet-Brigadier General Robert C. Buchanan, commanding the Fifth Military District, sharply criticized the practice by officers of preferring charges against enlisted men without investigating adequately whether there was sufficient evidence to warrant a trial. He cited the case of a soldier who had been acquitted of an offense after having been confined for more than seven months, although the officer preferring charges could easily have discovered that they were unfounded. "Such flagrant injustice," he concluded, "must not be repeated."[10] A month later, General Buchanan issued an order advising the officers in his command that they were responsible for the charges they preferred, and that if these charges were found to be false or frivolous, or preferred without proper investigation, the officers were themselves guilty of a military offense and could be prosecuted. The General further drew attention to the frequent mistakes that were made in charging as "absences without leave" and "disobedience of orders," offenses which were simply neglects of duty. "It is not just to the accused," Buchanan declared, "nor does it promote the interests of the service, to represent an offense other than it is, or to multiply it by charges describing it under different heads, for the sake of securing the infliction of greater punishment."[11]

Since even the slightest breach of discipline could become the basis for court-martial action, the number of army trials reached staggering proportions. Each year, "a large per cent of the enlisted men of the Army" were tried, and during some years there were almost as many cases before the courts as there were enlisted men.[12] A soldier could be brought before a military court for such offenses as missing a roll-call through oversleeping, or appearing at parade with a wilted collar or unbuttoned blouse. "For every neglect of duty of any kind," came a complaint from Fort Sill, Oklahoma, in 1882, "every man is brought to trial." [13] It was said that there were few soldiers who had not been confined in the guardhouse, awaiting trial, at one time or another during their term of service. The large number of court-martial trials had a most adverse effect on the public. Critics of the Army observed sarcastically that the operation of courts had become the chief activity of the service, and that there must be something wrong with an organization which could exist only with the aid of incessant court-martialing. "Whatever else may fall short in the army," said the New York *Times* in 1888, "it is sure to get a full supply of courts-martial." And a year later, the same newspaper reiterated:

> The crop of military trials never fails, barren of other incidents as garrison routine may be, and when it is noted that during the last fiscal year there were 13,542 trials of enlisted men, in an army averaging only 24,110, it is quite evident how much time and energy are consumed in the business.[14]

In 1885, General O. O. Howard, in his annual report as commanding officer of the Department of the Platte, commented on the large number of enlisted men's trials that had taken place within the department during that year—2,056 cases of men tried out of 3,008 men. He contended that it would be wrong to infer from this that the discipline of the command was poor. Rather, he insisted, the numerous trials arose solely from the fact that the court-martial had become the only legal means of punishment for the slightest infractions of regulations. The General was confident that if every post commander and field officer were empowered to handle summarily the many cases that arose out of the ordinary activities of a garrison, or in the field—with their powers properly limited—the court-martial lists could be reduced by two-thirds and the discipline of the Army improved. He warned that courts-martial, by becoming too common, lost their effect and also undermined an officer's sense of responsibility and care for his command. While he admitted that it was obviously necessary to check any tyrannical exercise of power, he maintained that when this restraint went too far, as was the case under the Army's legal system, the organization became weak and clumsy.[15]

The fact is that at many posts there were not always enough eligible officers on hand to constitute garrison courts, much less general courts-martial. In 1870, Major D. G. Swaim wrote to Congressman James A. Garfield that officers were so scattered over the plains with small detachments that at no point "were there a sufficient number available for a general court."[16] The large number of cases, the dispersal of the troops, the scarcity of officers, and the delay involved in sending officers from other posts—all combined to render it impracticable to convene courts promptly. Men would be kept in detention awaiting trial for greater periods than they might have had to serve if they had been promptly tried and sentenced. This was a hardship both on the internee and his comrades, who had to perform his duties as well as their own during his long absence.[17] One officer wrote in 1867:

> Nothing strikes terror into the mind of the evil-doer so effectually as prompt punishment, yet in our Army men often lay in the guard-house for months before they are brought to trial. This is simply unjust and would be considered indefensible by every officer had not custom taught us to disregard it.[18]

And as late as 1890, Captain W. E. Birkheimer, an assistant judge-advocate, pleaded for prompt trials for enlisted men in these words: "Unnecessary delay in bringing offenders to trial is oppression; it adds in a questionable manner to the punishment of the guilty and imposes injusice upon those who are found to be innocent."[19] The extent to which this was carried on as shown by the record of trials in the Department of the Platte for 1889. Of the 1,638 trials by minor courts, 1,014 involved only a forfeiture of pay. Of the remaining number, forty-five resulted in acquittal, twenty-seven in a reduction to the ranks, one in bar of trial, and nine in reprimands, leaving a balance of 542 trials that had confinement included in their sentences. Thus, over one thousand men were subjected "to the inconvenience and disgrace of confinement" not imposed by a sentence of a court.[20]

When the court finally assembled for trial, the fate of an accused soldier rested with a group of officers who were selected without regard for their qualifications for this duty. Yet they possessed the combined powers of a judge and jury. They heard testimony, ruled on all questions of law, determined the guilt or innocence of the defendant, and in case of conviction, pronounced the sentence. The officcer detailed as the trial judge-advocate acted, in "Poo-Bah" fashion, as prosecutor, recorder of the proceedings and legal adviser to both the court and the accused when the latter had no legal aid of his own.

One of the serious shortcomings of the Army court system during this period stemmed from the fact that the regulations never provided for an adequate body of trained legal officers. Not only did the Act of June 23, 1874, eliminate the office of Assistant Judge-Advocate General, which had been created twelve years earlier, but it also reduced the corps of judge-advocates from eight to four, by the process of attrition. Since there were not enough officers in the corps to permit the detailing of one to each department, much less to each post, the task of performing the trial judge-advocate's multiple duties fell to an officer detailed for that purpose—usually a newly commissioned officer.[21] Judge-Advocate General Swaim complained of this tendency to appoint the "youngest and least experienced of the subaltern officers" to serve as judge-advocate. With the necessary legal volumes rarely available, it is not surprising that trial records were seldom free of errors and irregularities.[22]

The placing of such extensive legal powers in the hands of men who had neither formal legal training nor ready access to trained legal advice was one of the most frequently criticized aspects of the Army's judicial system. General A. H. Terry noted in 1876 that in civil life, legal training was considered indispensable both on the bench and at the bar. Yet in most cases tried in the Army, neither the members of the courts nor the representatives of the government before these courts were versed in the law. "And yet," he went on, "these courts have very extensive powers. They may impose sentences which touch the liberty of men for terms of years, which even touch men's lives."[23]

Actually, however, court-martial duty came so frequently that officers, whether they were qualified or not, soon acquired an acute distaste for it. "I have been on a court-martial again today," Lieutenant Hugh L. Scott, Seventh Cavalry, wrote to his wife from Fort Sill in 1889, "which has at last finished its labors. It has hung on till everybody is tired of it." Another officer was quoted in 1892 as saying: "The most tedious and thankless work an Army officer has to do is court-martial duty." A third officer, after serving for more than a week, sought to express his grievance in a poem entitled "Midsummer Musings by a Member of the Court," which went in part:

> The worst of our dreary routine
> Upon the bleak frontier,
> Is to meet in solemn conclave
> And these stupid cases hear.[24]

After 1870, officers ordered away from their posts on court-martial duty received no *per diem* allowance for expenses while absent. "Not infrequently," said Secretary of War Robert Lincoln in 1883, "an officer is required to perform such duty under circumstances of considerable hardship in the extraordinary expenses incurred by him." The assignment to this duty was therefore regarded by officers as an unjust burden, and their primary concern was to get the trial over as quickly as possible. Such feelings were hardly conducive to a thorough consideration of all the issues and circumstances involved in a case.[25]

The actual court-martial itself was opened by the judge-advocate with a recital and detailing of the charges. He then proceeded to examine the witnesses in support of the charges. Until 1878, an accused soldier could not legally testify as a witness before a court-martial. The Act of March 16, 1878, made persons charged with crimes and offenses competent witnesses. If the accused took the stand as a witness, it was with the understanding that he must answer relevant questions and be subject to cross-examination, even if the answers would tend to incriminate him.[26]

The furnishing of counsel to the accused was not required by law, but in a general court-martial case, an application to the court for such counsel was invariably granted. Even when the soldier could afford to hire a civilian lawyer, such counsel had no official standing in the court. He was heard, if at all, as a matter of courtesy. He was forbidden to participate in the proceedings, except through the accused or in writing.[27] Although a soldier was permitted to act as his own counsel, few enlisted men were sufficiently familiar with the rules of evidence to be able to conduct their own defense. Assistant Adjutant-General Samuel P. Breck referred to "numerous cases where soldiers have pleaded guilty to offenses they did not commit, through ignorance of their rights and lack of proper counsel."[28]

Article 90 in the code of 1874 reiterated the provisions of the old code requiring the judge-advocate of a court-martial to consider himself, to a certain extent, a counsel for the accused, in addition to his role as prosecutor. His participation in this capacity was to be limited to objecting to leading questions directed at witnesses and to questions addressed to the prisoner, the answers to which might tend to incriminate him.[29] But Judge-Advocate General Swaim insisted that the multiple duties of the judge-advocate invariably created confusion in the minds of the accused soldiers. Thus, many of them, convinced that the judge-advocate was required to act as their counsel, confided their defense to him. When convicted, they sought a remission or disapproval of the sentence, on the ground that they had been deceived or misled by the advice of the judge-advocate during the trial.[30] Others went further and contended that it was utterly inconsistent to expect the same individual, no matter how well intentioned, to protect the legal rights of the accused as fervently as he pursued the prosecution. Captain Thomas Wilhelm, Eleventh Infantry, commented:

God had not made man so sublimely balanced as to deal out even-handed justice to all concerned, where it becomes the duty of an individual at once to convict and acquit a prisoner for the same offense.[31]

The fact that the judge-advocate was permitted to retire with the court for consultation was also decried. The purpose of this practice was to allow the judge-advocate to give advice on points of law.[32] But Acting Judge-Advocate General G. Norman Lieber felt strongly that he should be excluded from the secret sessions of the court, where the accused was unrepresented, and where he might, by a word, an inflection or a gesture, even unwittingly, influence the judgment of the court. The New York *Times* agreed that this feature of the court-martial procedures was "manifestly unfair to the man being tried."[33]

Before a court-martial deliberated on the judgment, the judge-advocate read over the entire proceedings of the court. He then collected the votes of the members, beginning with the youngest. The junior officers were required to vote first, in order that they might not be influenced by their seniors. The Articles of War required a simple majority in all cases, except for the death sentence, which required a two-thirds vote. The decision of the court-martial was actually no more than an opinion, for the proceedings, findings and sentence were subject to review by the officer who had ordered the trial and appointed the court. The judgment of the court, therefore, was not announced in open court, even when the accused was initially found not guilty.[34] In March, 1873, the New York *Tribune* published a lengthy communication from "an occasional correspondent," who wrote from Washington and criticized various aspects of the Army's judicial system. To allow an accused person to linger in doubt and anxiety after the court had passed judgment, he said, was reminiscent of the practices of the Inquisition. It certainly did not belong in any code, civil or military, of the nineteenth century. He further contended that it was improper for the same officer to both convene the court and review its proceedings. An officer in this position was bound to have opinions about the merits of the case against the accused, since the offense had taken place within his jurisdiction, and perhaps even against his own regulations. These opinions, in turn, might influence him in his selection of the members of the court. And should this body reach a finding or sentence that did not conform to his idea of justice, the commanding officer, who was only human, might find it difficult, if not impossible, to conceal his disappointment or disapproval. In order to avoid coming into conflict with their commanding officer, members of the court might, quite unconsciously, be inclined to please him rather than "to mete out his strict due to the prisoner." "Is it not evident," the correspondent concluded, "that the convening and reviewing officer should be one far removed from the influences of the *locus criminis?*[35]

Five years later, an officer wrote an angry letter to the *Army and Navy Journal* in which he charged that courts-martial were subjected to a variety of influences. He insisted that if the records of the military courts for the past eight years could be exposed to the public, it would be aghast at "the gross display of partiality and utter disregard of right and justice they manifest." Not even the proceedings of the Star Chamber or of the most autocratic courts of Europe of the past would reveal "more flagrant wrongs" than those that had been committed since 1870 and that were still a constant occurrence in the administration of military justice.[36]

In October, 1889, the *Eastern Argus* of Portland, Maine, published an interview conducted by its Washington correspondent with an officer who was identified only as "a general of high rank." In it, the anonymous general called the garrison court "about the most severe court in the world"—the instrument through which officers and noncommissioned officers vented their spite against unfortunate privates. "Indeed," he concluded, "if the history of garrison courts-martial for a single year could be made public in detail, I am afraid the country would be generally shocked by the revelation."[37]

Two months later, an enlisted man, writing to the New York *Times* from Jefferson Barracks, Missouri, added this contribution to the discussion:

> Any old soldier will always say it is better to plead guilty before a court-martial, for the charges have been preferred by an officer and if the court did not find him—the enlisted man—guilty, it would be a reflection on that officer, and there is too much Free-Masonry in the craft for that. Any man pleading not guilty would be punished anyway for the previous offense of occupying their valuable time by listening to testimony.[38]

Whatever the truth of the matter, there is no doubt that the nation's press, and probably the people as well, viewed the Army's court-martial system with a good deal of suspicion. In 1872, the Washington *Capital* said that the conclusion must be drawn that a court-martial and Judge Lynch's tribunal were one and the same thing. It insisted that Congress must either modify the military tribunals so as to make them safe, or wipe them out altogether. In November, 1886, the New York *Herald* reported that the Judge-Advocate General had noted that of the 10,224 cases tried by minor courts in 1886, only 281 resulted in acquittal. Two years later, *Harper's Weekly* declared: "There were some 12,000 trials of enlisted men by court-martial last year, not one in fifty resulting in acquittal." And in 1889, the Kansas City *Times* stated that no one could study the action of courts-martial without concluding that in many cases, members cared little about evidence, operating on the principle that if a soldier was charged with an offense, this was *prima facie* evidence of the man's guilt. The *Army and Navy Journal* admitted in 1886 that the opinion was widely held that the great majority of court-martial verdicts were "much in the nature of snap judgments, arrived at without much deliberation and often governed by prejudice and the influence of local surroundings."[39]

For many years, American military penal philosophy was dominated by the concept that severe punishment alone could preserve order and deter potential offenders. Therefore, the sentences imposed by the military tribunals reflected an emphasis on harsh and cruel treatment. Under the code of 1806, punishment by flogging was legal. Article 45 also gave courts-martial the authority to inflict "corporal punishment" upon conviction for drunkenness on duty. A number of other offenses likewise drew heavy penalties in the code. Disobedience, neglect, drunkenness, sleeping on guard, and desertion were some of the violations that were customarily punished by flogging "in a garrison ceremony" designed to impress the viewers and discourage crime.[40]

The elimination of the harsher forms of punishment was a slow process. Between 1806 and 1812, punishment by lashes was first limited to fifty strokes and then prohibited altogether. In 1833, however, lashes were revived as a punishment for desertion.[41] A familiar sentence for deserters who were apprehended and convicted in the years before the Civil War was "fifty lashes on the bare back, well laid on with a raw hide; to be indelibly branded on the left buttock with the letter 'D'; to have his head shaved, and to be drummed out of the service."[42]

In 1830, the death sentence for desertion in time of peace was abolished. Between 1830 and 1860, the forms of punishment included compelling the prisoner to ride a wooden horse; forcing him to walk around a ring from reveille to retreat, carrying a thirty or forty-pound log, or a weighted knapsack; requiring him to wear a twenty-four-pound ball and chain attached to his right ankle and a band of iron fitted with prongs around his neck; "bucking" and "gagging"; and suspending the prisoner by the thumbs or ordering him to be "spread-eagled."[43]

In September, 1850, three soldiers were tried for and found guilty of "mutiny" and "positive and wilful disobedience of orders" and sentenced by a court-martial held at Fort Constitution, New Hampshire, to be kept at hard labor by day and in solitary confinement by night, for one year, without pay. The sentence also provided for each prisoner to be restrained by a permanently attached ball and chain and to wear an iron collar around his neck with seven pointed prongs seven inches long projecting from it.[44] General Winfield S. Scott, the Commanding General of the Army, remitted the latter portion of the sentence, saying that it "would inflict a punishment cruel and unusual and consequently illegal."[45] Nevertheless, on November 6, the citizens of Portsmouth and adjacent towns assembled in a public hall in that city to protest against the punishments imposed by military courts. The meeting adopted a memorial calling upon Congress to undertake a general revision of the military justice code and the Army disciplinary system. Under the existing rules and regulations, it declared, the military courts exercised enormous power over the lives of the soldiers and this authority was too often exercised "in a most arbitrary manner, and sometimes with extreme cruelty." Punishments inflicted by these courts, the memorial went on, were frequently far out of proportion to the offenses involved and even petty misdemeanors were tried by courts-martial at great cost to the public treasury. It continued:

> It has recently been made known to your memorialists that courts-martial inflict upon privates in the army punishments as severe and cruel as to outrage the feelings of humanity. The law which authorized the infliction of corporal punishment (except in cases of desertion) by stripes and lashes has been repealed; but certain courts-martial evade the intent and meaning of the repealing act by punishing corporally with heavy instruments of torture far more intolerable than the lash. It cannot be believed in the nineteenth century that the degradation of the *man* can have a tendency to make him a better *soldier*. That punishment should be proportionate to the offense, and that good order in the army would be promoted by wise and humane rules of discipline more effectually than by that barbarous severity which was practiced in former times, seem to be the generally admitted doctrines of enlightened reason. . . . . .[46]

As the years passed, the more severe forms of punishment were gradually abandoned. "Bucking" was abolished in 1853, and Congress, on August 5, 1861, again prohibited flogging as a form of punishment, despite the predictions of many officers that the elimination of the lash would result in insubordination, relaxed discipline in the ranks, and an increase in crime.[47]

Since flogging was now forbidden, courts-martial would draw upon the customs of the service for a form of "corporal punishment" that would fall within the description contained in the 45th Article of War. Thus, the accused would be sentenced to carry a loaded knapsack for a period of time, to stand on a barrel, and to suffer other penalties which resulted in bodily pain or fatigue, "provided the same were not excessive or physically injurious." Soldiers were also "branded" (indelibly marked), had their heads shaved and were drummed out of the service for a variety of offenses.[48] On January 13, 1872, the *Army and Navy Journal* drew "the special attention of officers serving upon courts-martial and to officers reviewing their proceedings" to the remarks of General Irvin McDowell in the case of several soldiers who had been found guilty of desertion and sentenced to imprisonment, dishonorable discharge and to be marked indelibly with the letter "D" one and one-half inches long. He said, in part:

> It is true that it has been customary to mark indelibly the body of certain prisoners, as it was once the practice to brand them on the face with a hot iron; but such punishment . . . has become so abhorrent to the present state of society that it is not too much to say that if it were generally known to be still insisted upon in the Army, Congress would be allowed no rest until it abolished it, even if it had to abolish the Army along with it.[49]

The Act of June 6, 1872, made it illegal for a court-martial to order the branding or tatooing of any soldier. This same act provided that the word "corporal" be stricken from the 45th Article of War. A few months later, the *Army and Navy Journal* published a letter from an officer who reported that a week earlier he had been required to carry out a part of a soldier's sentence that directed "his head to be shaved and to be bugled out of the garrison." The officer asserted that even if the punishment were legal—about which he had serious doubts—it was barbarous and "unworthy of the progressive ideas of the present era." He hoped that the publication of his letter would attract the attention of the authorities and succeed in getting "man's inhumanity to man" eliminated from the military code.[50]

The influence of the advocates of the punitive principle was even better reflected in the length of the prison terms imposed by general courts-martial of that period. There seemed to be no limit at all to the power of a court-martial in imposing sentences of imprisonment. The courts seemed to operate with the expectation that the reviewing authorities would reduce their sentences.[51] In January, 1872, General Irvin McDowell, commanding the department of the East, cited the records of his department for the past three years, which showed that in almost half the cases of sentence to dishonorable discharge accompanied by long confinement, the department commander had found it necessary to reduce the term of confinement, and ultimately even the reduced sentence had been entirely remitted, in response to "the earnest application of the prisoner's officers," who felt this would be for the benefit of the service.[52] Two years later, the *Army and Navy Journal* observed that the reviewing officer was too frequently compelled to modify the excessive severity of the sentences imposed by the military courts. These sentences, it went on, "like the Draconian Law," were self-defeating, because of their disproportion in relation to the offenses. The magazine asserted that if it were to insert weekly a report of every case of unduly severe sentences inflicted on enlisted men, it would have to be enlarged and the patience of its readers would be exhausted.[53]

Under the penal code of 1806, penalties were not graded in accordance with the degree of guilt or the seriousness of the violation. Instead, courts were given great discretion in imposing sentences. This aspect of the court-martial system, with all its accompanying injustices, continued to plague the Army throughout the nineteenth century and was one of the most frequent sources of complaint against American military justice. Among other things, it resulted in differences in the kind and extent of punishment for the same offense and the same degree of guilt. Some courts preferred to resort to corporal punishment; others to stoppages of pay. Prison sentences for the same offense varied widely.[54] "It has been a matter of surprise to me," wrote one officer in 1871, "that the administration of military justice (which is frequently a good deal less than justice) instead of being governed by written law, should have been left to the caprice of many variously constituted minds for so long a time." A year later, a correspondent writing to the New York *Tribune* expressed his belief that the "anomolous and arbitrary way of punishment" was one of the principal causes of desertion, for it was impossible to expect discipline when the soldier knew that punishment was a matter of whim. Thus, he concluded, for the very same misdemeanor by which one soldier was fined the full extent of his pay for four months, another would lose it for three or six months.[55]

In the same year, Secretary of War William W. Belknap reported that an examination by the Bureau of Military Justice of the records of trials occurring in the different military departments had revealed the inequality of sentences imposed by different courts for identical offenses. The report stated that in one department, the sentence for desertion varied from one to five years' imprisonment, while in another, one year was considered ample. Since the prisoners who had been differently treated were often thrown together, the injustice became "manifest to the sufferers." The result, the Secretary said, was that the culprits were hardened rather than reformed. He was convinced that the service would be greatly benefited and its morale improved by the adoption of a code providing specific penalties for well-defined offenses, with minimum and maximum limitations.[56] Early in 1873, the *Army and Navy Journal* endorsed this recommendation and expressed the hope that it might see the day when the Army was provided with "some well-arranged system of punishments" to supplant the irregular system then in effect. And a year later, Colonel N. H. Davis, of the Inspector General's Department, wrote to the Chairman of the House Military Committee: "A penal code of punishment graduated to the character and magnitude of offenses should be established for the guide of courts-martial to better insure even justice."[57]

The revision of the Articles of War in 1874 provided little relief for this long-standing problem. In a few particular cases, the revised military code indicated precisely the amount or nature of punishment to be imposed by the court-martial. But thirty-two of the thirty-four articles under which enlisted men could be tried left the extent of punishment to the discretion of the court.[58] Acting Judge-Advocate General G. Norman Lieber declared that no other civilized country had a code of penal laws which gave such enormous powers to the persons entrusted with their execution. He noted that the range of punishment by confinement was limitless, extending from a day to a lifetime. Moreover, no matter how grave or trivial the offense, there was no minimum or maximum limit. As a consequence, he concluded, different standards of punishment prevailed in the different departments, and there was no uniform system governing the entire Army.[59]

In 1879, the *Army and Navy Journal* declared that the inequality of sentences of general courts-martial and the need for a new regulation in that area were strikingly brought home in two cases occurring in the Department of Texas. One private was tried for abusing and threatening the life of a comrade, found guilty and sentenced to dishonorable discharge and confinement at hard labor for one year. A second private was tried for drunkenness on guard, using disrespectful and insubordinate language to his commanding officer, and kicking at his superior. He was found guilty and sentenced to confinement at hard labor for twenty years. General E. O. C. Ord, the Department Commander, approved the sentence in both cases, but reduced the longer sentence from twenty years to two. "Perhaps there may have been cases more in point than the two referred to as to the inequality we have mentioned," the service journal continued, "but there seems to be no doubt from a review of the court-martial records of the past few years, that a system in sentences is much needed, and the abolition of the haphazard style now so much in vogue."[60]

The frequency with which the complaints continued to be heard about the wide divergences of punishment for similar offenses indicates that "a system in sentences" was indeed needed. It was not uncommon for soldiers to be confined in the same guardhouse for identical offenses, with one serving a sentence twice or even three times as severe as the other. They had been tried by different courts, each using its discretion as to the extent of punishment for the common offense.[61] "No wonder Private Bayonet loses faith in justice," wrote one soldier in 1877, "when he finds that Private Ramrod receives only one month's imprisonment for precisely the same offense for which he received three." The constant occurrence of such contrasting verdicts impelled General Hancock to comment that "the evils of our present system are very striking." And the Kansas City *Times* queried: "Is it any wonder that soldiers consider these courts-martial a farce, a mockery of justice and an institution that trifles with their lives and liberty, when justice is dealt out so unevenly?"[62]

In the single instance of desertion, there were wide variations in punishment. Two soldiers would be arraigned before a general court, each charged with this crime, committed under similar circumstances. The first would receive a sentence of confinement for six months or one year, while the second would be condemned to three, five or more years in the military prison.[63] Captain Arthur Murray, acting judge-advocate of the Department of the Missouri, observed in July, 1889, that the severity of the sentence depended more upon the post at which a court was convened than upon any circumstances connected with the accused's desertion or previous service. "That this is the only inference that can be drawn from the various sentences given," he concluded, "indicates that something is radically wrong in the present system of court-martial punishment."[64]

On July 5, 1894, J. L. Bradley, a prisoner at Fort Leavenworth Military Prison, wrote a letter to General Howard, then commanding the Department of the East, pleading that his sentence be reduced from four to two and one-half years. He told of fellow prisoners who had "the same charges and often times they have two or more desertions and who only receive two years or two and a half years." "Sir," he went on, "taking all in all, I often ponder over this question of Court Martial and I humbly bow to the the majesty of the Law but at times I cannot refrain from exclaiming 'Oh God, this cannot be justice in a land where justice, right, and liberty are supreme.' "[65]

Nor was the problem confined to cases of desertion alone. In 1887, the New York *Tribune* published a special dispatch from Washington under the heading "Injustice in the Army—Widely Different Sentences for the Same Offense." The correspondent noted that there had been a great deal of comment in Army circles about the wide disparity of sentences for similar offenses and that there was general agreement that this represented a serious injustice to the soldiers. He cited two recent cases at Fort Sill in which one man was dishonorably discharged and given a two-year period of confinement in a military prison, and another just six months in a post guardhouse to return again to duty, for the very same offense. The correspondent reported that "more than one Army man" was convinced that a system that would permit such injustice to the enlisted man deserved "to be taken up by the roots and destroyed to prevent further growth."[66]

It was not only the inconsistency of the punishments inflicted by courts-martial that provoked sharp criticism. Even in those cases where the sentences for similar offenses were uniform, they were considered unduly severe. In the 1874 revision of the Articles of War, the punishments of branding, tattooing and flogging, already abolished by acts of Congress, were prohibited. Several articles authorized the death sentence, but the court, in its discretion, might impose such other punishment, limited by the customs of the service, as it deemed proper.[67] The Troy *Daily Press,* in 1892, expressed the view that the Articles of War inflicting the death penalty were contrary to "the genius of republican institutions." "The capital offenses," it went on, "read to the average civilian more as though they were enacted by the Russian than the American government. They are a scandal to our civilization." In the same year, an officer expressed disappointment that, from the viewpoint of humaneness, so little was accomplished in the revision. He felt that an opportunity had been missed to bring the discipline of the Army "into harmony with the advance of civilization," and that the work had been performed "with but slight conception of the true needs of the service." [68]

Early in 1883, the New York *Tribune,* among other newspapers in the city, commented on the "heavy sentence for a minor offense" imposed on Private Thomas Benson. This enlisted man was tried by a general court-martial in December, 1882, for repeated violations of the 32nd Article of War, governing absence without leave, and for the specific offense of having been so absent from November 26 to November 28. The other offenses for which he had been punished were included in the specifications. Benson was found guilty and sentenced to be dishonorably discharged, to lose all his pay and allowances, and to be imprisoned for three years at hard labor. In view of the fact he was serving his fourth enlistment and held three regular discharges, General W. S. Hancock, the reviewing officer, reduced the term of imprisonment to one year. "It is all well," declared the *Tribune* editorially, "to maintain strict discipline in the Army, but there is neither reason nor justice in punishing a man more severely for a trivial offense than if he had deserted outright. There are also grave objections to punishing even a soldier twice for the same fault."[69]

Several months later, Private Charles Rose sent a communication to General Howard in which he related his case and pleaded for consideration. He stated that on January 25, 1884, he had been tried by a general court-martial at Fort Omaha, Nebraska, on the repeated charges of absence without leave. He attributed his transgression to the fact that he had yielded to the temptation of drink, for which he was extremely sorry. He had pleaded guilty and had asked for mercy from the court. "I am now serving a three months sentence," he went on, "which will expire M[ar]ch 14th, 1884. From the fact that the back charges were brought up against me in this last case, I am afraid it would influence the court, and induce it to inflict a severe punishment upon me. I would respectfully ask the Dep't Comd'r if he deems it just to use these back charges against me. Also that in reviewing the proceedings of the court to deal as Lenient as he deems consistent. If I am fortunate enough to Escape severe punishment in this case I will promise future good behavior and perform the duties of a soldier."[70]

In December, 1884, the Kansas City *Times* reported the case of a soldier tried on charges of drunkenness, disrespect toward his commanding officer and disobedience of orders. The court, it said, found him guilty, and although he had served for two and one-half years without any trouble, he was sentenced to be dishonorably discharged from the service and to be confined at hard labor for a period of six years. "It is almost impossible to believe," the newspaper concluded, "that the Army contains officers who have so little regard for justice and mercy as those who compose the court before which the trial of this soldier was had. . . . As long as so little regard is had for the rights of men who happen to be so unfortunate as to appear before these military courts . . . just so long will they be looked upon with disgust instead of respect."[71]

Five years later, the same newspaper reported that a court-martial at Camp Pilot Butte, Wyoming, had sentenced three men to four years' imprisonment, although they had been absent from their command for less than twelve hours and had not been more than fifteen miles away from camp. The *Times* was at a loss to understand how officers could sit in judgment on the liberty of one of their fellow men and, without the least disturbance to their sense of justice and charity, impose so harsh a sentence. At about the same time, the House Military Committee listed the case of a recruit of one week's service who deserted from a recruiting depot and remained absent for about three months before surrendering himself. He was sentenced to dishonorable discharge and confinement in prison for three years.[72] Adjutant General John C. Kelton summed it up in his annual report for 1889 when he wrote: "Too harsh and unequal punishments awarded by courts-martial under the Articles of War and the customs of war, are undoubtedly too prevalent and frighten many good soldiers into desertion."[73]

The indiscriminate imposition of fines, coupled with confinement in the guardhouse, was also "a serious and much commented upon evil."[74] Punishment meted out by the minor courts was usually in the form of fines ranging from five dollars to a month's pay, or confinement to hard labor under the supervision of the post guard for a period of up to a month's time, or both. A soldier who made thirteen dollars a month was not likely to find the Army attractive when he was fined as much as ten dollars for failing to stand at attention, being a minute late for roll call, or because "the heels of his boots did not reflect his company commander's face at Sunday morning inspection."[75] It is not surprising that enlisted men came to regard a garrison court-martial as a body of officers whose sole function was to relieve them of a considerable part of their meager monthly pay. "Should a 'Bunky' steal from him," wrote one soldier, "he would immediately thrash Bunky or at least make an effort in that direction; but he cannot thrash the Government or a garrison court, and feeling his loss grievously, he deserts. On the borders, the land of Montezuma gains a citizen, and the United States loses a soldier."[76] Judge-Advocate General D. P. Swaim agreed: "The practice of imposing forfeitures of comparatively large sums of money, by sentences of court-martial, against the pay of enlisted men, is demoralizing in the extreme to the Army."[77]

The proceedings, finding and sentence of a court-martial did not become effective until they were acted upon by the reviewing authority— the commander who had convened the court. The sole exception was a sentence of death, which, in time of peace, could not be executed without confirmation by the President. The charge was voiced that post commanders invariably approved the findings of the garrison courts, either because they felt that a maximum sentence served as a warning to others, or, in some cases, because it was convenient to have a large working party available in the guardhouse. Captain S. W. Groesbeck, acting judge-advocate, Department of Dakota, wrote in 1888 that where a post commander was inclined to approve all cases, regardless of "the individual character of the man back of the cold record of the court," the administration of military justice became merciless, and the number of trials increased.[78]

If the sentence was disapproved by the reviewing officer, without remanding the record to the court for reconsideration and revision, the proceedings against the accused were terminated and he was ordered released. In many cases where the sentence was approved, the reviewing officer exercised his power to pardon offenders or reduce the punishment. The fact that a soldier had been held under arrest for an unreasonably long period before trial was often cited as a ground for the reduction of sentences. A reviewing officer did not have the authority to increase the punishment set by a court. However, when a court in his judgment appeared to have erred in any respect, the reviewing authority might reconvene the court for a reconsideration of its action, with suggestions for its guidance. A finding of acquittal could be returned for reconsideration. Similarly, a sentence could be sent back for revision upwards. Should it concur in the view submitted, the court could proceed to remedy the error noted, and might modify or completely change its finding.[79]

Prior to 1881, the proceedings of a court-martial could undergo only one revision. Thereafter, however, the reviewing authority was able to return the finding and sentence to the court as often as he pleased, and seek to have the original decision altered, even a finding of not guilty. In 1896, the *Army and Navy Register,* criticizing this procedure, noted that the reviewing authority, in requesting revision, often sent along elaborate arguments covering the merits of the entire case, which were reviewed by the court in closed session. The accused was excluded, had no knowledge that such proceedings were being held, and was given no opportunity to reply, explain or protest. "At this rate," the service journal concluded, "how long will it take to bring the administration of justice in the Army, through the medium of courts-martial, into utter contempt?"[80]

When a sufficient number of proceedings reached the reviewing authority to justify the issuance of an order promulgating them, such an order was published and sent to the troops. It was only then that the accused, still in confinement, learned whether or not he was guilty, and if guilty, the extent of his punishment.[81] One soldier wrote in November, 1866:

> Officers are trying to discover the cause of the numerous desertions from the regular service. Perhaps the following case may assist them to a decision. A private in my company . . . was placed in the guard house and charges preferred against him in May, 1866. Two weeks since the proceedings of the General court-martial in his case were published to the company. The court acquitted the prisoner. An innocent man confined seven months.[82]

A year later, another soldier described the treatment of prisoners at his post in Dakota, relating how it frequently took more than six, and often nearly ten months from the time the accused had been placed in confinement to the time he heard his sentence. He insisted it was enough "to crush the manhood of any man" to be confined for many long months and then discover that he had been found innocent or guilty of some petty offense for which he had already been punished ten times over what he deserved. "What is there left for him," he asked, "but to desert the first opportunity he gets?" And in the same year, an officer pointed out that as the law then stood, men were kept in confinement and at hard labor until the proceedings of a court were promulgated. "If it was only for a few days," he went on, "it would not matter; but where it is five or six months it is a great wrong, especially so where the prisoner had to wait some three or four months before trial."[83]

The revision of the military code in 1874 did not provide a remedy for this shortcoming. In 1878, an officer declared that men whom the officers at the post knew to be innocent, and who had been so adjudged by a court and by the reviewing officer, were working every day in company with convicted felons, until the verdict of their innocence might return from some distant city, releasing them from unjust and undeserved punishment. "This crying abuse," he concluded, "has existed too long already. It is contrary to every sentiment of right and justice."[84]

The soldier who was found guilty and ordered confined also suffered injustices as a result of these prolonged delays, since he did not begin to serve his sentence officially until the day the decision was promulgated in orders. The intervening time he had served in the guardhouse was, in many cases, lost to him.

A department commander might, at any time at his discretion, remit the unexecuted portion of the sentence of any soldier confined in his command if such sentence was imposed by a court-martial convened by him or by a predecessor in command.[85] The papers of General O. O. Howard contain numerous applications for clemency from wives of enlisted men confined in guardhouses under his command. In pathetic terms, the petitioners describe the hardships besetting them and their children. "I am the wife of John Mangel late Private Company E 7th Inf. now in confinement at Fort Omaha, Neb. under sentence for one year," wrote Mary Mangel on January 27, 1886 from Fort Fred Steele. She did not complain of the justice of the sentence, but begged the General to consider her case. She had been left with two infants, one eighteen months and the other four months old, and she was now penniless. It was only through the kindness of the commanding officer, who gave her quarters, and through the charity of some of the enlisted men at the post, that she was able to survive. Since her husband had forfeited everything, which she felt was sufficient punishment for the offense he had committed in a state of intoxication, her situation was now almost hopeless unless the General would have pity on this helpless family and restore to them their father and husband.[86]

There was no provision for a writ of error or for the appeal of a sentence of a court-martial. The Judge-Advocate General was expected to correct any irregularities in court-martial proceedings, but his duties, power and authority over these tribunals were not clearly defined by law. Where he found defects in the conduct of a trial, he was supposed to submit a report of the case to the Secretary of War, with such recommendations as he felt the interests of justice demanded. At that point, the functions of his office ceased. The President and the Secretary of War could reduce the sentences of military convicts, but they had no corrective power or authority conferred by law over court-martial proceedings, except where the court had been appointed by the President.[87]

There was considerable difference of opinion in the Army about the wisdom of having a separate legal department for the service. This department—the Bureau of Military Justice—had been created in 1862 and was retained in the reorganization after the war. It consisted of a Judge-Advocate General, with the rank of brigadier-general, and an Assistant Judge-Advocate General, with the rank of colonel. Together with the corps of judge-advocates, who operated under their general direction, these officers had the responsibility of providing legal advice to the military commanders.[88] In 1869, General McDowell stated that while the Bureau had been of benefit to the Army by "contributing a sort of code of practice," nevertheless, since the Judge-Advocate General was "more lawyer than soldier," many of his decisions had been harmful. But a correspondent, writing to the New York *Tribune* in 1873, insisted that the establishment of the Bureau had represented genuine progress. However, he went on, it functioned under serious handicaps. Proceedings could be revised only after they became *faits accomplis,* and its recommendations were not binding on the courts. "There are cases on record," he concluded, "where the Judge-Advocate General has shown that the judgment of the court was wrong; yet the court adhered to its findings, and its sentence was carried into effect."[89]

In 1876, the House Military Committee submitted to a number of officers the question: "Might not the Bureau of Military Justice be dispensed with, without injury to the service?" The responses revealed the sharp division of opinion that existed. On the one hand, it was contended that there was absolutely no need for a legal department in the

Army. The service had gotten along without one before the war, this argument ran, and it could get along without it now as well. The majority of offenses committed by soldiers, especially during peacetime, were easily handled by the military code and regulations. Moreover, it was said, the Bureau had been harmful to discipline, since few of its officers were familiar with the "customs of the service." It had done further harm by converting some valuable young officers into indifferent lawyers. Even if its members were competent lawyers, there would still be no use for it, for the judge-advocates selected for trials from among the officers of the Army performed better than those appointed from the ranks of the legal profession. What the Army needed was even-handed justice, not the tricks and subterfuges indulged in by lawyers eager to display their deftness with the law.[90] "Lawyers introduced in the Army," said General W. T. Sherman, "have not improved discipline or increased the measure of substantial justice." And Lieutenant-Colonel Richard I. Dodge, Twenty-third Infantry, insisted that the legal branch of the Army had done more to ruin the discipline of the service "than all the whiskey-sellers of the land." "It has added nothing to the dispensation of justice," he concluded, "and but little to the knowledge of law."[91]

But opponents of this view were equally vigorous in asserting that the Bureau and the corps of judge-advocates could not be eliminated without serious injury to the service. Their influence, it was argued, had greatly increased the knowledge of the principles of law among the officers, and for this reason alone, the Bureau had justified its existence. Moreover, the military code was a part of the law of the land, and there was no reason why it should be less governed by correct principles than the other branches. Indeed, in view of "the despotic character of all military institutions," a review of cases by competent legal authority was all the more essential. Otherwise, the military law would vary in practice with the peculiarities of opinion of a hundred different courts-martial and a dozen different military commanders. The officers of the corps of judge-advocates exercised this function of legal scrutiny, and it was on their professional advice that the department commanders acted. Without them, there would be no means whatever by which legal knowledge could be brought to bear in the examination of cases before the reviewing authority took action.[92] "This is a government of law," said General Albert E. Meyer, chief signal officer, "and in the Army, where especially law is too apt to be ignored or disregarded, competent law officers are, in my opinion, absolutely necessary." Major Samuel Breck, assistant adjutant-general, was convinced that the Bureau had rendered a great service to the Army in correcting irregular practices of the courts, and "especially in the care and pain taken that justice is done to enlisted men." And General W. S. Hancock echoed: "Inasmuch as the military is a more arbitrary and despotic system than the civil, so is uniform and even-handed justice more necessary in it. But we are far from securing it in our code, even with our judge-advocates. Without an efficient corps of them we shall be still further from it."[93]

The Army's legal department survived the attack of that year. In time, the name was changed to the Judge-Advocate General's Department, but there still remained a good deal of prejudice against specialized legal training in the Army. "I have long thought," observed General Howard in 1885, "and I say it without wishing to reflect upon the worthy officers of that department, that the special machinery of a department of justice could be dispensed with without detriment to the service. This would lessen the tendency to magnify the distinctive work of courts-martial which are a source of shame and disrepute."[94]

In July, 1892, the New York *Times* called for a board of review to examine court-martial decisions, similar to a court of appeals in civil jurisprudence. It felt that there was no more reason "for imputing special accuracy of judgment" to the military than to the civil court. While recognizing that there were reviewing officers who could reverse or modify a sentence, the newspaper felt that this was "not quite the same as another hearing and a regular presentation of the case."[95]

When the sentence of the court was confirmed and the convicted soldier finally began his confinement, he found further cause for complaint. Prior to 1875, when the United States Military Prison was officially declared "open for business," military prisoners were confined in penitentiaries, state prisons or post guardhouses. In 1862, Congress limited confinement in penitentiaries and state prisons to soldiers convicted of certain felonies. This was reinforced by Army general orders five years later, prohibiting such confinement "for purely military offenses."[96] In April, 1871, Judge-Advocate General William Holt stated in a decision that a sentence of imprisonment in a penitentiary for desertion was improper, since it violated the act of 1862. Nevertheless, a year later, Secretary of War Belknap declared in his annual report that the Department had been compelled, because of the absence of proper detention facilities, to confine prisoners guilty of purely military offenses in state prisons, where they were forced to associate "with the vilest felons in the country," and where they were subjected to humiliating and degrading treatment. "Many men," he concluded, "who might, under different treatment, again become useful soldiers, are thus yearly added to the criminal classes."[97]

In November, 1873, the *Army and Navy Journal* published a moving appeal from a correspondent in behalf of the thirty-two military prisoners serving in the state penitentiary at Huntsville, Texas. He had recently visited "that awful prison" and had personally witnessed "the terrible punishment dealt out there to our poor defaulting soldiers." He found them confined with assassins and murderers, "whose hands were still gory with the blood of their human victims." Various forms of torture were regularly inflicted on them at the whim of a guard, with the result that a two-year term became a life sentence.[98]

In the years after the war, most military prisoners served their sentences in the guardhouses located at military posts. These were usually single prison rooms which seemed to have been designed to make the life of the prisoner as uncomfortable as possible. Sanitary facilities and health conditions were often at the lowest level. The prison rooms were overcrowded, poorly lighted and ventilated, and so inadequately heated that during the winter the occupants suffered terribly from the cold.

There was neither a rehabilitation program nor any opportunity for recreation or education. Moreover, the guardhouse room was used as both a detention center and a prison, and there was no separation of the different types of inmates.[99] Major Thomas F. Barr, Judge-Advocate of the Department of the East, reporting on a visit to the prison at Castle Williams in New York Harbor in Janary, 1871, complained of the "promiscuous and indiscriminate confinement in large rooms of all classes and grades of offenders." Major Barr also noted that since all prisoners were assigned to the same type of fatigue duties—such as policing the camp grounds—the sentence of confinement at hard labor meted out to the more serious offenders lost its meaning and effectiveness. He concluded his report with the recommendation that a military prison be established for the confinement of soldiers sentenced to imprisonment and hard labor.[100]

There had been considerable agitation by military leaders for the establishment of such prisons since the end of the Civil War. In two consecutive annual reports, for 1867 and 1868, Adjutant General E. D. Townsend had called attention to the need for a better military penal system and proposed the establishment of several Army prisons throughout the country.[101] Supporting this proposal, the New York *Times* stated: "These military prisons promise so much good for the service that it is desirable that Congress should take early action upon the suggestion made by the Adjutant General."[102]

However, it was not until March, 1873, that Congress passed a law authorizing the Secretary of War to organize a mixed civilian and military board of five members to plan the establishment and administration of a federal military prison at Rock Island, Illinois. Prisoners were to be employed at such trades as were deemed suitable for their health and reformation, and the articles manufactured by them could be sold for the benefit of the government. The act also provided that prisoners were to be furnished with wholesome and sufficient food, good clothing, clean bedding, suitable ventilation and adequate bathing facilities, as well as with newspapers and books. In no case was any prisoner to be subjected to whipping, branding, or the carrying of weights. There was provision, too, for the restoration to the service of those whose conduct in prison merited it.[103] An officer writing to the *Army and Navy Journal* in February, 1874, greeted the new legislation in these words:

> Ever since my entering into the Army, the condition of prisoners sentenced to long terms of imprisonment in our post guardhouses had forced itself on my attention, and I hailed with joy the passage of this act as a step in the right direction at the hands of a humane government.[104]

Although Congress failed to make the appropriation necessary to implement the act, Secretary Belknap, on May 31, 1873, appointed a provisional board of three officers with instructions to visit the best state prisons in order to promulgate regulations for the new institution. This preliminary board was dissolved in October, 1873, at which time the mixed board authorized by Congress was established. The two civilian members—Rev. E. C. Wines and Z. R. Brockway—were leaders in the movement for modern penology in this country. They agreed to devote their time to board duties without compensation until the appropriation was made.[105]

In 1874, the law was amended to abolish the civil commissioners. In the same year, the location of the prison was changed from Rock Island to Fort Leavenworth, Kansas, and it was prescribed that buildings already erected should be modified for use by the prison. Secretary Belknap therefore visited Fort Leavenworth and selected three old stone buildings, then in use as quartermaster storehouses, to be remodeled as a prison, for which Congress appropriated $100,000. Finally, in 1875, the first United States military prison was set up at Fort Leavenworth, separate from the fort proper. As quickly as accommodations could be provided, long-term military prisoners were transferred there from the various penitentiaries, state prisons and post guardhouses.[106]

The prison was conducted in most respects like a state penitentiary, although entirely under military control. Very few prisoners were returned to the Army, for it was soon discovered that the original plan of restoring them to the service did not work out in practice. The policy, therefore, became one of teaching the men trades that would fit them for civil life.

The prisoners could reduce their terms by earning five days each month for good behavior. They were not paid for their labor. When released from prison, each was to be given five dollars as a start in civil life.[107]

The military prison proved vulnerable to attack from both outside and within the service. The industrial program created hostility among various groups of workingmen who felt that their conditions were threatened by prison competition. Nor was the prison a very popular institution among officers of the Army, many of whom complained regularly of what they considered the mild treatment of the prisoners at Fort Leavenworth. Indeed, there was a saying in the Army that the only soldiers who were well cared for were the inmates of the military prison and those of the national cemetery. Officers insisted that it was hardly conducive to discipline for "evildoers" to be sent at great expense thousands of miles to a military prison, where they were, in some respects, treated better than the members of the guard, leaving behind the dirty and disagreeable work of the military posts to be performed by "the well-behaved and faithful soldiers."[108] One officer observed:

> The prisoners are pampered, not punished in the way they should be. They are not made to feel that they are in disgrace and on their discharge they go back to their friends—as if returning from some honorable school institution. The Army is not intended as a reformatory for bad men. That duty rests upon other organizations in the community.[109]

This argument was rejected by the defenders of the institution. In 1886, Adjutant General R. C. Drum asserted that the true feelings of the prisoners toward confinement at Leavenworth were indicated by their persistent efforts to obtain release—that in that year alone, he had received over six hundred applications for clemency.[110] And three years later, Adjutant General John C. Kelton wrote:

> The statement which appears to be current in the Army that the prison service of deserters is made too pleasant at Fort Leavenworth, and that offenders prefer to be convicts to serving out their term of enlistment in the ranks, is, if true, a serious reproach to the officers of the post and companies from which they deserted; but as this statement is not borne out by any established fact, it is probably not true and does great injustice to the men who enlist, as well as to the government. On the contrary, every effort of the prisoner shows utter discontent with prison life and anxiety to either secure pardon or effect his escape.[111]

CHAPTER III

THE ENLISTED SOLDIER, HIS OFFICERS
AND THE COMMUNITY

Another aspect of military life during this period that aroused a considerable amount of concern had to do with the relationships between commissioned and enlisted personnel, and with what was generally considered the inadequate opportunities provided soldiers for advancement in the service.

The regulations prescribed that soldiers were to obey the lawful orders of their superiors. Military authority was to be exercised with firmness tempered by "kindness and justice." Punishments must, in all cases, conform to law, and officers were forbidden to abuse or injure those under them.[1] Orders issued by General Grant in 1866 called upon commanders of departments and regiments to carefully investigate the state of discipline and the treatment of enlisted men by commissioned officers in their command, "with a view to preventing harsh and arbitrary treatment and illegal punishments."[2]

There was no uniformity in Army discipline. It varied widely throughout the service, depending upon the individual characteristics of the officers who administered it. On the one hand, there were many officers who felt that in order to retain men in the service and make them function efficiently, it was necessary that they be treated with fairness and understanding. These officers were convinced that the performance of the soldier would improve as he saw that his officers were genuinely concerned about making his life in the Army as tolerable as possible. While they believed in strict discipline, these officers opposed harsh measures designed to impress the troops with the meaning of authority. They demanded maximum effort from those in their command, but behaved with restraint and allowed nothing to be done that would tend to degrade the men.[3] "The soldiers of this post," wrote an enlisted man from Fort Sill in 1875, "are especially favored by having officers who interest themselves personally in the welfare of the men—the commanding officer in

59

particular being always ready to extend every possible encouragement to the men in any sensible amusement." [4] Three years later, Major James S. Brisbin, Commanding Officer, Fort Ellis, Montana, wrote to General W. T. Sherman that there had been no desertions for a long time from the troops stationed at that post. He attributed this fine record largely to the manner in which the soldiers were cared for. While discipline was strictly maintained, he noted, the officers did not forget that "soldiers, like themselves, are men, and should have granted to them every privilege consistent with the good of the service."[5] And a correspondent from Fort Bliss, Texas, who signed himself "Perfect Bliss," reported in February, 1882:

> We have had very few desertions from here. The commanding officer, Colonel Pollock, is liked by the men, and no one can complain of the duty. About one mile from the post there are numerous saloons, but drunkenness is the exception, and we have rarely more than one man in the guardhouse at a time. Discipline is strict; but the men have many privileges.[6]

On the other hand, there were officers who believed that only the most rigid discipline could control the kind of men who made up the bulk of the Army.[7] In 1868, an officer admitted that many of his colleagues often risked their commissions by summarily inflicting such punishments as tying by the wrists and thumbs, "bucking" and "gagging," and even striking their men. He justified these practices on the ground that existing regulations and the long delays in court-martial proceedings left the officers no alternative if they were to have any discipline in their commands.[8]

Soldiers complained of the frequency with which their officers set aside the rule book and invoked arbitrary measures and punitive methods of punishment. In August, 1871, the *Army and Navy Journal* told of receiving reports of "illegal and unjustifiable" punishments inflicted upon enlisted men. Five months later, the *Journal* again referred to the numerous communications it had received complaining of the treatment of enlisted men at the hands of officers. On the basis of these letters, it said, it was impossible to doubt that there were officers in the Army who grossly abused their positions to the serious injury of the service. It cited a letter it had recently received from a discharged soldier as proof of the manner in which some officers callously disregarded the army regulations regarding the rights of the men. This man—an infantry soldier of two enlistments—told how men were sworn at, threatened, and even, on occasion, struck in the face by their officers, while unable to obtain redress for their injuries.[9]

In July, 1873, the *Journal* reported that it had received a copy of the proceedings of a court-martial convened at Fort McKavett, Texas two months earlier, in the case of Captain Theodore J. Wint, Fourth Cavalry, who was tried for "conduct to the prejudice of good order and military discipline." According to the finding of the court, this officer, annoyed at the conduct of one of his soldiers, handcuffed the man and had him suspended from a wall, keeping him in that position alone and unattended for forty-five hours, day and night, except for short intervals for meals. At the end of this ordeal, when the soldier asked for permission to visit the hospital for medical treatment, the captain refused, saying, however, that he might have a day's leave from stable duty to cure himself.

Captain Wint was found guilty and sentenced to be publicly reprimanded. In approving the proceedings and finding, General Christopher C. Augur, commanding the Department of Texas, condemned this "cruel, illegal and unnecessary punishment of a soldier." "What young man of spirit—the very ones required in the Army," he asked, "are going voluntarily to subject themselves to the possibility of being tied up and otherwise arbitrarily punished, on the mere whim and caprice of others?" The *Army and Navy Journal* approved of this reprimand, and went on to state that it was humiliating that General Augur had been compelled to impress upon his officers that they were under the control of law and authority—"as much so as the humblest soldier."[10]

Along the same lines, soldiers complained that company commanders too often appointed as non-commissioned officers men who did not hesitate to use the severest measures to keep the soldiers in line. As a result, a host of grievances arose against the conduct of these non-commissioned officers, particularly the first sergeants. They were accused of subjecting the men under them to all sorts of persecution with no recourse to justice.[11] After undergoing such treatment, the *Army and Navy Journal* declared in 1873, it was not surprising that soldiers should "finally forget their obligations and abandon the service altogether."[12] "Fully one-half the numerous desertions of our Army," wrote an old soldier in November, 1866, "are caused by the petty tyranny of non-commissioned officers." In October, 1867, another "old soldier" contended that the men were deserting in large numbers because they were treated "as dogs—spoken to like dogs, cursed at and sometimes kicked." During a long service, he went on, he had seen such things happen a thousand times and he could say without hesitation that "a large number of desertions are due to the rough-riding and unendurable tyranny of non-commissioned officers." [13] In 1872, General E. O. C. Ord declared: "The non-commissioned officer has almost entire and continuous control over the men, and if, as is often the case, these petty officers are bullies, drunkards, or tyrants, the men desert wholesale." And in 1883, Lieutenant Henry Romeyn, Fifth Infantry, related the case of a soldier being tried for desertion who offered as his defense the fact that he was regularly bullied and abused by his first sergeant. His requests for permission to appeal to the company commander were repeatedly rejected, and when he finally did appeal despite the sergeant's prohibition, he was denied redress "because he had come in defiance of orders." Witnesses corroborated his claim that the first sergeant had assured him that he could desert without fear of being hunted, while, if he remained, things would be made "hotter than h—l for him." Although he was not sought, he was accidentally recognized six months after he deserted and was sentenced to two years' confinement. "The man who drove him to the crime went unpunished," concluded Lieutenant Romeyn, "and out of seventeen desertions from the post (eleven of them from the same company) in a few months, five of those captured told similar stories, and with a fair show of truth."[14]

Enlisted men also complained that officers demanded from them the performance of duties that had no relationship to their position as soldiers.[15] In 1880, a soldier writing from Fort Assinboine under the name, "White Slave," told of the men in his company being assigned to work in their officer's garden, "digging like slaves," and added: "If any men taking warning by this letter and try to make a living in plain clothes instead of enlisting in the Army, the object of the writer will be accomplished."[16]

Before 1870, the regulations permitted an officer to employ a soldier as a servant with the latter's consent. Some soldiers complained, however, that they were given no choice in the matter and were compelled to perform jobs that were humiliating to them.[17] On February 19, 1869, the New York *Tribune* printed a communication from a deserter who charged that an officer of his company had had him imprisoned when he refused to serve as a menial, keeping him in the guardhouse without food until he was forced to yield. He concluded:

At times, I felt like dying—the situation was so humbling to me who went into the army for love of my country, only to have to black a brute's boots and look after him when a return blow was death. It was hard, harder than the charge on Wagner, where I was. Self respect was destroyed, it was misery. So, Mr. Greeley, I deserted, and glad I did it, and only sorry I did not do it sooner and defy the consequences.

In 1870, Congress declared it unlawful for an officer to use an enlisted man as a servant under any circumstances. However, soldiers complained that not all officers complied with this restriction. Officers, on the other hand, argued that they were left with little alternative, since they had to serve in localities where it was impossible to obtain civilians to work as servants for any length of time. They insisted, however, that wherever soldiers were so employed, it was with their consent, and that they were compensated for their work.[18] But the *Army and Navy Journal* saw no grounds for equivocation on this point when it declared in 1882: "The law forbidding the use of a soldier as a domestic servant should be strictly enforced, for nothing is more calculated to take all the ambition from a recruit and make him do as little as possible during the term of enlistment than to find himself turned into a lackey."[19]

Officers were also accused of failing to provide for the comfort and well-being of their men. Some were said to have no concern at all for the conduct of their company kitchens and mess halls. Others, it was charged, confined their contact with the men to visiting the company when it appeared for parade or inspections, communicating at all other times through their first sergeants.[20] A soldier of twenty-eight years' service wrote to the New York *Herald* in October, 1882: "Soldiers do not jump at conclusions, but they are certain of this, that were our officers as directly and as deeply concerned in the matter of soldiers' rations and cooking as the enlisted men, it would take but a short time to settle the question to the entire satisfaction of all concerned."[21]

The absence of officers from their companies on staff or other special assignments imposed an additional hardship on the troops. This was particularly true in the case of company commanders, who were responsible for the morale as well as the efficiency of the men in the ranks. A company deprived of the services of its captain for any length of time was regarded as an "orphan company."[22]

Paragraph 167 of the Army Regulations of 1881 provided that, except for unusual circumstances, captains were not to remain detailed to duties separating them from their companies for any considerable time. Nevertheless, in 1883, Adjutant General Drum reported that there were 102 line captains absent from their commands—nearly 24 percent of the whole number of line officers of that grade."There is scarcely any doubt," General Drum declared, "that the absence of captains from their companies, for long periods, leads to much discontent on the part of the men."[23]

If the absence of officers from their companies brought discontent, sometimes their presence had the same effect. Complaints were continually being heard about officers who lost their tempers, were high-handed and lacked any understanding of human nature. They would take delight in addressing their men in rude and insulting terms and would deliver all their orders in a bullying tone, as if a refusal, rather than obedience, was expected.[24] In 1867, an "Ex-officer," who was then an enlisted man, declared that the chief causes of desertion were "the inefficiency and unfitness in every respect of certain officers to command." Three years later, a reporter for the New York *Herald* stated that he had been advised by well-informed soldiers that the hostility toward the Army among the enlisted men sprang basically from the "tyrannical, rude, unsympathetic and insufferably snobbish" conduct of their officers.[25] In 1875, an officer declared:

> There is no small amount of damning and cursing enlisted men by officers, and if a few of this class could be brought before a general court and punished, it would do much good . . . . Because a man happens to enlist, it does not follow he has lost all his former spirit, and such tones and styles disgust him.[26]

And Samuel B. Holabird, assistant Quartermaster General, echoed in 1882:

> What chapter could be written about the soldiers' grievances without including the army cranks? We have known such severity that men dreaded a Sunday morning inspection more than they did an enemy . . . . Fairly good men, men of the greatest courage, have been driven to desertion and the life of a desperado . . . under the mistaken notion that Spartan discipline was thereby enforced.[27]

It was also noted critically that a company commander had the power to issue a discharge "without character" to any man leaving the service.

This type of discharge had exactly the same effect as a dishonorable discharge in preventing the reenlistment of a soldier and marring his subsequent career in civil life. Unlike the latter, however, it did not require a court-martial sentence.[28] "I have known cases," wrote Colonel Richard I. Dodge, "where really good men were discharged 'without character' by captains who allowed personal ill-feeling or the remembrance of some personal disfavor to stand in the way of justice."[29] There was no recourse against a company commander who gave a discharge without expressing the "character," since this was merely the opinion of the officer.

It is true that the 35th Article of War in the code of 1806 was designed to protect the subordinate officer and soldier from unjust treatment. It provided that any such individual who considered himself wronged by his captain or other officer could complain to the regimental commander. The latter was required to summon a regimental court-martial to hear the complaint. After the decision of the court on the merits of the complaint, either party could appeal to a general court-martial. However, the burden of proof rested on the complainant, and if the charges were adjudged "groundless and vexatious," he was to be punished at the discretion of the court-martial.[30] This provision was held responsible for preventing many soldiers from availing themselves of this regulation. In 1867, an officer complained that the article had degenerated into mockery. "If some more practical method of appeal cannot be devised," he went on, "it were better the inferior officer or soldier had none at all." Two years later, another officer declared that it would be difficult to find an officer in the Army who could not relate the injuries he had suffered from a superior officer, at one time or another in his career, and how he "bore his wrongs quietly rather than hazard the chances of redress under the 35th Article." And in 1873, the West Point correspondent of the New York *Herald* wrote:

> The soldier has no redress. If his persecutor is his captain he must appeal through him to the colonel; the captain sees the colonel first and explains the matter, and generally the enlisted man receives severer punishment for his folly. And when restored to duty from punishment the life of that soldier is hard indeed.[31]

When the Articles of War were revised in 1874, Article 30 of the revised code referred only to complaints of soldiers, and under it an enlisted man was permitted to make formal complaint of mistreatment by pressing charges against any officer. The procedure, however, was the same as in the past: the burden of proof rested on the complaining soldier and if the charges in his appeal to the general court were found to be "groundless and vexatious," he was similarly liable to punishment at the discretion of the court. Enlisted men complained that recourse to this article often "boomeranged" and was made the basis for charges against them instead.[32] In 1888, Captain S. W. Groesbeck, acting judge advocate, Department of Dakota, referred to "the unmeaning, because rarely used, thirtieth Article of War."[33]

Inspecting officers were required to announce at all posts they visited that the troops would be given an opportunity to present any well-grounded complaints without their officers being present. It was the duty of inspectors to investigate all such complaints and report on them. Soldiers complained, however, that the commands were too often "spruced up" for the inspecting officer's visit, and that the men did not feel free to air their grievances, since experience had taught them that they might have an even more difficult time of it after the inspector had departed.[34]

The army system of discipline was subjected to widespread criticism in civilian circles. In February, 1869, the New York *Tribune* called for a sharp reduction in the number of officers in order to protect the enlisted men. It referred to "a sickening list of abuses" in the Army on the frontier, and argued that a reduction by one-third of the officers would leave "a body having fewer members capable of such enormities." "We believe in taking care of the Army," it concluded, "but the first men in it to command our sympathy are the men in the ranks." And in May, 1872, the New York *Sun,* in an editorial titled "Desertions from our Demoralized Army," said: "In the West such are the barbarities to which the men are subjected that many of them, in preference to submitting, escape to the Indians, and fired by their wrongs, become worse foes of the whites."[35]

The application of the Army caste system was another feature of its social structure that produced a steady flow of critical comment. Obviously, no one expected equality between officers and men, but the complaint was constantly heard that a double standard of treatment existed. This was particularly true, it was said, in the matter of military justice.[36] It was charged, for example, that enlisted men could do nothing forbidden by the code without suffering severe penalty, while officers were apparently able to flout the regulations with impunity. In 1877, a noncommissioned officer, writing from Camp Douglas, Utah, said: "Cases occur daily, and are becoming too frequent, where the Regulations provide one law for both, where it is set aside in favor of the officer." [37] While enlisted men were punished even when they were only slightly under the influenece of liquor, intoxicated officers were said to be permitted to go on sick report without being charged with any offense. "I have seen officers more than once too drunk to perform their duty, go unpunished," wrote a first sergeant in 1867, "when the poor private would be fined and confined for the same offense, without fail."[38] The *Army and Navy Journal* asserted that such disparity of treatment could only serve to undermine the morale of the Army and injure its discipline, and went on:

> All the courts-martial, guardhouses, stocks and balls and chains in the world will not convince Private Brown that he ought to be punished for drunkenness when he sees Major Boosey and Captain Fuddleston going to their quarters at night from the post trader's store, arm in arm, and endeavoring to walk straight. No discipline, however strict, can knock the ideas of justice out of the American soldier's head, and discipline must suffer under such state of things.[39]

There was also the contention that there was a similar disparity in the treatment accorded the two groups when they were charged with offenses. An officer's pay continued from the time of the accusation until the sentence was approved, while that of a soldier was cut off as soon as charges were filed. Officers were not confined to the guardhouse as enlisted men were, but were placed in arrest in quarters pending trial. While a time limit of forty-eight days was set, within which an arresting officer had to be either brought to trial or released, no such time limit existed for enlisted men.[40] Judge-Advocate General D. G. Swaim regarded this differential treatment as "unjustly discriminatory." "I cannot understand," he went on, "why such a distinction should be made among any class of persons amenable to military law."[41]

In addition, officers were tried by their peers—fellow officers—but neither privates nor non-commissioned officers were eligible to serve as members of a court-martial. In 1873 and again in 1878, General E. O. C. Ord recommended a change in the military law so that two soldiers of similar grade would sit as members of the court in the case of a trial of an enlisted man, to aid "in securing a fairer trial for the soldier."[42] Advocates of this type of innovation noted that the practice had long been in effect in the German Army, where it was said to have functioned successfully. "That a man is entitled to be judged by his peers," said the Minneapolis *Tribune,* "is an essential principle of military justice, even in a country like Prussia, notorious for the stern discipline of her Army."[43]

The critics maintained that the discrimination carried over into the area of punishments, as well. "We all know," wrote an officer in 1867, "that courts-martial are as a rule lenient to officers." Four years later, another officer remarked sarcastically that if one were to judge by the decisions of courts-martial, the officers never offended while the enlisted men were all "dashed rascals." And the *Army and Navy Journal* felt that the Army would never be what it should until officers serving on courts-martial were governed only by a sense of justice, and, abandoning "class feelings and class interests," extended "impartial justice to all under the law."[44]

The absence of any social contact between officers and enlisted men was a subject of considerable controversy in military circles. There was no law or regulation forbidding such association; rather it was a matter of custom inherited, like many other features of the military caste system, from the English model. Many officers considered it necessary to insure the proper maintenance of authority. It was even defended on the ground that it furnished a protection for the enlisted men against the possibility of favoritism. Nor, it was argued, was such social distinction confined only to the Army—it existed in all walks of life.[45] A correspondent writing to the *Army and Navy Journal* in 1890 said: "God never intended that there should be an equality, nor will there be any more in the Army than in civil life." And the *Journal* itself declared:

> There is no throne and no aristocracy in this country, and no claim to superiority which anybody is compelled to recognize, but there are differences, and these differences divide men in the service as they do everywhere out of it. . . . The merchant does not invite his employees home to dine with him when the day's work is done, the bank president does not keep open house for his tellers and bookkeepers. . . .[46]

But there were military men who felt that even though there had to be a difference in status between the officers and enlisted men, to carry this to the extreme of absolute social separation was hardly conducive to either discipline or efficiency. They further contended that while the mili-

tary caste system accurately reflected the class distinctions of British society—after which it was modeled—it ran counter to the spirit of a de-
mocracy such as ours.[47] A correspondent who signed himself "Egalite"
wrote to the *Army and Navy Journal:* "It [the Army caste system] is
an exotic, evil growth and of blighting tendency, and I think its existence
in our Army helps to estrange the native-born citizen from its ranks."[48]

Newspapers throughout the country joined in characterizing the gulf
between enlisted men and commissioned officers as an affront to American institutions. The New York *Herald* said that the social line that sep-
arated privates from officers was of a nature "to effectually deter any
young man of self-respect from enlisting." The Chicago *Tribune* declared that the denial of protection and privileges afforded to officers
made the soldier "a slave," rather than a free man. The *Henry George
Standard* maintained that the distinction between officers and men in the
Army was essentially the same "as that made in the worst days of European monarchies between high-born nobles and base-born peasants."
And the Cincinnati *Commercial Gazette* called the gulf between officers
and men "as uncrossable as the lines of caste in India." "The German
Army under Imperial government," it concluded, "is a free and easy de-
mocracy compared with the Army of the United States."[49]

The difficulty in achieving a commission was also a source of complaint for enlisted men. The act of 1854 authorized the granting of commissions as second lieutenants to non-commissioned officers who were
found qualified upon examination by a board of officers. General orders
issued in the same year as the initial legislation directed that one-fourth
of the annual vacancies should be filled from among the non-commissioned grades. This same formula (after the assignment of West Point
graduates) was reiterated in an order of the Secretary of War in 1867.[50]

In spite of these directives, the number of enlisted men receiving commissions did not reach the 25 percent figure called for. Thus, from 1867
to 1878, exclusive of West Point graduates, 295 men were appointed
second lieutenants, of whom only thirty-six—about one-eight—were
promoted from the ranks, with the remaining 259 being civilians with or
without previous military service.[51] In 1872, General Ord stated that few
young men "of intelligence and ambition" enlisted any longer, since the
prospects of promotion from a sergeancy to a commission were "just
about none at all."[52] Soldiers complained that regardless of how long or
faithfully an enlisted man might serve, or how intelligent and capable he
might be, the door to a commission was virtually sealed to him. In 1871,

a correspondent wrote to the *Army and Navy Journal,* asking: "Is appointment to commission by enlisted men only a thing of the past, and is paragraph 77 RAR [Revised Army Regulations] only intended to gull the credulous?"[53]

Enlisted men also objected to the practice of granting commissions to civilians with little or no military experience. If West Point did not turn out a sufficient number of graduates to officer the Army, they argued, there were many capable soldiers who could better fill these vacancies than civilians, whose only qualifications for commissions often were their political friends in high places.[54] In November, 1874, the announcement of the appointment of a dozen civilians as second lieutenants brought a sharp protest from a non-commissioned officer, who noted the failure to include a single soldier on this list, despite the fact that it had been drawn up at the very time when the heroic deeds of enlisted men on the Southwest frontier were being praised. Almost three years later, another enlisted man inquired as to why the legitimate rewards due soldiers were being denied them and were being bestowed on civilians instead. "Let the giving of commissions to worthy enlisted men be a genuine fact instead of a dead letter," he concluded.[55]

In response to this sentiment, Congress passed the Act of June 18, 1878, providing for the promotion of meritorious non-commissioned officers to the rank of second lieutenant. This law stipulated that non-commissioned officers who had rendered outstanding service for at least two years should receive priority, immediately after the graduating class of the Military Academy, in filling officer vacancies. If any vacancies remained after these two sources had been exhausted, they could be filled by civilian appointments. Recommendations for promotions of eligible non-commissioned officers were to be forwarded from the company commander to the regimental commander, and then to the department commander. The latter officer was to convene a board of five officers annually for the purpose of examining the candidates as to their general fitness for advancement. The report of this board was to be forwarded to the Secretary of War by June 1st of each year. The general order implementing this law limited candidates to unmarried men between twenty-one and thirty years of age, and listed the subjects to be covered by the examination.[56]

The Act of 1878 was hailed as a genuine step forward in the effort to provide a means of advancement to men in the service. Every enlisted man, it was said, now carried a commission in his knapsack and could, if competent, rise to the highest grades in the service—provided the intent of Congress was fulfilled and external influences rejected. "There is sufficient ability, tact and experience among the enlisted men of the Army," wrote one soldier, "to fill all vacancies not filled by the graduates of the Military Academy. If there is encouragement so to do, the enlisted man will prepare himself for promotion."[57]

In 1880, Adjutant General R. C. Drum noted that the beneficial effects of the new law on promotions had already been demonstrated by the fact that a total of twenty appointments had been made of non-commissioned officers since it had gone into effect. "This powerful spur to the ambition of young men entering the ranks," he went on, "will tend to still further elevate the morale of the Army." Two years later, the *Army and Navy Journal* declared that the service now presented as good an opportunity "for the well-disposed young man as the average of occupations." And in 1887, the *Army and Navy Register* stated that it was now recognized that commissions could be won through meritorious service in the ranks. "It is well known," it continued, "that there are today many young men who are endeavoring to prove themselves fit for a commission by service in the ranks."[58]

The figures did show an increase in the percentage of appointments of non-commissioned officers. Thus, from 1878 to 1892, the percentage of such appointments from the ranks, exclusive of West Point graduates, rose to over 30 percent—123 out of a total of 366.[59] However, the contention was still heard that civilians were being favored over the men in the service. "I know as an incontrovertible fact," wrote Henry Schindler, the military affairs specialist of the Kansas City *Times,* "that appointments to the Army are often made at the solicitation of politicians—simply on the ground that friends must be gratified and that political capital may not be made from a refusal to comply."[60]

It was also charged that sons or relatives of officers and politicians, having failed to obtain commissions from civil life, would enlist in the Army for the sole purpose of becoming officers. If they could not secure a commission, they would use their influence to obtain a discharge. These were hardly the kind of men, the critics said, that Congress intended to reward.[61] "The present system," declared Secretary of War Redfield Proctor, in 1890, "gives a great opportunity for favoritism. Doubtless there have been cases of it, and there is danger that the abuse may become a serious one."[62]

The fact that eligibility for examination was limited to non-commissioned officers was also a source of criticism. Since opportunities for promotion to these grades were often limited, a large number of potentially qualified enlisted men were prevented from even applying for commissions. "Every man who commands troops," declared an officer in 1889, "is in favor of the abolition of this distinction, and to make this alteration would not only prove highly beneficial to the service, but would also bring it into far closer sympathy with the spirit of American institutions."[53]

If the soldier felt that he could look forward with little hope to a reward for his years of service while he was on duty, his prospects for a comfortable life after retirement were hardly brighter. Until 1885, the only provision made for the care of retired enlisted men was the Soldiers' Home in Washington, D.C., to which soldiers who had either been disabled in the line of duty or had served for twenty years in the Regular Army were admitted. This institution, which was established in 1851, had to rely for its support on funds contributed by the men themselves —through stoppages or fines levied against soldiers by courts-martial; through forfeitures for desertion; from the unclaimed estates of deceased soldiers; and finally, through a deduction of 12½ cents each month from the soldiers' pay.[64]

Enlisted men expressed indignation at being taxed to meet an expense that they insisted should have been borne by the government, especially since so few of them would ever have an opportunity to utilize it.[65] In 1878, a group of enlisted men asked that the money used for the Soldiers' Home be applied for their benefit in the service. Many officers agreed that such a step would make it possible for the men to enjoy decent quarters, libraries, gymnasiums, and better conditions generally, without any additional expense to the government.[66]

It was also admitted by officers that an important reason why so few soldiers reenlisted after their first term of service was the fact that there was no provision for a pension which would enable men who had served long and faithfully to live decently in their declining years.[67]

Except by death or the expiration of time, it was extremely difficult for an enlisted man to withdraw honorably from the service. Unlike the practice in European armies, there was no provision for the purchase of discharge. Honorable discharge prior to the expiration of the five-year term of service could only be obtained through a physician's certificate of disability, or by order of the President, Secretary of War, or the commanding officer of a Department, usually on the application of a senator or congressman.[68] In 1871, Secretary of War Belknap noted that the appeals to the Department for the discharge of soldiers were "almost numberless." In 1889, the *Army and Navy Journal* called for relief for "those unhappy Congressmen" and others who, it said, were pestered almost to death with requests to get friends and relatives out of the service.[69]

The few who were able to obtain their release by "pulling strings" only served to aggravate the discontent of the many who had no such influence. "Under the present ruling," said Colonel Richard I. Dodge, Eleventh Infantry, in 1887, "nothing is easier than to get into the service, nothing harder than to get out of it. . . . To the soldier, tired out and disgusted with the service, desertion now offers the sole means of escape. It is not a matter of marvel that desertion is common." Three years later, a correspondent to the New York *Times* wrote: "Desertion is not an honorable means of getting freedom, but in a great many instances men are actually driven to it, not having the influence necessary or grounds sufficient for the procuring of a discharge."[70]

When a soldier died in the service, a sum of $10 was allotted by regulation to provide for burial expenses.[71] To give a deceased comrade a fitting burial, therefore, the members of his company would tax themselves to permit the purchase of a better casket than the plain pine box furnished by the Army. "Only yesterday," came a report from Fort Leavenworth to the Kansas City *Times* in August, 1894, "the members of Company G, Twelfth Infantry, buried a comrade whose remains were placed in a casket costing forty dollars, not a cent of which was furnished by the Government, and this is the second death within the same company in less than a month. Here is a total of $80 taken from the pay of the soldiers of that company, certainly a severe strain. . . ."[72]

The combination of the physical and social conditions under which the Regular Army soldier served in the years after the war influenced the attitude of the public toward the Army as a profession. In 1883, the New York *Tribune* characterized the private soldier as little more than a convict who ran the risk of being killed, and felt that under such circumstances, it was not surprising that he should desert. "What is surprising," it concluded, "is that there should be any enlistments." Six years later, the St. Louis *Globe-Democrat* asserted that the record of 40,000 desertions in sixteen years, with peace prevailing, was sufficient evidence that there was something radically wrong with our military system. "It is not to be believed," it went on, "that such a large number of men would have quit the service in that way without strong provocation; and, indeed, there is plenty of testimony to the effect that desertion is often the only hope of escape from serious personal wrong and oppression."[73]

This feeling about the service was reflected in the view that most citizens held concerning desertion from the Army in peace-time. In fact, the sympathy of many people was so completely on the side of the deserter that they even assisted him in his efforts to flee the service by protecting him, despite the thirty-dollar reward offered for his apprehension and delivery. "If a soldier deserts near a town or settlement," wrote an officer in 1883, "you will hardly find a person who would not offer the deserter shelter and conceal him for the military authorities until all chance of recapture is passed."[74] Indeed, in many localities, the man who apprehended a deserter or furnished information leading to his arrest was regarded with contempt and the arrested party as a martyr.[75]

Military men expressed serious alarm over this public attitude. General John M. Schofield, Commanding General of the Army, in a letter to Secretary of War Redfield Proctor, wrote:

> Let the doctrine be inculcated that the obligation of the soldier is no greater than that of the industrial employee, that the former has as much right to quit his colors as the latter to go on strike, and who can tell when the emergency may arise which will appeal to the sympathies of the common soldier in favor of his brother laborers, when he will put in practice the doctrine taught him and join in the strike with his fellows to better their common condition.[76]

The attitude of the civilian public toward the military service carried over to its opinion of the soldier himself. In August, 1868, the *Independent* asserted that "a respectable American citizen" would no more think of joining the Regular Army "than he would volunteer for the penitentiary." In 1877, the New York *Sun* referred to the rank and file of the Regular Army as consisting of "bummers, loafers, and foreign paupers." Ten years later, the New York *Herald* contended that in the case of national need, the country could hardly afford to depend upon "the poor shiftless waifs" who had been compelled by desperation, poverty or shiftlessness to find refuge in the service.[77]

It was impossible for the soldiers to be unaware of or insensitive to these aspersions. In September, 1877, a veteran soldier wrote: "Let a regular soldier go into any of the cities of the states and you will see all the citizens stick up their noses." And in May, 1878, Private David Barrow wrote to the New York *Herald* from the frontier that no one was thought of as poorly in that part of the country as a soldier. "There are only two creatures who look upon a soldier here without scorn and contempt, and they are little children and dogs," he complained.[78]

There were some in the nation, however, who maintained that the proper target for such "scorn and contempt" was not the soldiers, who had performed every public duty required of them with honor and credit —but rather the inequities of the military system. Instead of complaining about the men in the Army, they said, a determined effort should be made to render the service more attractive to the man in the ranks.[79]

In the late 1870's, and throughout the '80's and '90's, such an effort was made. It took the form of a series of reforms and improvements in the conditions of military service for the enlisted men, which shall engage our attention in the ensuing chapters.

CHAPTER IV

THE ARMY REFORM MOVEMENT, 1880-1886

The years following the Civil War were marked by efforts on the part of Congress and the military authorities to institute reforms that would render the service more attractive to the men in the ranks. The progress made during this period—though limited—touched upon many phases of service life and laid the groundwork for the more significant reforms that were to follow.

This movement for reform was temporarily halted by the drive for economy and retrenchment that followed the panic of 1873, which was accompanied by a sharp decline in the number of desertions. These dropped from almost 8,000 in 1873 to less than 2,000 in 1876. Meanwhile, the number of reenlistments increased nearly threefold. In fact, as a consequence of economic pressures, so many men now sought to enter the ranks that it became necessary to place restrictions upon recruiting for the general service.[1]

Sober analysts realized, however, that this was only a temporary phenomenon, and that once the nation's economy improved, the problem of desertion would once again present itself. "It is generally admitted," said General Irvin McDowell in June, 1879, "that at no previous period have so many intelligent, educated and worthy recruits entered the service as during the last few years, and it is the duty of all concerned to try to make the conditions of the service . . . such that these men will cheerfully remain loyal to the Government they have sworn to faithfully serve."[2]

Starting in 1880, and largely as a result of the efforts of Adjutant General R. C. Drum, new attempts were made to improve the conditions of the enlisted men. To begin with, recruits were kept at the depots for longer periods, and were thus better prepared to assume their duties when they joined their permanent units. Under this arrangement, too, it was possible to discharge undesirable recruits or those who had been im-

77

properly enlisted before sending them to distant stations at considerable expense.[3]

The soldier's complaints about his clothing also received some measure of attention. The issue of the objectionable gray flannel shirts was discontinued. Helmets were substituted for the dress caps, and cork summer helmets were provided for men stationed in warm climates. In January, 1881, a general order was issued directing that certain specified articles considered necessary for the comfort and cleanliness of the men —clothes, hairbrushes, combs, towels, needles and thread—should be available for sale to the troops by the Subsistence Department at all military posts. At the recruiting depots, the newly enlisted soldiers were also able to purchase plates and cups, knives and forks, and buttonsticks and brushes. As soon as the provisions of this order were carried into effect, the practice of entering stoppages against the pay of enlisted men to reimburse post traders was discontinued. And in April, 1882, another general order provided that suspenders, handkerchiefs and toilet articles were to be sold to the recruits on credit at the depots by the Subsistence Department.[4] "In our young days," said the *Army and Navy Journal,* "the recruit was looked upon as an obnoxious animal . . . with no beneficent military authority to provide for his many wants down to a pocket handerchief. We live and learn."[5]

Some attempts were also made to render the soldier's life in garrison more bearable. In 1881, oil lamps replaced the candles in the barracks and reading rooms.[6] The *Journal* greeted this innovation as "a step from the dark ages towards modern civilization." And an enlisted man expressed his pleasure in verse:

> So if "fiat lux" the order is,
> And candles are shown the door,
> Round the bright kerosene twenty men will be seen,
> To one at the trader's store.[7]

Other efforts were made to improve the conditions of the enlisted men. They were encouraged to participate in sports, such as baseball, football and lacrosse. In 1881, the New York *Herald* reported that Colonel J. C. Kelton of the Military Division of the Pacific was taking steps to introduce "a series of athletic sports" throughout the division, and expressed the hope that these admirable efforts would, before long, be felt throughout the entire Army.[8]

One reform that was destined to assume great and even controversial importance dealt with the provision of a place for the men to spend their off-duty hours. In the fall of 1880, a group of officers at Vancouver Barracks, Oregon, conceived the idea of setting up an amusement center for the benefit of the enlisted men, patterned somewhat after the English canteen system. They obtained the consent of the post commander, Colonel H. A. Morrow, for this project, and on November 29, 1880, the center, which came to be known as the coffee canteen, was formally opened. It consisted of a reading room, a room for games, and a lunchroom—all decked out to present an attractive, home-like atmosphere—and it was received with such enthusiasm by the men that it soon became a model for similar centers at other posts in the Department of the Dakotas. Leading officers in that Department viewed it as a practical and valuable plan for meeting a long-recognized need in the Army—that of providing the men with some satisfying outlet instead of hard liquor and gambling.[9]

In several of the posts, temperance societies were formed. "The enlisted men of Company F, 17th Inf.," came a report from Fort Sisseton, Dakota, in January, 1881, "have reflected credit on themselves in their noble purpose of abstaining from the use of intoxicating liquors." And four months later, the surgeon at Fort Sully, Nebraska, reported that seventy soldiers there had taken the abstinence pledge and were holding social gatherings.[10]

The movement to promote temperance in the Army seemed to have received a powerful impetus by an order issued in February, 1881 by outgoing President Rutherford B. Hayes prohibiting the sale of intoxicating liquors at military posts and stations. The temperance adherents in the service hailed the order as "the greatest blessing ever bestowed upon the Army."[11] On March 10, 1881, the Cheyenne *Daily Leader* published a petition to the President signed by over two hundred enlisted men stationed at Fort D. A. Russell, Wyoming, asking that the order be continued in force "for the best interests and entirely in accordance with the wishes of the enlisted men of the Army." A correspondent writing to the Cheyenne *Daily Leader* from Fort Saunders, Wyoming, praised the men at Fort Russell for taking the lead in supporting the President's order and suggested that copies of the petition be printed and forwarded to every company in the department for signatures. He warned that the post traders would attempt to have the order revoked and that unless the enlisted men put up a strong fight, they would most likely succeed.[12]

This warning proved accurate, for the post traders, sensing the loss of a substantial source of income, launched a campaign to have the order completely cancelled, after having succeeded in having it clarified to permit the sale of light wines, cider, beer and ale. In November, 1882, all the post traders were circularized to contribute to a compaign fund for this purpose. After being given a schedule of suggested contributions, graded according to the size of the post, the traders were urged to prepare applications to the Secretary of War asking for "the revocation of the obnoxious order," if possible with the support of the post commander.[13]

However, it was not only the post traders who opposed the temperance order. Many soldiers insisted that it was unfair to impose total abstinence upon enlisted men while others were under no such restriction. And they considered it naive to assume that men who wanted to drink would be prevented from doing so by such an order.[14]

Events bore out this prediction, for the post traders soon added to their stock of allowable liquors an unlimited number of almost purely alcoholic preparations which they sold as essences, perfumes, patent medicines, and even as red ink. And as had been feared, too, the restrictive order was a virtual invitation to liquor vendors to set themselves up near Army posts and dispense "the vilest concoctions" of liquor to the men. Their establishments became a menace to the soldiers' health—both internally and externally—for the drunken brawls that took place there, complete with knives and pistols, resulted at times even in death.[15] In 1886, a correspondent wrote from Fort Bridger, Wyoming:

> The whiskey ranch located about three miles north of here was burned to the ground. . . . The burning of this ranch is the best thing that could have happened for the benefit of this garrison, and now all the companies are "present or accounted for" at reveille.[16]

The Army's system of trial and punishment was also affected by the reform movement. In 1880, a general order was issued decreeing that every regimental and garrison court-martial must have an acting judge-advocate, instead of assigning one of the members of the court to that function, as had previously been the case. A year later came another general order impressing upon officers the need for more careful inquiry into cases of enlisted men brought to trial for desertion. The point was made that the unauthorized absence of a soldier did not constitute desertion unless it was accompanied by an intention to remain away without returning. This intent must be proved in order to sustain the charge. "The entry on the descriptive list of a soldier that he has deserted," the order cautioned, "is not proof of the crime, but merely evidence that he has been charged with its commission." Judge-advocates were instructed to refrain from advising enlisted men charged with desertion to plead guilty and throw themselves at the mercy of the court, if they had simply been absent without leave and could present a reasonable defense. And in 1882, a decision was handed down by the Judge-Advocate General and concurred in by the Secretary of War, making it illegal for a soldier to be sentenced to carry weights.[17]

In spite of these modest advances, much still remained to be done to make life in the service attractive. This was brought home sharply by the fact that the number of desertions once again rose sharply. In 1880, the figure stood at just a little over 2,000, and Adjutant General Drum commented enthusiastically that desertions appeared to have reached an even level. But during the next four years, the number of desertions began to climb steadily, reaching a figure of 3,678 for 1884. In addition, the reports from recruiting stations indicated that the Army was finding it impossible to attract a sufficient number of acceptable recruits to make up its losses. In fact, because of the pressing need for men to fill up depleted commands, it even became necessary to abandon the practice of keeping recruits at the depots for longer periods.[18]

Some observers attributed this disappointing turn of events to the better times that had followed the temporary economic setback of 1880.[19] But numerous reports in both the service and general press placed responsibility for this reversal on alleged neglect and mistreatment of the men. "There is no end of the reports that began some time ago about dissatisfaction among soldiers," commented the New York *Herald* on August 27, 1883. A correspondent to the *Army and Navy Journal,* writing over the signature "Justice," complained that the decision making it illegal to sentence a man to carry weights was being disregarded, and that men at frontier posts were still being forced to carry logs weighing from twenty-five to thirty pounds, even with the mercury at 90 degrees in the shade.[20]

In May, 1882, the New York *Sun* sent a reporter to Fort Hamilton to ascertain from the soldiers themselves why so many men were deserting from that post. Soldiers informed him that they resented the way in which they were being treated by their officers, and that they were being used as lackeys, compelled to do all sorts of dirty work at the private residences of the officers.[21]

Three months later, the New York *Telegram* assigned one of its men to do a similar report on the Army post at Willets Point. After a careful canvass of the men, the reporter found that they were thoroughly dissatisfied with the poor rations, inadequate housing, overwork, persecution and lack of privileges—all of which, they said, served to make life at the post little better than imprisonment. There was also much resentment expressed against the officers, who were accused of treating the soldiers "more like dogs than men."[22]

The *Telegram* observed editorially that unless a remedy was speedily found to prevent desertion, "the standing Army of this country will be an institution of the past and will have died a natural death." At about the same time, the New York *Graphic* declared in a lengthy editorial that something had to be done to discover why men in the Regular Army were deserting every day, and so fast that it was impossible, at times, to get as many as a corporal's guard to represent a company.[23]

It was not only the press that was so deeply concerned with the increase in the number of desertions. Within the Army itself, the subject provoked the most earnest consideration. In no previous period in its history did the problem of desertion and the proposals for solving it receive such serious attention. It became the favorite topic of discussion within the service, figuring prominently in the annual Army reports and in articles and letters appearing in service publications.

Participants in this broad symposium were generally divided into two main schools of thought. One group felt that the complaints were gross exaggeration, that while there were defects in the service, they were easily curable, and that only the threat of the most severe punishment would serve as a deterrent to potential deserters. Their proposals for achieving this included increasing the reward for the deserters' apprehension, thus making capture more likely; confining them in post guardhouses at hard labor, instead of in the more congenial surroundings at Fort Leavenworth; and finally, causing their bodies to be marked indelibly with the letter "D" to prevent them from reenlisting in the service.[24]

On the other side were those who claimed that fear of punishment alone was not enough to keep a man in a service that he found both abhorrent and disreputable. Rather, they felt, the answer lay in eliminating those conditions and features of the service that bred desertion.[25]

These two points of view were brought sharply into focus in an exchange of letters in July, 1888 between General O. O. Howard, Commanding the Department of the Pacific, and Assistant Adjutant-General Colonel John C. Kelton. Replying to the former's request for permission to hire a civilian to apprehend deserters in the San Francisco area, Colonel Kelton expressed "the convictions of one who has made desertion and it causes and prevention, a serious study for years" that "the idea of *stamping* out desertion in the Army by *punishing severely the few deserters who may be apprehended* is utterly absurd." Instead, he said, "I would use every means to *remove the cause* of desertion." And he then proceeded to list a series of proposals that ranged over every phase of Army life: granting the soldiers "some right of appeal for the wrongs they daily suffer at the hands of their officers"; permitting them to claim their discharge after three years and to purchase it at any time, upon three months' notice; scaling penalties to fit the crime; improvement of the soldier's ration; and finally, abolition of the "iniquitous" and "corrupting" company fund.

If these provisions "for the welfare of the soldier" were made, Colonel Kelton said, he "would give not the slightest attention to the deserter —neither by offering reward for his apprehension nor sending anyone in pursuit." "In nine cases out of ten," he went on, "the deserter is not the proper person to arrest—it is those who compelled him to desert who should be arrested."[26]

Beginning late in 1882, and for several years thereafter, both the military authorities and Congress instituted a series of changes "for the welfare of the soldier."[27] This movement for army reform coincided with the civil service reform movement, which reached its peak during these years.[28] In November, 1882, a systematic attempt was made, for the first time, to investigate the subject of desertion. A general order from the Adjutant General's office directed that a Board of Survey be convened in each desertion case for the purpose of ascertaining the cause of the soldier's leaving. Enlisted men of his company were to be invited to tell all they knew about the the soldier who had fled and his probable reasons for having done so.[29]

Although this order was hailed as a genuine attempt to get at the root of the evil, the findings of the Boards were considerably less informative than had been anticipated. "The reports do not serve the purpose for which they were required," wrote Captain J. G. Ballance in 1889, "and have deteriorated into mere perfunctory and hence unreliable statements of opinion, and entail an amount of labor not commensurate with any supposititious results."[30] To some people, this failure was not at all surprising. After all, they said, the officers of the garrison who made up these Boards were hardly the persons best qualified to undertake such an examinatiton, since the findings might very well reflect on their own conduct.[31]

In February, 1885, Congress finally passed a retirement law for the enlisted men of the Army. Under its provisions, any man who had served thirty years could, upon his own application to the President, be placed upon a retired list with the rank held at the date of such retirement. The law further provided that the retired soldier should thereafter receive three-fourths of his pay and allowances.[32] The New York *Times* felt that Congress could hardly make better use of the public money. The *Army and Navy Journal* reported:

> The rank and file of the Army received, with unbounded satisfaction last week, the good news that at last provision has been made for them when their days of usefulness are passed. Faithful soldiers have now something to look forward to, and another inducement for the performance of duty during the allotted period.

And a corporal sent his "thanks for the retirement law" from Fort Laramie, Wyoming. "Its effect," he wrote, "will at once make itself manifest among all classes of honorable enlisted men. . . . A man who has served fifteen, twenty or twenty-five years need not look to a future which at best assumes the features of mendicancy, i.e., the Soldier's Home."[33]

Legislative provision was made, too, for the physical well-being of the men. A building program was inaugurated to convert temporary wooden structures into permanent barracks and quarters. In providing for the headquarters of the Military Department at Fort Snelling, Minnesota, Congress authorized permanent buildings of brick and stone. The same was done for the headquarters at Omaha, Atlanta and San Antonio, and at Forts Reno, Riley and Leavenworth.[34] The policy of gradually assembling troops in greater numbers and dispensing with small posts was pursued in earnest, and larger garrisons became the rule in a number of departments. In addition, the construction of several new posts, such as Forts Sheridan near Chicago, Logan near Denver, and Crook near Omaha, was authorized. In 1887, Congress appropriated over a half million dollars for the enlargement and improvement of military posts, and in the following year almost a million and a half dollars was made available for this purpose and for the general repair of barracks and quarters.[35] The *Army and Navy Journal* congratulated the members of Congress on their "more liberal spirit" toward the Army. "The new post," came a report from Fort Robinson, Nebraska, in 1887, "would strike with astonishment the visitor to the wretched frontier garrison of years ago."[36]

In January, 1887, the Army and Navy General Hospital was opened at Hot Springs, Arkansas, with eighteen beds for officers and sixty-four for enlisted men. Several months later, Congress provided for a hospital corps to be made up of men specially trained for this work. The recruit for the corps was to be selected and enlisted by the medical officer, or transferred from the line upon application by the medical officer. He was then to be sent to a post or company of instruction for drill, discipline and education. Two companies of instruction were provided for—one at Fort D. A. Russell, Wyoming, and the other at Fort Riley, Kansas. Here, all were set up as soldiers and taught the practical details of first aid to the wounded and the principles of nursing.[37]

In 1884, a *Soldier's Handbook,* prepared under the supervision of Adjutant General Drum, was issued to the enlisted men. It contained extensive extracts from the Regulations and Articles of War, indicating what was required of the soldier under his contract of enlistment. "This compact and useful volume," said the *Army and Navy Journal,* "ought to be appreciated by the rank and file of the Army and is a step in military education not to be underestimated."[38]

In July, 1887, a system of monthly payments was inaugurated by the Paymaster-General at twenty-five posts. The posts selected were those in the vicinity of the paymasters' stations and were chosen because the additional payments could be made at no appreciable extra cost. In the succeeding years, this system was extended to more isolated posts, and by 1891, the list had been increased until it embraced seventy-six military posts.[39] This change in the method of paying troops met with widespread approval. "The good effects of monthly payments to troops," said the Leavenworth *Times* in February, 1888, "are shown by the fact that out of a garrison of more than 500 men (at Fort Leavenworth) not a single man has been confined to the guardhouse for disorderly conduct or drunkenness. This one thing alone speaks volumes for the changes from bi-monthly to monthly payments."[40]

A great boon to the enlisted soldier in this period was the appointment of Samuel B. Holabird as Quartermaster-General on July 1, 1883.

During the time that he served in this capacity, he did much to improve the condition of the soldiers. He was instrumental in introducing a number of changes in various articles of clothing and equipment. The range of sizes of trousers and blouses was increased. Interlined canvas overcoats, caps and gloves, arctic overshoes and woolen mittens were issued to the men at Northern posts. Suspenders, fatigue jackets and trousers were added to the clothing allowance. A sewed shoe of two kinds, one for dress occasions or garrison duty, and another for active service in the field, replaced the unpopular brass screwed shoes, and sewed boots of a revised pattern were issued to mounted men. Overcoats were improved in style and were provided with detachable hoods. Barracks bags, made from dyed shelter tents, were issued to the men.[41] During the next two years, other "radical reforms" were made in the matter of soldiers' clothing. "The clothing now issued to the enlisted men," wrote one soldier in 1887, "is good in quality, ample in allowance, and at the rate our Quartermaster General is improving it, it will soon fit."[42]

In 1885, the enlisted men at the San Antonio post were authorized to wear white linen trousers on guard and parade, as well as on fatigue duty. A year later, permission was granted to all enlisted men to wear straw hats of a type to be prescribed by their department commanders when off duty, on fatigue duty or at target practice. And the following year, white linen collars were distributed among the men to be worn with their uniform dress coats. These were not added to the supply table, but an arrangement was made whereby the soldier could buy them from the government at about nine cents apiece, instead of paying the post trader more than three times that amount.[43] And finally in 1888, General Holabird announced that cotton duck clothing would thereafter be issued to troops in the Departments of Texas and Arizona. The New York *Times* welcomed this announcement as "a successful grapple with conservatism."[44]

General Holabird also tried to achieve greater comfort for the soldiers in their quarters. Army bunks were equipped with wire mesh springs— a decided improvement over the old-style slats. Mattresses, hair pillows, sheets and pillow cases replaced the hay-filled bed sacks and pillows, while lockers were furnished in which men could store their belongings; and chairs and tables were provided for their further convenience. The sanitary condition of a number of military posts was improved by the introduction of steam laundries, as well as improved water and sewage systems. At several stations, facilities were provided for year-round bathing.[45]

In June, 1890, General Holabird was retired from active service. The Kansas City *Times* expressed the feelings of many in and out of the service when it wrote: "The years during which General Holabird occupied the important post of Quartermaster-General were fruitful of many reforms in the Army."[46]

Another source of general dissatisfaction in the ranks was removed in January, 1889, when a general order from Army Headquarters abolished the post and regimental funds. The Quartermaster Department was now charged with the duty of buying books, papers and periodicals for post libraries, and instruments for regimental bands.[47]

The operation of the recruiting service was also subjected to careful examination. In 1884, an order was issued directing all recruiting officers to demand that applicants for enlistment present evidence of good character and information about their employment during the six months preceding their enlistment. If a recruiting officer had any reason to question an applicant's character, he was authorized to reject him. All men who looked as if they were hard drinkers were to be turned down.[48] The Kansas City *Times* greeted this directive as a significant reform, stating: "It is much better to enlist one out of every twelve that presents himself, than to enlist eleven who will desert shortly after."[49]

In October, 1889, a general order was issued further amending the army regulations relating to enlistments. Recruiting officers were now required to obtain an authentic personal history of every candidate. After an applicant had passed the medical examination, he was to be retained on probation for six days at the recruiting station. During this time, the recruiting officer was required to look into his background and to reject him if the investigation showed that he was not fit to become a soldier. Great care was to be taken to prevent the enlistment of minors without the consent of their parents, as well as of men who had families dependent upon them for support. A later order required that recruits be kept at depots for four months after enlistment. Commanders of the several depots were instructed to show special consideration to recruits at the outset of their military careers. The manner of conducting recruits to their new stations was also improved by requiring that an officer from the post where they were to be stationed accompany them to their destination.[50]

Steps were also taken by military commanders to revise the Army's judicial system. In orders from headquarters appointing general courts-martial, authority was almost invariably given to the court to "sit without regard to hours."[51] In 1883, General C. C. Augur, in command of the Department of Texas, set forth a scale of punishments as a guide to officers serving on courts-martial in his Department. This was a step toward standardizing punishment for similar offenses and had an immediate salutary effect. Two years later, the same officer attracted attention by his disapproval of a court-martial sentence which prescribed the punishment "walking in a ring twenty feet in diameter while carrying a log weighing twenty pounds." "Such punishment," declared the General, "is a great waste of manpower; something useful ought to be found for prisoners to do instead of such idle exercises."[52]

In 1884, a general order was issued which directed that the sentence of a court-martial involving confinement should be considered as beginning from the date of the promulgation of the sentence in orders, unless otherwise stipulated by the court or the reviewing authority. A year later, a new rule was introduced requiring that men be recorded as having deserted only after they had been absent for at least ten days, unless the company commander had conclusive evidence of the absentee's intention not to return. Thus, a soldier who had stayed away for a few days on a spree was now able to return to duty without inviting a possible charge of desertion.[53]

In 1886, the War Department issued an order forbidding the confinement of a soldier except on the order of an officer who had previously inquired into the offense. Post and company commanders were cautioned to use careful judgment in bringing cases to trial. Also in 1886, a general order advised judge-advocates that evidence of previous convictions could only be introduced after a decision had been reached on the particular charge before the court, and then only to determine the amount and nature of punishment.[54] The *Army and Navy Register* considered this a step of great importance which demonstrated that "the spirit of reform" had entered an area where many changes were needed.[55] In the following year, judge-advocates were informed that they must advise accused soldiers of their right to testify under oath in their own behalf. In that year, too, the Judge-Advocate General decreed that soldiers arraigned before general courts-martial should not, except for compelling reasons, be tried by fewer than thirteen officers. It was felt that the rank and diversity of views of that number might further the impartial administration of justice.[56]

In May, 1888, the War Department ordered that men confined in the guardhouse while awaiting trial by courts-martial were not to be sent out to work with prisoners serving sentences. And on July 6, 1889, a general order was issued which stated: "That the proper amount of punishment is the least amount by which discipline can be efficiently maintained, is a principle of recognized validity in the administration of military justice." It further stipulated that punishments for the same offense should be uniform and "without vindictiveness."[57]

In 1886, Lieutenant Colonel W. Winthrop, Deputy Judge-Advocate General, published his important book entitled *Military Law*. The *Army and Navy Register* said that such a work had long been needed, for it detailed the growth of "our military jurisprudence" in the years since the war. It urged that "this admirable work" be placed in the hands of every Army officer. On March 27, 1886, the Sidney (Nebraska) *Telegraph* reported: "The officers at Fort Sidney meet daily and devote an hour to the study and discussion of military law, taking as a text Winthrop's treatise on military law, a recent work, which is esteemed as of great value to the military profession."[58]

In July, 1887, a pamphlet was issued from the headquarters of the Department of the Platte, which contained valuable information for courts-martial and judge-advocates. The publication was prepared by Lieutenant Colonel Thomas F. Barr, Deputy Judge-Advocate General. A year later, Captain Arthur Murray, Acting Judge-Advocate of the Department of the Missouri, prepared a 72-page pamphlet with "some excellent instructions" for courts-martial and judge-advocates which General W. Merritt had published for the officers of that Department.[59]

Attention was also directed toward rendering life at the military posts less monotonous and more attractive. In March, 1889, a revised edition of the Army Regulations was issued, Paragraph 160 of which prohibited commanding officers from employing troops, when not in the field, as working parties or on chores that interfered with their military duties, except in cases of necessity. On June 18, 1889, an allowance of tableware and kitchen utensils, provided for under Paragraph 277 of the new regulations, was officially announced in a general order issued to the troops.[60]

The time schedule for events making up the soldier's day was also revised. Tatoo roll call, which required that the men stand formation at 9 p.m. each evening and which was a long-standing "gripe," was abolished. Unless detailed for duty, they were free from the time of retreat until 11 o'clock.[61] To the Kansas City *Times,* the new directive furnished striking evidence of the march of reform in the Army. "Let the good work go on," it earnestly appealed.[62]

Amateur theatricals and minstrel performances were frequent occurrences at a number of posts during the fall and winter months. Gymnastic exercises, field sports and athletic games were encouraged. "There is no greater safeguard against the breaches of discipline," commented General Howard in 1886, "than to create for the men, when not occupied with their duties, means of harmless amusement and recreation."[63] A report to the *Army and Navy Register* in 1886 paid tribute to Lieutenant M. O. Parker, Ninth Cavalry, for his initiative in organizing a brass band at Fort Washakie, Wyoming, as a means of enabling men "to while away the long winter evenings and break the monotony of garrison routine." "Taken all together," the correspondent concluded, "it is another evidence of the fact that any effort made toward an amelioration of the condition of our soldiers, who are thus placed so many miles from civilization, will receive its suitable reward."[64]

Whenever the transportation fund permitted it, regiments so entitled were given a change of station. During the month of June, 1884, the Twenty-third Infantry left New Mexico for the Department of the East and was replaced by seven companies of the Tenth Infantry. In the same year, there was a change of station for nearly all the troops in the Department of the Columbia. On June 26, 1884, the Vancouver *Independent* described the departure of the Twenty-first Infantry in these words: "The band played once more one of its best pieces and then the crowd dispersed, the people having by words expressed their kindly regard for the Twenty-first, from which they part with regret."[65]

In 1885, the Second U.S. Artillery was ordered south to the Gulf coasts and the Third Artillery took its place in the Department of the East. The Fifth Cavalry went to the Department of the Missouri, taking the place of the Ninth Cavalry, which went to the Department of the Plate. "We are glad to see," said the *Army and Navy Journal,* "the 'Army Transportation' appropriation put to such good uses."[66] On July 21, 1886, Cheyenne *Daily Leader* reported:

> The Ninth Infantry left this morning on two immense trains for New Mexico and Arizona. A thousand people were at the depot to see the regiment off. It has been stationed here for seventeen years. . . . Many members of the regiment married in this city. The part-

ing of the people and soldiers was touching. The band played "Auld Lang Syne."[67]

In 1888, the most elaborate "house moving" in years was undertaken by the Army. It included all regiments which had not had a change of station for seven years. Some of the transfers involved journeys from the Atlantic to the Pacific, and from the Northern territories to the Gulf. Units that had served for years in Texas and Arizona were shifted to the Dakotas, Colorado and Montana, while those which had been stationed in the regions of the blizzards were sent to Texas and Arizona.[68]

In February, 1889, the system of Army education received a decided stimulus with the issuance of regulations requiring the establishment of schools at every post. Attendance at these schools was made compulsory for men in their first enlistment and for those in their second enlistment who did not have an elementary education. The privileges of the schools were also extended to those older soldiers who desired to take advantage of them. Time devoted to instruction was to be taken from that allotted to military duties. Commanding officers were urged to encourage attendance at school, and Adjutants-General of Departments were directed to render annual reports "setting forth specifically the failure or neglect of any post commander to take interest in or facilitate the operations of the schools." This was followed in 1890 by the granting of an allowance for text books, maps, globes and school supplies.[69]

An even more drastic change was heralded in March, 1889 with the report that the new Secretary of War, Redfield Proctor, was preparing a General Order which would abolish Sunday inspections and dress parades in the Army. The news of the projected change aroused strong opposition from a number of prominent officers who felt that a day of leisure at military posts would do more harm than good. General Sherman, although on the retired list, thought it a matter of such importance that he lodged a vigorous protest. However, Commanding General of the Army John M. Schofield favored the change, and Secretary Proctor therefore submitted the proposal to President Harrison.[70] It was issued on June 8, 1889 as a Presidential Order. As such, it would be difficult for a future Secretary or officer in command of the Army to revoke it. By this order, the customary weekly inspection was shifted from Sunday to Saturday morning. Saturday afternoon was made a half-holiday to be devoted to sports and recreation. No work was to be performed on Sunday other than guard and police duty.[71]

Another significant development during this period was the extension of the canteen system to many new posts. On December 15, 1884, an amusement center was opened for the troops at Fort Sidney, Nebraska, largely as a result of the efforts of the post commander, Colonel H. A. Morrow. Coffee, sandwiches and other light refreshments were sold at low prices, and thereafter, the sale of beer in limited amounts was permitted. Billiard tables, games of all sorts, books, newspapers and magazines were provided, and a band furnished music three evenings a week. By November, 1886, the profits accruing from the operation of the canteen reached the sum of $3,000. This money was applied to furnishing the canteen, replenishing the stores, paying attendants, making company quarters more comfortable, helping the band, and subsidizing entertainment at the post. But the most noteworthy achievement of the caneen was its effect on the morale of the men. In the five and one-half months preceding the opening of this center, there had been 193 confinements in the post guardhouse. For a similar period immediately following its opening, there were only seventy-three confinements—a drop of 62 percent.[72]

The successful operation of the canteen at Fort Sidney led to the establishment, in 1886, of similar centers at a number of other posts in the West, as well as at David's Island, New York and Columbus Barracks, Ohio. However, the War Department had not yet expressly authorized the canteens; it had only allowed them to exist without specific authority. It was becoming clear that, sooner or later, a definite attitude would have to be taken, for the two establishments—the canteen and the trader's store—could not flourish side by side.[73]

In July, 1888, the canteen suffered a setback when Secretary of the Treasury A. S. Fairchild ruled that canteens selling tobacco, cigars and malt liquors were liable for the federal tax imposed on these articles, even though their sale was restricted to enlisted men. It was further ruled that the canteen did not come under the provisions of the law authorizing the purchase of supplies at cost from the Subsistence Department.[74] But the severest blow came three months later, when the War Department issued an order forbidding the sale of wine, beer or other alcoholic beverages in canteens, and directing that they be conducted so as not to infringe upon the vested rights of the post traders. The latter were to retain the exclusive privilege of trading at posts where they had been appointed.[75] Many officers protested this directive bitterly, claiming that wherever the canteens had been adopted, drunkenness had decreased and discipline had improved markedly. They urged the War Department to rescind the restrictions on the canteens. "Breaking up the canteen," wrote an officer from Fort Robinson, Nebraska, "has sent the garrison back to the old pay day times, filling the guardhouse to the utmost capacity."[76]

In response to these protests, the War Department initiated a thorough investigation into the respective merits of the two systems. Department and post commanders were asked to submit reports on the subject, and the Department finally decided early in 1889 in favor of the canteen. The license of the post trader was to be revoked if this should be found desirable, after an adequate opportunity had been afforded him to dispose of his stock and fixtures. At posts where no post trader was established, the canteen was authorized forthwith.[77]

On February 1, 1889, rules and regulations for the establishment and operation of post canteens were issued. They set forth the purpose of canteens—to supply the troops with articles for their use, entertainment and comfort, at moderate prices, and to afford them facilities for recreation and amusement. The sale or use of hard liquor in canteens was strictly prohibited, but commanding officers were authorized to permit light wine and beer to be sold, in order to discourage the men from seeking intoxicants outside the post. No liquors of any kind were to be sold to an intoxicated person. Gambling was strictly forbidden. Each canteen was to be managed by an officer assisted by one or more enlisted men. A committee of commissioned officers, or "canteen council," was to supervise all the affairs of the canteen and to submit a monthly report on its operations. The regulations also required semi-annual reports regarding the functioning of the canteen, together with critical comments of the post commanders. Profits accumulating after authorized expenses had been met were to be distributed among the several companies and detachments contributing to the canteen, to be used as part of the company funds.[78]

The first semi-annual reports of the canteens were uniformly favorable and confirmed the wisdom of the War Department's action in fostering their extension. On September 27, 1889, the Army Regulations were modified to deprive post traders of the exclusive trading rights they had previously enjoyed on the reservations to which they had been appointed. The canteens were now permitted to make sales at cost of all commodities required by officers and soldiers, thereby cutting off the traders from the profitable sale of staple articles. At the same time, their right to sell light wines and beer was restricted to sales in unbroken packages, thus ending their retail traffic in alcoholic liquors. This last provision was practically a death blow to the traders, for with the growth of new towns in the vicinity of Army posts, the business of the post trader had fallen off to a point where his revenue was derived largely from his license to sell beer and wine.[79]

The order was greeted with widespread enthusiasm in the ranks of the Army. "The canteen system has come to stay," wrote one soldier, "and slowly but surely we are progressing to a condition of things when the enlisted man will not have to pay through the nose for every article he is obliged to purchase at the post." And the *Army and Navy Journal* echoed: "The sooner the canteen system is made universal throughout the Army, the better."[80]

The canteen now had every advantage, including the open support of the War Department, free buildings for its use and the wholehearted backing of the members of the garrison. Where the canteen flourished, the trader's store declined and usually disappeared. By January, 1890, fifty-seven canteens were operating successfully in the Army and the institution could be regarded as permanently established.[81] "Less than a year has elapsed since this new policy was announced," said the New York *Times*, "yet canteens have already been established at a great many posts and are steadily increasing in number." An enlisted man at Fort McKinney, Wyoming, described the satisfaction of the soldiers at his post over the successful operation of the canteen in these words: "Soldiers are human, and something must be done to appeal to their humanity, and this allowing them to get together for amusement is a part of this humanity."[82]

Those who advocated the introduction of the canteens, as well as of all the other Army reforms instituted in this period, were considerably encouraged by the fact that during 1885 and 1886, there was a gradual decrease in the number of desertions—from the unusually large total of 3,672 for 1884 to 2,927 for 1885 and 2,090 for 1886.[83] The New York *Sun* called this "the most promising feature in the current condition of the Army," and the New York *Times* hailed the figures as "most remarkable."[84]

In military circles, this gratifying development was attributed in great measure to the efforts that had been made to improve the conditions and prospects of the enlisted men. An officer writing from Fort Sill, Oklahoma, commented enthusiastically on the feeling of cheerfulness and satisfaction that now prevailed among the men there. "The experience of this post," he went on, "goes to show that it pays the Government to make the enlisted men comfortable in their quarters and surroundings. . . . In this respect the soldier is like a domestic animal—the better cared for, the more efficient and willing he becomes."[85] Adjutant General Drum commented in 1886: "I have no doubt that this great decrease since 1884 . . . is not a mere coincidence but evidence that the Army at large recognizes and appreciates the active interest in their behalf by the constituted military authorities and Congress." And the *Army and Navy Journal* observed: "Desertion is now on the decrease and the many inducements now held out to faithful service are slowly but surely achieving the desired result."[86]

CHAPTER V

THE ARMY REFORM MOVEMENT, 1887-1892

It is one of the ironies of the history of the Army in the post-Civil War years that whenever its authorities began to congratulate themselves upon their success in combatting the problem of desertion, the pendulum swung in the opposite direction. The period following the reforms instituted in the 1880's was no exception, for no sooner had the press and the military finished proclaiming the beneficial effects of these changes than the number of desertions began once more to mount. This rise began in 1887, and by the end of the fiscal year, June, 1889—a three-year period—the number had risen by almost a thousand to a figure of 2,835.[1]

Keen disappointment was expressed both inside and outside the service over the fact that the encouraging developments of the previous two years had not continued, and that all the intensive efforts to improve the welfare of the enlisted men had not provided a lasting solution to the Army's most vexing problem. The New York *Tribune* found it difficult to understand why, despite the many reforms that had been instituted for the benefit of the men, there should still be nearly three thousand desertions in a single year. "There can be no doubt of the desirability, if not the necessity of some action by Congress," it concluded. And an officer complained bitterly that unless some means were found to bring these recurrent waves of desertion to an end, the Army would "soon be in such bad odor as to stink in the nostrils of the whole nation."[2]

As always happened when the desertion rate took a turn for the worse, discussions of the problem and its remedies once again engaged the attention of the country as a whole, no less than the Army. In nearly every issue, service journals and other periodicals featured the views of both military men and civilians on this subject. As usual, too, these views presented a varied picture of the reasons why desertion still plagued the Army authorities.[3]

Some felt that the increase was merely proof that the country was prosperous again, and enjoying full employment. Thus, "one of the high officials of the War Department" was quoted in the St. Louis *Globe-Democrat* in November, 1889 as saying ruefully that "while the Army may well regret the increased desertions as a means of reducing its efficiency, the people of the United States have cause for congratulation." On the other hand, if times were hard and workingmen found it difficult to make a living, they would be willing to endure the discipline and rigors of Army life in return for shelter, clothing, food and pay. "If we had a panic in this country," he went on, "and hard times were pressing upon every branch of industry, the Army would find an abundance of recruits."[4]

However, there was a considerable body of thought, particularly among the officers, which held that neither economic conditions nor reforms could strike at the root of the desertion problem—the hard core of incorrigibles who made up the bulk of the deserters. General Howard had expressed this view as early as 1885, when he wrote: "If we take bad men we cannot always reform them. Bad men will desert."[5] There were even some deserters who were candid enough to admit that this was often the case. A prisoner awaiting trial for desertion at Fort Porter, New York, wrote to General Howard, commanding the division of the Atlantic, in 1889, setting forth the details of his desertion from Fort Custer, Montana. He had, he said, been treated very well and liked the service. He related how one day, after pay day, he was approached by another soldier who asked him to desert. He refused, but then, he went on:

> We went to the sutler store, and liquor got the best of me, and sir I done what I never would have done if I had not been influenced by an older man, whom I afterwards found was an old deserter, who had made a regular profession of coming in the Army for winter. I deserted with him, but my conscience troubled me so much, that I came here and surrendered to the officer of the day. . . .[6]

There was another reason advanced for the persistence of the desertion problem—particularly during this period. With the growth of towns in the vicinity of formerly remote posts, and the establishment of larger stations near cities, it had been hoped that there would be an improvement in the public attitude toward the soldier. Instead, however, the men found that they were still regarded as little better than social outcasts. When they went to town after hours, they were often ostracized and humiliated; either forbidden to enter respectable places of entertainment, or, if allowed, plainly shown that their presence was not desired. To most citizens, it was considered axiomatic that a respectable girl would not be seen in public with an enlisted man. Indeed, soldiers were even reluctant to accompany their own daughters into town, for fear of besmirching their reputations.[7]

In March, 1890, the citizens of Mobita, Texas, a town close to Fort Elliot, sold tickets to the men at the post for a grand ball to be held on St. Patrick's Day. However, when the soldiers presented themselves at the door of the ballroom, they were refused admittance. The indignant men returned to the post and held a meeting, where they passed the following resolution:

> Whereas, in consideration of the contemptible insults which the enlisted men of this post were the recipients of at the hands of the Mobita citizens on March 17, 1890, it is
>
> Resolved, That each and every enlisted man hereby pledges his word and honor that he will not buy from any merchant within the precincts of the said town any article of goods which he may have exposed for sale; and he further pledges his word and honor that he will avoid all kinds of monetary transactions and association with any person or persons who claim to be citizens of Mobita.[8]

This public humiliation and degradation was considered by many to be a potent factor contributing to desertion. General George A. Crook placed the blame for the still numerous desertions upon the people themselves, and specifically upon "their attitude toward the unfortunate private soldier." "A man loses his pride and self-respect," he said, "when he finds that he is despised by the people he meets, that he is shunned by his former associates and is no longer regarded as their social equal."[9] An officer, who had himself served in the ranks for more than five years, wrote in a prize-winning essay on the subject of desertion: "The uniform of his country is theoretically a thing to be proud of, but practically a badge of disgrace. One must wear the uniform of the enlisted man to feel the truth of this, and I have felt it . . . ."[10] And Private Will Stokes, whose poetic efforts earned for him the title of "the American Kipling," was moved to comment bitterly on the popular opinion of the men in the ranks:

Oh, what's the use o' mincin' things—it's
    plain enough to us—
A sojer or a sailor, now, ain't wurth a
    darned cuss,
An' when he joins the Service, be it plainly
    understood
His name is most emphatically Mud! Mud! Mud!

.   .   .   .

We do not claim admission to the
    Patriarchangel's Ball,
But when they bar our entrance to a
    bloomin' music hall—
O tempora! O mores! it is time to
    make a kick—
Such un-American treatment makes me
    Sick! Sick! Sick![11]

.   .   .   .

Some observers felt, however, that it was hardly surprising that civilians regarded enlisted men as their social inferiors. After all, they said, this was no more than an echo of the position of Army officers who, in the words of Colonel James Montgomery Rice of the Illinois National Guard, constantly sought "to impress upon everyone, everywhere and always the immensity, permanency and impassability of the gulf which socially exists between the men who fill the offices and the men who fill the ranks, and then expect the citizen to accept the enlisted man as a social equal."[12]

But the continuation of the caste system was not the only feature of Army life held responsible for the recurring desertion dilemma. Despite the steps that had been taken to improve the conditions of the soldier, the view was expressed that the major grievances—over pay and food —still remained unresolved. "It cannot be expected," said Captain W. E. Hoffman, Ninth Infantry, in 1889, "that a man should be content to give his lifetime for $13 a month and no prospects for the future."[13]

As for the food, the complaints about its inadequacy still persisted. In 1887, Captain J. G. Ballance noted that men serving in Texas had found it necessary to contribute $12,000 of their own money that year to supplement the food provided by the government. "It is impossible for anyone to doubt," he concluded, "that this is one of the most important causes of desertion." And two years later, the *Army and Navy Journal* echoed:

> All the efforts to improve the condition of the soldier and make him contented with his lot will come to naught if this most important item, wholesome and nutritious food for his stomach and plenty of it, is neglected.[14]

Another factor held responsible for the increase in desertions was the practice of utilizing troops to perform the necessary labor involved in carrying out the Army's extensive construction and improvement program. Major E. V. Sumner, Fifth Cavalry, in an analysis of the large number of desertions from Fort Riley, Kansas, in 1887, declared that the men at that post were embittered by the daily toil involved in the tearing down of old quarters, the construction of new buildings and the improvements made in the water and sewage systems.[15] In the same year, an officer wrote from Fort Niobrara, Nebraska:

> The task of making the place comfortable has demanded constant and excessive fatigue duty during the most severe weather of last winter, and this has been the means of at least quadrupling the usual proportion of desertions.[16]

And two years later, a soldier from Fort Sill complained that there was so much labor for the troops there that the men had to eat their supper by candlelight. "And yet," he exclaimed, "the question is asked, 'Why do men desert?' Let them come to this post, and they will soon learn the cause."[17]

But by far the cause most often assigned for the rise in desertions was the arbitrary treatment of the men by their officers. As we have seen, this was the conclusion reached by Adjutant-General John C. Kelton, in his annual report for 1889.[18] This opinion was also reflected in a host of communications to both the service journals and the civilian press. The correspondents charged the officers with negating the effects of all the reforms enacted by the War Department by making life miserable for the men under them. In many cases, the offenses of which the officers were accused were in direct violation of existing orders.[19] For example, it was charged that men awaiting trial were still put to work alongside of convicted offenders. "I know that here the guardhouse routine is the same at present as it has been for the last ten years," wrote an "Old Soldier," "and if general orders are disregarded with impunity by those in command, how can they expect to receive to their orders, the implicit obedience which is the first duty of a soldier?"[20]

Even where commanders did not actually violate regulations, they were accused of interpreting them in such a way as to inflict the greatest hardship on the men. A soldier writing from Fort Sill complained that the post commander had issued orders closing the post library and canteen to enlisted men after 9:30 p.m., while permitting officers, their families and guests to remain until 11 p.m. Thus, despite the abolition of the tattoo roll call, soldiers were practically forced to retire at 9:30, since they could hardly be expected to sit around in their quarters after the lights had been turned out.[21]

The complaint was also heard that orders were issued restricting behavior in the post canteens, which was in violation of the whole spirit in which the canteens had been conceived. The men would be forbidden to sing, tell stories or otherwise enjoy themselves, even though such actions involved no breach of discipline.[22] "It cannot be expected," wrote one soldier from Fort Riley, "that a canteen can be run on the same plan as a Sunday school, nor is it possible to make men who always expect to have a good time, at least once a month, and who can have it in a decent way outside, observe Mr. Cushing's rules just because they are in a canteen."[23] According to a report from Fort Totten, Dakota, a company commander at that post actually used a telescope to observe the movements of his men and took a special delight in detecting the slightest infringement of his own restrictions, many of which were illegal.[24]

Accusations of "rough and oppressive treatment" of soldiers by "non-coms" and officers continued to be voiced.[25] On December 4, 1887, the New York *Herald* published a letter from a prisoner at David's Island, New York Harbor, who complained that while in confinement in the guardhouse, he had been beaten by the sergeant of the guard with the butt end of a rifle "for no just cause." "If one of your reporters," he went on, "came here and had a talk with the enlisted men, he would learn much that would surprise the many readers of the *Herald* and would enlighten the public in regard to the United States Army." And nine days later, the same newspaper printed a communication from a prisoner at Fort Union, New Mexico, charging that the tyranny of his captain had driven him to desertion after over three years of service.[26]

The following year, under the heading, "A Grave Injustice," the Kansas City *Times* related the experience of Private John C. Dudley of Fort Riley, Kansas. This soldier was arrested for having used disrespectful language and for having refused to work when ordered to do so by his troop commander. To force him into obedience, "the authorities at Fort Riley made a 'spread eagle' of him for two hours," and when he still refused to do as ordered, he was tried by a court-martial and sentenced to confinement for four years and six months—a sentence that was approved by the department commander. The newspaper bitterly condemned both the use of "a relic of barbarism" and the disproportionately severe sentence for the offense committed.[27]

On May 6, 1889, the St. Paul *Pioneer Press* published a letter from a sergeant at Fort Pembina, North Dakota, who charged that desertions were caused in many instances by "abusive and overbearing officers." "Of course," he went on, "all officers are not hard. The really mean officer is in the minority, but one of these mean ones in a post will be the cause of more dissatisfaction and desertions than all other causes put together." A month later, the New York *Sun* published a lengthy communication from a soldier at Fort Douglas, Utah, in which he detailed the misconduct of "officers in the United States Army who are such in name only," and charged that these officers "have driven many good men to desert." "It is high time," he concluded, "that the reading public be made acquainted with at least a few of the causes which lead so vast a number to desert the service every year."[28]

Just a few days later, the Kansas City *Times* carried a letter signed "Enlisted Man," in which the correspondent complained that the men at Little Rock Barracks, Arkansas, were tried and fined heavily for the most trivial offenses. Thus, a soldier who might open a button or two of his blouse while visiting the nearby town on a hot day would be court-martialed and fined $8 to $10 for this dereliction, while the officers were seen regularly in town dress in part-military and part-civilian clothing, in tennis clothes and even in jockey suits. Such treatment, the writer contended, was responsible for the many desertions from that post.[29]

On July 13, 1889, the *Army and Navy Journal* published a dispatch from Bismarck, North Dakota, under the caption "Knock Down by a Cavalry Captain." It related an incident that occurred among the troops of the Eighth Cavalry from Fort Yates who had been sent to participate in the Constitutional Convention ceremonies. On the day following the cermonies—July 5—while the troops were awaiting a train back to the fort, Captain E. G. Fechet, the officer in command, ordered a drunk and boisterous soldier—Private Dugen—to sit down and keep quiet. When his order was not obeyed, the captain seized a rifle from a soldier standing nearby and struck Dugen on the head, cutting open his scalp and slitting his ear from top to bottom. After his ear was sewed up, Private Dugen was taken aboard the train.

Persons who had witnessed the attack "were inclined to censure the captain severly for his action." But five officers of his unit came to his defense and insisted that he was justified in acting as he did to prevent "open mutiny in his command." Another officer at the post took the opposite view, and the incident provoked considerable controversy.[30]

It had hardly subsided when the Army was subjected to a new barrage of unfavorable publicity in the form of a series of articles on conditions and treatment of recruits at Jefferson Barracks, Missouri. The articles were published in the St. Louis *Post-Dispatch* and were written by one of its reporters—Frank L. Woodward—who had spent three months at the post as a recruit. As a result of his experiences as a soldier, Woodward made some highly sensational charges concerning the treatment of the men by their officers. He said that the officers were unnecessarily cruel and overbearing; that the food was unfit to eat; that vermin infested the quarters; that men were placed under arrest on the most trivial charges and confined in the guardhouse which was indescribably filthy. Worst of all, he charged that soldiers were treated brutally by non-commissioned officers without as much as an investigation.[31]

Coming when they did, the Woodward articles unleashed a storm of new criticism against the Army, as well as a rash of letters from soldiers, ex-soldiers and even deserters, purporting to verify the reporter's account.[32] Equally vehement, however, were the denials from the post officers who called his assertions "brutally false and malicious." Even some enlisted men wrote to deny accusations Woodward made against specific non-commissioned officers.[33]

Although a court of inquiry appointed by President Harrison to investigate the causes of desertion at Jefferson Barracks found that Woodward's more sensational charges could not be substantiated, it also established that there was sufficient substance to his account to warrant remedial action. Quartermaster-General Holabird made a personal visit to the post, as a result of which plans were drawn up for a thorough renovation of the barracks and the guardhouse. A new mess hall, fitted with all modern conveniences, was ordered built and improvements were made in the cooking and distribution of the food. A library was installed for the use of the recruits, and a canteen was established.[34] "Jefferson

Barracks, the well-known recruiting station in Missouri, will probably never again fall into the condition which recently provoked a court of inquiry," said the New York *Times*. And the St. Louis *Post-Dispatch* felt "a reasonable pride in its successful efforts in the direction of much-needed reform."[35]

But although the *Army and Navy Joural* expressed the hope that the prompt reaction of the War Department to the Jefferson Barracks disclosures would put an end to the unfavorable publicity the Army was receiving in the press, the reports continued.[36] On February 18, 1890, a story that shocked and angered the nation appeared simultaneously in the St. Paul *Globe* and the Chicago *Tribune*. It concerned the case of a Private Dell P. Wild, who was serving a sentence in the guardhouse at Fort Snelling, Minnesota. In an interview with correspondents from the two newspapers, Wild told of having been ordered by his first sergeant at Fort Yates, South Dakota, to deliver a canvas to the quarters of Lieutenant Matthew F. Steele during the previous October. When the officer ordered him to climb up and nail the canvas on the roof of a shed, Wild refused, stating that he had not enlisted to act as a servant. There followed an angry exchange during which Lieutenant Steele allegedly called Wild a deserter, cursed him, struck him and finally had him put under arrest. On November 5, he was brought to trial for disobeying the command of an officer and for conduct prejudicial to good order and discipline. When Wild discovered that Lieutenant Steele had been assigned to act as judge-advocate, he protested that a fair trial was impossible under these circumstances. This objection was overruled on the ground that a judge-advocate could not be challenged. Wild then turned to Lieutenant Steele and asked him to step down of his own accord, which the officer refused to do.

After a trial which Wild claimed was rushed through so that he was given practically no opportunity to present his side of the story, the court found him guilty of disobedience and insubordination and sentenced him to dishonorable discharge from the service, with loss of pay and allowances and imprisonment for one year. General Ruger, the Department Commander, approved the sentence. On January 11, 1890, Wild, shackled hand and foot, was sent off in an open sleigh to Bismarck, North Dakota, where he lay ill in a cell for two weeks, after which he was removed to the prison at Fort Snelling. Wild closed his story to the reporters with the following statement:

I am now working out here in the stone quarries, about twelve hours a day, and at the end of the year I'll be turned loose without a cent and dishonorably discharged. If I violated the twenty-first article of war, Lieutenant Steele violated the thirteenth article, which provides that an officer who strikes one of his men shall be cashiered from the service.[37]

The publication of Wild's story evoked much resentment against the Army and its officers. From one end of the country to the other, the cry was raised that the Army was "a disgrace" and "a blot upon the republic," led by officers whose brutality rendered them "unfit companions for any man or woman." It was pointed out that the presiding officer at Wild's trial was the same Captain E. G. Fechet who had himself assaulted a private only three months before. On that occasion, Lieutenant Steele had come to the captain's defense when he was criticized for his conduct. Now the captain was returning the favor. It was no wonder, the critics claimed, that the men in the ranks revolted and fled from the Army as from a plague.[38]

While there were some voices raised to justify the action of the officer and the court as necessary for the maintenance of military discipline, the Wild case produced so much public agitation that President Harrison summoned Secretary of War Redfield Proctor to the White House on February 20 to discuss all its implications. On the following day, the Secretary issued an order remitting the unexpired portion of Wild's sentence on the ground that it was "excessive in a very marked degree." At the same time, Proctor also noted that no action had been taken against Lieutenant Steele, "whose breach of discipline was of an aggravated nature," and stated that he felt strongly that the selection of Steele as judge-advocate had been "grossly improper." "The President," the order concluded, "does not believe this case to be, nor does he think it just to the Army that it should appear to be, a fair illustration of the administration of military justice."[39]

Four days later, Secretary Proctor ordered Lieutenant Steele to be tried by a general court-martial for conduct prejudicial to good order and military discipline by striking Private Wild and using insulting language.[40]

These actions of the Secretary were warmly commended by the press as having "vindicated a poor soldier's rights."[41] The *U.S. Army Visitor,* a publication of the U.S. Army Aid Association of New York City, which was active in providing religious and education materials for the Army, hailed the Secretary's announcement in a lengthy editorial:

> The Enlisted Man is not a *"galley slave"* nor a "lackey," but has rights and privileges in which he must be protected. His first lesson is obedience, truly; but his superiors have no right to provoke him unduly to wrath, and because he sins to subject him to punishment out of all proportion to the offence; and we are glad that the Secretary of War has ordered that his attention be called to cases of this character. . . .
> We owe a deep debt of gratitude to our soldiers. They have often defended our shores; nor, like other armies, the tools of ambiltious tyrants or usurpers, have they ever turned their swords against the lives or liberties of those whom they were sworn to defend; and, therefore, their comfort, their material happiness, their moral and religious welfare, should be a grateful country's anxious care. . . .

Meanwhile, as had often happened in the past on such occasions, the release of Private Wild let loose a flood of stories in the newspapers of alleged mistreatment of soldiers by officers. Many of the correspondents said that they had been encouraged to speak up as a result of the President's action and in the hope that they might add the weight of their experiences to the drive for reforms in the service. "Every day brings new cases of cruelty and injustice that were suppressed at the time but are now being dragged into light," said the San Francisco *Chronicle.*[43] So great was the deluge of such stories that an officer of "rank, reputation and experience" felt constrained to deny that the officers were as guilty as they were charged of abusing the soldiers under them. In an interview published in the St. Paul *Pioneer Press,* he asked:

> Don't you believe that if they did so, their lives would be in danger? They live in the midst of their men day and night from one year's end to another, often dependent upon them for safety and always for comfort. Whatever may be said of army officers, they are not, as a rule, fools, as the conduct imputed to them would make them out to be. . . .[44]

On March 6, 1890, the term of Lewis Carter, a Negro soldier who had been sentenced by a court-martial in 1885 to ninety-nine years for desertion, robbery, assault and rape, was reduced to six years by order of the President, after having been earlier reduced to twenty-five years by the reviewing officer.[45] A few days later, Private John J. Dudley, whose case has been previously cited, was ordered released by Secretary Proctor.[46] At the end of the month, the *Army and Navy Journal* reported that since the action in the Wild case, nearly a hundred sentences had been either remitted or reduced, with others still to be reviewed.[47]

It was in this atmosphere that the court-martial of Lieutenant Steele opened on March 18, 1890, in Chicago. The court consisted of thirteen officers, and both their number and their rank were regarded as indicative of the importance attached to the case by the War Department. In addition to a large contingent of officers from the Illinois National Guard, there were also present reporters from newspapers of Chicago, New York and other cities.

Lieutenant Steele pleaded not guilty to the charge and to each of the specifications. He asserted that whatever he had done had been for the good of the service and the maintenance of discipline. Testimony was presented to the effect that Lieutenant Steele had first requested and then ordered Wild to help him place the canvas on the shed—a public building at Fort Snelling—and that the latter had refused in a disrespectful, sullen and insolent manner. When asked if the lieutenant had offered his assistance, Wild admitted that he had but maintained that Steele was doing the work for himself, and that he, Wild, had enlisted to be a soldier, not a servant.[48]

The defense devoted much of its case to proving that Wild was an untrustworthy person and a poor soldier. Testimony was introduced to the effect that he had previously served in the Army under the name of Ward. His troop commander called him the most insolent and insubordinate man in his command. His comrades testified that they would not believe him under oath, and his record of convictions by court-martial and confinements in the guardhouse—195 days inside of sixteen months—was presented to the court.[49]

On the other hand, witnesses testified that Lieutenant Steele was an excellent officer. The post commander at Fort Yates, Colonel Edwin C. Townsend, declared that he considered him one of the very best young officers in the Army. "I once had to send a troop of cavalry to suppress an incipient outbreak among the Indians," he said, "I selected Lieutenant Steele, and the Indians were back on the reservation inside of twenty-four hours."[50]

On April 10, it was announced that the court had found Lieutenant

Steele guilty of striking Private Wild and using abusive language, and sentenced him to be reprimanded and restricted to the limits of his post for three months. The court said it had been lenient on account of the great provocation under which Lieutenant Steel had acted and his excellent character as revealed in the evidence. General Schofield, the reviewing officer, approved the findings and administered the reprimand, which went in part:

> A temporary loss of self-control in dealing with mutinous conduct of a soldier has already resulted in subjecting Lieut. Steele to punishment of public and official censure, to which little can now be added by formal reprimand. The lesson taught by this incident is instructive to all young officers of the Army by showing them the absolute necessity of self-command as a qualification for the command of men. Abuse of subordinates by words or blows is not to be tolerated under any circumstances. . . .
>
> It is proper to remark in connection with this case that Lieut. Steele committed an unfortunante mistake in acting as prosecutor in trial of soldier with whom he had had personal difficulty. This resulted from the accidental circumstances that Lieut. Steele was J. A. of an existing court, before which this case was sent to trial. . . . A nice sense of propriety and due appreciation of self-interest should suggest to an officer the wisdom of requesting to be excused from duty of prosecutor under such circumstances. Such request would, of course, be respected by the commanding general who appointed the court.[51]

The General's reference to "formal reprimand" was occasioned by an erroneous report that the reprimand would be administered publicly in the presence of Lieutenant Steele's command, which would have been considered a far more severe punishment.

The decision of the court in the Steele case evoked widely divergent reactions. On the one hand, the sentence was angrily denounced as a travesty on justice. The fact that Wild was a disreputable character, the critics contended, did not at all lessen the seriousness of Lieutenant Steele's offense.[52] And they characterized his punishment as laughable. The Minneapolis *Tribune* observed sarcastically that the sentence meant little more than that for three months, Steele would not be able to dance with the young ladies in St. Paul, but would be free to attend the frequent social affairs at the Fort.

On the other hand, the sentence was defended as flowing inevitably from the facts that came to light at the trial, which indicated both Lieutenant Steele's excellence as an officer and Private Wild's weaknesses as a soldier. But even those who supported the decision endorsed the important principle enunciated by General Schofield that an officer who had an interest in a case should not be permitted to act as judge advocate in that case.[53]

The public agitation aroused by the Wild case was instrumental in hastening the adoption of a number of reforms in the Army. On March 18, 1890—the day the trial of Lieutenant Steele opened—a general order was issued directing that in all general court-martial cases, the accused soldier would, upon his request, have a suitable officer assigned to him as defense counsel.

Two weeks after the court decision in the Steele trial was made public, a bill was submitted to Congress and subsequently passed empowering the President to prescribe and define the limits for court-martial sentences in time of peace.[54] Four days after he signed this measure—on October 1, 1890—President Harrison signed a second bill which instituted summary courts for the trial of minor offenses in time of peace. Under its provisions, within twenty-four hours after arrest, enlisted men charged with offenses previously under the jurisdiction of garrison or regimental courts-martial were to be brought before a court consisting of the officer second in command at the post. However, the accused soldier had the option of requesting trial by a regimental or garrison court-martial, if he so desired.[55]

The *Army and Navy Journal* greeted the legislation with enthusiasm. "At last the Army will have the 'summary court' it has so long desired," it wrote, "in place of the cumbersome and tedious system of garrison courts." A year later, the Omaha *Bee* gave a facetious picture of the operation of the summary court in this account: "A cavalryman is galloping along. Summary court officer hails him. 'Hello, is your name Smith?' 'Yes, sir.' 'Were you absent from roll call last night?' 'Yes, sir.' 'Three dollars!' 'Yes, sir,' the soldier keeping right along at a gallop."[56]

On February 27, 1891, President Harrison issued the long-awaited code of punishments to implement the law passed five months earlier. The maximum punishment for desertion without surrender was limited, except under special circumstances, to confinement at hard labor for from one to two and a half years, according to the deserter's length of service. Another section provided that soldiers awaiting trial by summary court were not to be kept in the guardhouse, but should be confined in quarters under arrest until the verdict was announced, unless restraint was considered necessary.[57]

The *Army and Navy Journal* welcomed the appearance of the code and observed that with this reform, Secretary Proctor's administration of the War Department had become "one of the most progressive in the history of the Army." And a year later, Judge-Advocate General Lieber, in his annual report, paid tribute to the code as having brought about the disappearance of "the former great disparity in punishments in the different military departments." [58] Another improvement in the administration of military justice was the Act of Congress of July 27, 1892, excluding the judge-advocate from the closed sessions of a court-martial.[59]

An important measure passed by Congress on the recommendation of Secretary Proctor was the bill approved on June 16, 1890, optimistically entitled "An Act to Prevent Desertion and for Other Purposes." Its two most important features were the addition of a pound of vegetables to the daily ration of the enlisted men and the provision, for the first time, that a soldier could purchase his discharge after serving for at least one year. The amount required varied with his length of service. At the end of three years, he was entitled to a three-month furlough and the right to claim a free discharge. The act also provided for the retention, until the end of his enlistment, of four dollars a month from a soldier's pay for the first year. This sum, plus the interest on it, was to be turned over to the soldier on the day of his discharge, if he had served faithfully.[60]

The new legislation was widely hailed as an effective deterrent against desertion. The improvement of the ration alone was viewed as one of the best steps taken for the soldiers in many years. It was called "an unmixed blessing," and the feeling was expressed that barring downright incompetent cooks and utterly negligent mess officers, the soldiers should thrive on the new diet.[61]

In September, 1890, Commanding General of the Army John M. Schofield asked for opinions from all commanding officers concerning the amount of guard duty required at military posts. He announced that he intended to use this information to formulate a plan which would increase the "number of nights in bed" for each enlisted man. Accordingly, an order was issued directing that guard duty details be so arranged, wherever practicable, so as to assure soldiers of an interval of not less than six days between tours. Except in an absolute emergency, the men were not to be detailed more frequently than once in five days.[62]

In June, 1892, Congress passed a law which modified significant sections of the Act of 1878, which pertained to promotion to a commission. The new law—sometimes called the soldier's "Magna Charta"—provided that any unmarried enlisted man under thirty years of age who was physically sound, of good moral character and had served for at least two years, could present himself as a candidate for promotion to a department board of examiners. If he passed this body, he went before a general board at Fort Leavenworth, where he took a strictly competitive examination. Not only did this legislation open the door to commissions for the first time to privates, but it also enabled the soldier himself to initiate the application, rather than having to depend upon the recommendation of his commanding officer.[63]

Another effort was made, too, to insure the selection of more desirable recruits. In 1891, a basic ability to read, write and understand English was added to the list of qualifications for enlistment. The experiment was also initiated of extending recruiting to the smaller towns and villages, and the number of recruiting stations was increased fivefold. Wherever regiments were so located that they could send recruiting parties into towns and villages within a reasonable distance of the post, they were required to rely largely upon their own efforts for recruits. Under this new system of regimental recruiting, an officer and a small detachment of men moved about from place to place, giving practical demonstrations of Army life in the field and delivering a series of descriptive lectures on the improved conditions in the service, which were enlivened by attractive lithographic posters furnished by the War Department.[64]

Special praise was accorded to Secretary of War Proctor for having accomplished more good for the enlisted men than any "ten of his predecessors." So genuine was the feeling of gratitude toward the War Department head that on the eve of his visit to Fort Sherman, Idaho, a correspondent described the garrison as being "on the tiptoe of expectancy." "Everyone is anxious to see the man who has done so much for the service," he went on.[65]

The announcement of Proctor's resignation from his office to take a seat in the Senate in November, 1891, was received with sincere expressions of regret throughout the Army and the country generally. "Secretary Proctor," came a voice from Fort Assinboine, Montana, "in leaving the War Department will carry with him the best wishes of the Army for which he has done so much."[66]

Proctor was able to leave with the comforting knowledge that desertions for the year ending June, 1891, came to 1,503, a drop of 30 percent from the figures for the previous year. This heartening trend was continued during the following year under the administration of the new Secretary of War, Stephen B. Elkins. Desertions for the year ending June 30, 1892 fell to 1,382—by far the smallest number for any twelve-month period since the end of the Civil War.[67] The Philadelphia *Ledger* attributed this development "to the attractiveness of the service as compared with the severe conditions that surrounded the soldiers' life heretofore." And the New York *Times* said: "The condition of the Army may fairly be a cause for congratulations."[68]

CHAPTER VI

THE ARMY ON THE EVE OF THE
SPANISH-AMERICAN WAR

It could hardly be expected that the sweeping changes introduced into the Army during the Proctor administration would meet with unqualified approval throughout the service. But while some measure of opposition was expected, the military authorities must have been surprised at the intensity with which many officers attacked the reforms. From the commissioned ranks came the complaint that the first casualty of the reform movement was Army discipline, and that while its soldiers were undoubtedly better provided for than before, its effectiveness as a fighting machine had been seriously impaired. Officers bemoaned the fact that privates now showed less respect for a commissioned officer than they had previously shown for a non-commissioned officer. They sarcastically envisioned the day when officers would have to say "please" in issuing orders, and when silver platters would be provided on which company commanders could leave their cards, inviting their men to see them at their convenience.[1]

Other officers complained that they were reluctant to exercise their legitimate authority, for fear of incurring the wrath of the War Department or the criticism of the press. "The old officers," one wrote in November, 1890, "are generally of the opinion that the Army is going to the ————."[2] About six months later, an "old officer" commented that in his twenty-six years of service, he had never seen the Army in such poor condition. The men, he said, carried out their assigned tasks as if they were doing the officers a favor, while authorities in Washington conveyed the feeling to the officers that they did not enjoy the support of their superiors.[3] In December, 1891, an officer wrote from Fort Robinson to the Kansas City *Times:*

> What we now need is legislation to protect the officer. I have been
> in the service a quarter of a century and have never seen discipline
> so lax as it is at present. It is now impossible to properly discipline

an insubordinate character. Officers are now at the mercy of their men, and severe field service will result in mutiny unless an officer jeopardizes his commission by going back to the old ways. An Army cannot be managed like a Sunday school, even in a republican country. The majority of the older officers are thoroughly disgusted.[4]

These attacks on the state of Army discipline were buttressed by an incident at Walla Walla, Washington, in April, 1891, which aroused considerable public excitement. It involved the lynching of a civilian gambler named A. J. Hunt by a crowd of Fourth Cavalry troops stationed at nearby Fort Walla Walla. The gambler had shot one of the troop's soldiers, and when he subsequently died, about fifty of his comrades stormed the town jail, forcibly removed Hunt and shot and killed him.[5]

This lynching was seized upon by the critics of Army reforms as indicative of the collapse of discipline in the service. In fact, when the post commander, Colonel Charles E. Compton, appeared before a court of inquiry investigating the incident, he attributed the tragedy to the fact that "within the last four years a new code of military ethics has been produced. . . . The old, unwavering loyalty of the soldier for his officer is fast disappearing, discipline is becoming irksome, restriction is being considered as an affliction and proper reproof has in some instances been deemed an insult and aroused anger."[6]

If the critics of reform needed additional ammunition, they found it in the unforeseen difficulties that arose in carrying out some of the changes. By far the greatest of these came about in connection with the Act of June 16, 1890, which provided an honorable discharge from the service at the end of three years or by purchase before that time. It developed that practically every man who was entitled to the three months' furlough after three years of faithful service took advantage of it. Commanding officers complained of constant changes in their company organizations which threw the service into a state of continued turmoil. And instead of returning to the Army after their furloughs, the bulk of the men took their final discharge.[7] "It is a deplorable fact," wrote a veteran officer, "that a large number of our best non-commissioned officers who have become, through years of hard service, efficient and trained soldiers, are daily taking advantage of late General Orders to be discharged."[8]

Moreover, many more men than had been anticipated availed themselves of the opportunity to purchase their discharges. Officers pointed out that for many new men, the term of service had practically become a period of one or two years. This situation was further complicated by the fact that, despite the most persistent canvassing, there was a marked falling-off in the number of recruits enlisted. While some reduction had been expected as a result of the greater selectivity in the choice of men, the decline was far greater than had been foreseen. For example, the enlistments for December, 1890, numbered about three hundred, as compared with nine hundred for the corresponding month of the previous year.[9] And even though recruits were now furnished by two methods, with the special regiments supplementing the general recruiting service, withdrawals from the service before the expiration of the regular term of enlistment began to exceed the number of recruits taken in.[10] Adjutant General Kelton described the condition as "discouraging," and Army officers expressed genuine concern over the problem of maintaining an enlisted force.[11]

On May 22, 1892, Commanding General Schofield announced that thereafter, the right to purchase a discharge would be limited to men who had served for at least eighteen months. However, this restriction did not prove very effective, and a year later, Secretary of War Elkins issued an order stating that requests for such discharges would not be granted unless they were based on valid reasons verified by officers. All former orders that conflicted with the new regulations were revoked.[12] While this action was undertaken as a means of halting the mass withdrawals from the Army, its effect was negated by an amendment to the Army Appropriations Bill sponsored by Senator Proctor in February, 1893.

This measure provided that thereafter, in peacetime, no man over thirty years could be accepted for enlistment. The section that created an uproar, however, was the one stipulating that no person was to be reenlisted if he had served for ten years or more or was over thirty-five —except for those who had served for twenty years or more. Although this amendment was inserted without the knowledge, much less the advice of the War Department, it was quickly passed by the Senate.[13]

The Senate's action unleashed a storm of opposition from both within and outside the Army. The critics of the amendment characterized it as unjust to the men in the ranks and harmful to the service, since it would deprive the Army of all its experienced soldiers and turn it into a body of raw recruits. The Kansas City *Times* called upon officers and enlisted men to deluge the members of the lower House with messages urging its defeat. "Delay may be dangerous," it warned. "Keep the telegraph wires hot between the post and Washington and load down the mail with letters setting forth the grave danger to the Army if Mr. Proctor's amendment is permitted to pass."[14]

In response to these protests, the House Committee on Military Affairs recommended a modified version of the Senate amendment which excluded from the ten-year restriction any men that the Secretary of War might authorize to be reenlisted. This change came as welcome news to the Army. The feeling was even expressed that the measure might accomplish some positive good by placing the men who desired to remain in the service on their good behavior.[15]

But the Army's relief was short-lived, for the modification was rejected by the Conference Committee, which recommended the original Proctor amendment but substituted the word "private" for "person," so as to exclude non-commissioned officers from its operation. Appeals were now directed to Congress urging the rejection of the Conference Committee's recommendation. They stressed the point that it was ridiculous to assume that a soldier who had served for ten years without acquiring his chevrons was not worth reenlisting. Instead, it was argued, some of the best soldiers served throughout their careers as privates; such men taught recruits the important lessons of obedience and faithfulness, while in times of emergency or danger, they were invaluable. Some felt that it would be better to have the Appropriations Bill defeated than to permit this objectionable amendment to stand.[16]

This time, however, the protests were unavailing, and the bill, together with the amendment, was adopted by Congress and signed by President Harrison. Its opponents called it the most vicious piece of military legislation ever enacted. Soldiers, they said, no longer had a lifetime profession, but were now just like factory employees, completely without security. One soldier urged his comrades to follow the example of the workingmen of the nation and form unions to protect their interests.[17] And the name of Proctor, which had so recently elicited nothing but praise as the enlisted man's benefactor, was now universally condemned. It was reported that at many posts, one could get up a fight at any time by merely mentioning the Senator's name.[18] "If the Vermont Senator," said the Kansas City Times, "should hear the words of condemnation coming from the lips of the enlisted men, he would wish that he had never been called to preside over the War Department, a step that finally aided him in getting into the United States Senate." And a soldier expressed his feelings on Proctor's amendment in verse:

> Poor old soldiers, lame and sick,
> Let them at work with shovel and pick,
> Broken hearted, old and gray;
> Proctor says they cannot stay;
> For we had this bill to pass
> To get men of a better class,
> For nine dollars and four retained
> Better men can be obtained.
>
> .   .   .   .
>
> Now let us live in hope until
> They do remove the Proctor Bill
> And every soldier breathe his prayer
> That he'll resign the Senator's chair.[19]

Soon after the passage of the bill, applications for discharge began reaching the War Department from soldiers who had reenlisted with the intention of remaining in the Army until they could be retired after thirty years. These men claimed their discharges on the gouund that the government had not kept faith with them. The ten-year law was also held responsible for the increase in the number of desertions—from 1,410 in 1892 to 1,632 in 1893.[20] In fact, the law was viewed as the cause of more dissatisfaction than any measure that had been introduced in years. "The older soldiers," observed one officer, "have resented the spirit of the law and their increased discontent has been communicated to the younger men."[21]

Although a concerted drive was launched to repeal the ten-year amendment, which was joined in by the President, the Secretary of War and the Commanding General of the Army, a far more potent factor in filling the depleted ranks of the Army was the panic of 1893. The depression that swept over the country filled recruiting stations with unemployed men seeking entry into the service. The New York *Times* reported that one result of the severe economic dislocation had been to give the Army all the recruits it wanted.[22] The Waterbury (Connecticut) *American* described the success of the recruiting effort in its area and went on:

> The prevailing hard times are proving to be beneficial to the Army.
> Many young men throughout the country who are out of work,

seeing privation and want staring them in the face, are enlisting in the Army, preferring that course to spending a short time in jail for some petty crime. The number of applicants at the New Haven station has nearly doubled within three months.[23]

And the *Army and Navy Journal* observed:

Not since the war can the oldest recruiting officer recall the time when there were so many applicants as during the past few months. Good mechanics, mill men and labouring men generally . . . are clamoring to get into the Army, and all because the financial stringency has taken away their means of earning a livelihood.[24]

With more than enough men available, the military authorities now felt secure enough to introduce several changes that they had long contemplated. In August, 1894, Secretary of War Daniel S. Lamont ordered the abandonment of the three Army recruiting depots at David's Island, Columbus, and Jefferson Barracks. Thereafter, recruits were to receive their initial training with their companies at the various posts.[25] That same month, Congress fixed the term of enlistment at three years and repealed the disputed ten-year clause. In the same law, it restricted enlistments in time of peace to citizens of the United States or those who had officially declared their intention to become citizens, and no persons, except Indians, who could not speak, read and write the English language were to be enlisted. Congress also provided for an end to the "retained pay" of $4 per month and extended the system of monthly payments to all posts.[26] The reduction in the reward for apprehending deserters from $60, adopted in 1890 to $10 was also indicative of the Army's new-found confidence. And in 1895, the military prison which had been established at Fort Leavenworth twenty-one years earlier, was discontinued and thereafter military prisoners were confined at the larger permanent posts.[27]

There was considerable favorable comment to the effect that the Army was now getting a better class of men than at any other time in its history. "Young men with characters corresponding to their fine physique, of such is the Army largely composed today," observed the Chicago *Herald*. It also noted that a larger percentage of native-born men than ever before now made up the ranks—more than 75 percent, according to a survey by the War Department in 1894.[28] The Inspector-General of the Army reported that never before were drill and discipline better nor contentment greater throughout the ranks of the Army.[29] There were even some optimists who went so far as to predict that the problem of desertion was now on its way to ultimate resolution. The annual report of Adjutant General Samuel Breck in 1897 reflected this feeling of euphoria, when he wrote:

> It is gratifying to report that the number of desertions from the Army during the past year has been lower than at any period during the last decade. While this serious military crime will perhaps never be entirely eradicated, yet the adoption of measures tending to guard the service against men of bad character, to increase the well-being, moral and physical, of the American soldier, together with the generally superior class of men now attracted to the ranks bid fair to relieve the Army from the unmerited odium cast upon it in the past by desertions.[30]

The General's optimistic report was dated October 19, 1897. Just ten days earlier, an incident was reported from Fort Sheridan, Illinois, that set into motion a chain of events destined to bring to the surface the deep suspicion that still existed in the public mind toward the Army. On that day, the Chicago *Tribune* featured the story of "the cruel and unusual treatment" of Private Charles Hammond. This soldier had been absent without leave for nine days from his post in Plattsburgh, New York and had given himself up at Fort Sheridan in order to avoid being charged with desertion. While the authorities at Sheridan were contacting his post, he was kept in the guardhouse.

The incident that touched off the outcry occurred when Hammond refused to work with the other prisoners, claiming that no charges had yet been preferred against him. When he persisted in this refusal, he was ordered brought before a summary court, and Captain Leonard A. Lovering, Fourth Infantry, the officer of the day, was sent to deliver him. Hammond refused to accompany Captain Lovering, whereupon the latter ordered him tied up and dragged to the court, with the captain prodding him with his sword.[31]

The *Tribune's* account of Hammond's experience, together with its interviews with soldiers who had witnessed it, was widely reprinted in the nation's press and aroused a storm of indignation reminiscent of the earlier response to the Wild case. "A people that maintains societies to prevent cruelty to animals," said the Chicago *Journal*, "will not maintain an establishment that sanctions cruelty to human beings." So violent was the reaction that the *Army and Navy Register* felt compelled to complain of "the malignity" of those papers that gave their readers the impression "that the service is officered by brutal, thuggish creatures . . . whose chief occupation is the untrammeled indulgence of their fury and malice."[32]

Reacting to these press accounts, Secretary of War Russell A. Alger, on October 11, directed that an inquiry be conducted into the incident. On the following day, acting with a dispatch for which "military annals furnish few parallels,"[33] the Secretary ordered Captain Lovering tried for conduct unbecoming an officer and gentleman. The latter exercised his right to choose a court of inquiry rather than a court-martial, and that body began its deliberations on October 21. Aside from the testimony of Lovering, who justified his actions as necessary to enable him to obey an order—to deliver Hammond to the court—the proceedings of the court of inquiry were notable mainly for the impassioned defense by Captain Robert H. Hall, post commandant, who spoke of the prisoner as "a mutinous deserter," and said: "If it was necessary to prod Hammond with a sword. . . . I regard it as perfectly justifiable." [34]

This defense of Lovering's behavior shocked even such a "staid and usually decently-disposed publication" as the Philadelphia *Public Ledger,* which wrote:

> It appears then, that the first reports of the way in which Hammond was treated were correct, and that the treatment comes under the head of justifiable military discipline. Flogging in the United States Army was abolished in 1861; but if this is the kind of discipline that has taken its place, and if this method of enforcing orders is necessary, it would be better to restore the flogging punishment. That really seems the more humane treatment and has the additional advantage that it can be conducted in seclusion and need not expose the cowardice of the offender and the brutality of his superiors to the gaze of the world. But there is evident need of reform in the methods of punishment in the Army if not in the character of some of its officers.[35]

On November 1, in accordance with the findings of the court of inquiry, Acting Secretary of War General Nelson P. Miles ordered Captain Lovering to be tried by a court-martial for conduct prejudicial to good order and military discipline. The trial began on November 22 and heard essentially the same evidence as had been presented to the court of inquiry, except that the defense sought to prove that Hammond was a disreputable character who had enlisted in the Army in order to avoid arrest for shooting a man in Michigan.[36]

The summation of Lieutenant Colonel Edward Hunter, trial judge-advocate, was featured in the press throughout the nation. In it, he called the attention of the court to the "considerable notoriety" that the case had achieved and stated that it involved "the dignity and respectability and humanity of the military service." He then warned the court:

> If you establish the fact that an officer may with impunity order any punishment he pleases to be inflicted on a soldier, you reduce enlisted men to a condition of servitude. That is what is meant by the false doctrine of being masterful. But it is the law that should be our master. There are rules published for the guidance of those who command, as well as those who may serve. These rules are well considered, appropriate to the conditions of our service, and a strict observance of their principles would go far to prevent catastrophes like the one we have investigated.

And he concluded with these words:

> This is time of peril to our order and to our tribunals. I think the things which the accused has done tyrannically ought to appear to you who have heard the testimony just as bitter and scandalous as they did to him who felt them. The finding delivered by this court will live long after taps have been sounded over the graves of the men composing this court.[37]

Lovering was found guilty and was sentenced to be reprimanded. The court said it was lenient on account of the outstanding record of Captain Lovering and the bad record of Private Hammond. Secretary Alger, while accepting the decision of the court, expressed his disappointment "that an offense so grave . . . should have been visited with so light a penalty." "There is no question," he went on, "but that Private Hammond deserved punishment for his conduct, but he should have received it in a lawful way." The Secretary ended his reprimand with this further criticism: "Under excitement men frequently do things which in cooler moments they recall with sorrow and regret; but this case is aggravated by the fact that after weeks of deliberation this officer evinces no regret for his wrongful acts." [38]

The case, however, was not yet closed. Secretary Alger had intended that his reprimand be given the widest possible publicity throughout the Army. The Washington correspondent of the Chicago *Tribune* reported that he was "determined to make the case a sort of Magna Charta for the private soldiers." He soon learned, however, that attempts were being made to suppress and bury his remarks. He therefore ordered that his statement be read in full to the garrison at every post in the United States.[39]

The *Army and Navy Journal* was not surprised at the fact that "there should be a difference of opinion on the question of discipline between the War Department and those actually on duty with troops." However, it went on to caution the officers that "those who legislate for the Army and those who ask for legislation must consider public opinion and the necessity for finding some way to reconcile the demands of discipline with American conceptions of the dignity of the individual man."[40]

Thus, on the eve of the Spanish-American War, after a quarter of a century of attempted reform, the Army still found itself in an unenviable position with respect to public opinion. It was not only that there remained a deep-seated popular feeling against the so-called caste system and the mistreatment of the soldiers by their officers. It was also the undeniable truth that as far as many of its most important aspects were concerned, the condition of the enlisted men continued to be a source of complaint, both within and outside the service. In spite of all the optimistic reports, the feeling persisted that the reforms had merely scratched the surface—that the United States Army, poised on the brink of its first major encounter in over thirty years, was still composed largely of soldiers who were basically underpaid, poorly fed, inadequately clothed, and governed by a system of justice that did not provide sufficient protection for men charged with military offenses.[41]

While the wages of all other workingmen had increased, the pay of the soldier had remained virtually the same since the Civil War. An officer of twenty years' service observed:

> That a young, strong man of good character will devote his life to such a poor prospect in a country as prosperous as ours is not to be expected. The outlook for him is one of poverty, deprivation and want. . . . The labouring man will go on strike and demand redress for his grievances; the soldier has no such means of making his dissatisfaction heard and simply deserts.[42]

The events of the Spanish-American War were to furnish the most dramatic proof of the fact that food and clothing still remained two of the Army's unsolved problems. The widespread criticism of the Subsistence Department during the war was presaged as early as 1895 when Captain H. B. Brinkerhoff complained of the meat served to the troops:

> About one-third of the fresh beef furnished to the soldier from the Subsistence Department is not beef at all, it is bone, and bone is not now, never was, and never will be beef.[43]

Captain Brinkerhoff was reprimanded for this criticism, but his comments were mild compared with the storm of protest that arose over the meat furnished the soldiers during the war.

As for the uniform, after all the improvements that had been made, it was still possible for a soldier to write in August, 1897: "It is high time the government issued an unlined blouse for summer wear. No one feels the need of it more than the poor enlisted men who are sweltering these hot days in the same blouse that is issued in the Dakotas during the most extreme cold weather."[44] This complaint was echoed in much more colorful terms by troops who suffered the tortures of wearing heavy woolen uniforms in Cuba in the summer of 1898.

And finally, with respect to the court-martial system, the *Army and Navy Register* was prophetic when it warned in August, 1896 that so long as "the lawlessness of courts martial" was "permitted to continue unrebuked," desertions would increase. "There is but one proper and efficient remedy for all this," it concluded, "and that is for Congress to take up the subject thoroughly and enact a complete Military Code."[45]

CHAPTER VII

THE NEGRO IN THE POST-CIVIL WAR ARMY

One of the most significant features of the post-Civil War Army—and one that is particularly relevant to the problems of present-day America —was the treatment of the Negro soldier. On the whole, the Army reflected the social attitudes of the country, not only toward the Negro, but toward other minorities as well. And, like the rest of the nation, the Army had within it those who adopted a forward-looking approach to the problem, and those who resisted any change in the traditional military structure.

Although Negroes had served in the Army during the Revolution, during the quasi-war with France in 1798, and during the War of 1812, they were effectively excluded from the Regular Army—not by any statute of Congress, but by a provision of the Army Regulations which limited enlistments to "free, white males." This restriction originated solely in the Army. The Act of December 10, 1814, only used the term "free" in describing the class of persons eligible for enlistment. Attorney General Edward Bates noted in 1864 that no act of Congres had ever "prohibited the enlistment of free colored men into either branch of the national military service," and Colonel William Winthrop wrote in his classic study of American military law that the insertion of the restrictive word "white" into the Army Regulations during this period was "a striking instance of legislation by an executive department."[1]

During the Civil War, the enlistment of Negro soldiers was expressly authorized, and several Negro regiments served in the Union Army in all branches of the line. At the end of the war, Negro soldiers constituted about 13 percent of the Army. However, in 1864, Colonel August V. Kautz noted that the enlistment of Negroes was "a peculiarity of the volunteer service," and had not yet been authorized for the regular service.[2]

After the war, the Radical Republicans insisted that the "blacks in blue" should be given a place in the regular military establishment of the

United States. On March 14, 1866, the Army Bill—S. 138—came up for discussion in the Senate. It provided that the line of the Army should consist of sixty-seven regiments—five of artillery, twelve of cavalry and fifty of infantry, with eight of the latter to be composed of colored troops. Senator Benjamin F. Wade of Ohio, "a determined defender of the Negro," proposed that two of the twelve cavalry regiments should be composed of colored enlisted personnel. His amendment was accepted, and the amended bill then passed the Senate "by the decisive and gratifying majorty of 27 to 5."[3] One week later, the *Army and Navy Journal,* in an editorial entitled "The Colored Troops," said:

> Ten regiments—eight of infantry and two of cavalry—are the colored forces the Senate bill contemplates. But the numbers are not really so much the subject of wonder as the fact of forming such regiments at all. For it seems resolved, however wisely, that the complexion is not henceforth to be put down in the recruiting officer's list of exemptions.[4]

This forecast proved accurate, for the distinction of "free, white" was omitted from the recruiting regulations when Congress, in 1866 and 1869, provided for four colored units—the Ninth and Tenth Cavalry and the Twenty-fourth and Twenty-fifth Infantry. Sections 1104 and 1108 of the Revised Statutes provided that the enlisted men of two regiments of cavalry and two regiments of infantry should be colored.[5] "The distinction of white has at last been omitted from the recruiting regulations," wrote General S. B. Holabird several years later, "and manhood alone, with proper restrictions as to age and physique, is the only qualification for service of our country."[6]

Despite the existence of numerous problems, the experiment launched in 1866 was a success. The morale of these units was high, and the desertion rate was only a fraction of that of white units. Their regimental bands came in for high praise.[7] In 1877, Chaplain George M. Mullins of the Twenty-fifth Infantry wrote from Fort Davis, Texas:

> The ambition to be all that soldiers should be is not confined to a few of these sons of an unfortunate race. They are possessed of the notion that the colored people of the whole country are more or less affected by their conduct in the Army.[8]

In a letter to General O. O. Howard in 1881, Colonel B. H. Grierson, commander of the Tenth Cavalry, described his troops as "one of the

best regiments in the Army." In 1889, Secretary of War Redfield Proctor wrote of the colored troops in his annual report: "They are neat,
orderly and obedient, are seldom brought before courts-martial and
rarely desert."[9] A year later, the nation's press praised the role played
by the troopers of the Ninth Cavalry during the Ghost Dance troubles
on the Pine Ridge Reservation, when four companies under Major Guy
V. Henry made several forced marches under blizzard conditions and
rescued elements of the Seventh Cavalry Regiment. The New York
Times said that the colored soldiers had shown themselves to be "fully
equal to any others."[10]

By the time of the Spanish-American War, the Negro soldiers had
won recognition both in garrison and in the field. In 1898, Colonel
Loomis L. Langdon declared that the colored men had fully "justified
the action of the Government in availing itself of their services."[11]

Still another attempt at including different racial groups in the postwar
Army was the enlistment of Indians as regular soldiers, instead of only
as scouts. Secretary of War Proctor, who had long been an advocate of
such recruitment, was convinced that if the program were properly managed, it would prove beneficial to both the Army and the Indians. His
idea was to assign men who believed in the possibility of progress and
civilization for the Indian as officers to these troops.[12] Endorsing this
view, the Army and Navy Journal said: "The accomplishment of objects
such as these must be conceded to be an aim not unworthy of the highest
aspirations of our Army officers."[13]

Early in 1891, a provision for the enlistment of two thousand Indians
was inserted in the bill for the reorganization of the infantry and artillery. Although Secretary Proctor worked hard for its passage, the bill
was defeated by a few votes in the House. Having failed to secure specific legislation for the recruiting of Indians as privates in the Army, the
Secretary issued a general order on March 9, 1891, authorizing the enlistment of one company of Indians for each of the twenty-six regiments
of white cavalry and infantry serving west of the Mississippi River.[14]
The New York Tribune praised Secretary Proctor's "good judgment" in
the recruiting of Indians as soldiers. And General Howard wrote: "If
the results of enlistment shall prove as good as they have with the colored element, they will be a success."[15]

By December of 1891, seven companies—three of cavalry and four
of infantry—had been fully and seven others partially recruited. In the
main, the officers assigned to these companies worked diligently to make

them efficient soldiers. Particularly noteworthy were the efforts of Lieutenant H. L. Scott, who viewed enlightened treatment of the Indian as a
trust.[16]

Early reports on the Indian experiment noted that encouraging progress was being made. The Indian soldiers were found to be eager to
learn and zealous in the performance of their duties. It was felt that if
this progress was maintained, the success of the project was assured.
"The outlook for the success of the experiment," said the Boston *Traveller,* "is certainly a gratifying one." The New York *Advertiser* expressed pleasure over the fact that the new policy was progressing so
promisingly. It was confident the nation would agree that it was far better to make soldiers of the Indians "than to cheat them first and extermi-
nate them afterward."[17]

However, the policy of utilizing Indians as soldiers proved decidedly
unpopular with many officers. The army, they argued, could not be expected to be a rehabilitation agency, or a center for social experiments,
if it was to perform its combat role effectively. There was enough good
material in the country, these critics maintained, without resorting to the
dangerous innovation of "enlisting savages" to defend the flag. "Is the
enlistment of barbarians to do our duty, the beginning of the end?"
asked one officer. "God forbid."[18]

Meanwhile, the experiment had taken a turn for the worse. Company
after company was disbanded, until only two commands remained in the
service, and these were consolidated in June, 1895, into one unit—
Troop L of the Seventh Cavalry, under the command of Captain Scott.
At the same time, orders were issued halting any further enlistments or
reenlistments of Indians. Even the consolidated troop fared poorly. As
the terms of its men expired, they were discharged. Soon the last of the
Indians had been retired, and the experiment came to an end.[19] *Battle
Flag,* a publication of the U.S. Army Aid Association, said that its failure provided "an interesting illustration of the relative aptitude of the
Indians and the Negroes for regular military service." "After a fair trial
the former are condemned," it went on, "while the latter have firmly established the reputation for soldierly qualities which they won in war
time."[20]

However, General Howard had a different opinion of the reason for
the difficulties. "One trouble with having regular Indian military companies," he wrote, "was that white soldiers would not serve under Indian
non-commissioned officers. . . ."[21] And General Hugh L. Scott, who

had devoted much of his time and energy to the success of the project, wrote years later:

> It seems a remarkable thing that British officers could make efficient soldiers of Egyptians, who have been slaves for three thousand years, but American officers could not make soldiers out of Indians, who had fought us successfully for a long period, and who when suitably armed and mounted were the best light horsemen the world has ever seen. The truth was that the army was angry at Gen. Schofield for mustering out the white men of the two troops in each regiment, and did not want the experiment to succeed. Innumerable obstacles were thrown in my way by unthinking officers, and support in Washington was withheld by a change of the Secretary of War.[22]

A great many national groups were also represented in the ranks, with Irish, Germans, Swedes and English predominating. "A man observing the Army," said the Sturgis (Dakota) *Record,* "can make a study of the immigrants in the United States that is interesting." And Poet-Private Will Stokes painted a colorful picture of the conglomeration of national groups that made up the American Army:

> Maginnis scowls at Johnny Bull, an' Yawcob
>   Meyer roars
> At Jean Duval; an' I have heard the
>   comp'ny "countin' fours"
> In seven different languages; on which
>   eventful day
> The captain burst a blood vessel, an'
>   fainted dead away.[23]

In 1891, Major Guy V. Henry aroused considerable indignation because of certain remarks attributed to him in an interview with a Washington *Post* reporter. After praising the fearlessness of the colored troops when he commanded, Major Henry was quoted as saying:

> Another thing about them that is to be considered; suppose there should be a Fenian outbreak or a riot of German Socialists, our white soldiers who are largely Irishmen and Germans could not be expected to fight their fellow countrymen with much zeal. But a Negro would not want anything better than a chance to kill some of his hereditary enemies, Germans and Irish. He knows they don't like him, and he likes them no better.[24]

The *Irish World,* one of the leading Irish papers in the United States, assailed Major Henry for seeking to inflame prejudice. "Know-nothing-ism," it said, "has been exorcised from our politics. It should find no refuge in the United States Army."[25]

Religious discrimination in the service also came under attack. It was charged, for example, that army chaplains were not assigned to the troops in proportion to the number of enlisted men of the various faiths. Critics claimed that while the great bulk of the enlisted men were Roman Catholics, the number of Catholic chaplains was very small. For many years after the war, there was only one Catholic priest among the thirty-four chaplains. It was reported that Catholic soldiers refused to attend chapel services altogether rather than attend services conducted by Protestant chaplains.[26]

On February 8, 1890, the *Army and Navy Journal* published a communication from a correspondent whose letter it described as bearing "the stamp of sincerity." "Two-thirds of the Army," he wrote, "are Roman Catholics, and would attend the Services of that Church if the opportunity was afforded them. But all the chaplains (with one exception) are Protestants, and while they complain that the men don't attend services, they never take into account that the men desire the services of their own Church." At this time, too, Major General John M. Schofield, commanding the Army, answered a complaint from Senator P. H. Plumb of Kansas, by writing: "Give the Army religious liberty and assist the men to obtain the religious ministrations of which they feel the need, and there will be the same interest in religion in the Army as elsewhere."[27]

The General's words provoked praise in both military and civilian circles. The New York *Freeman's Journal* endorsed his appeal with these words: "Let Uncle Sam be just to his Catholic soldiers; no one asks him to be generous; let there be religious liberty." General Schofield's statement drew support also from Rev. Edward B. Browne, the Rabbi of the Hebrew-American Congregation of Toledo, Ohio. He said that there were in New York City thousands of able-bodied Jewish men who would gladly enlist in the Army but who were kept from so doing by the absence of Jewish chaplains. Rev. Browne urged that the General favor the appointment of chaplains from "the *three* American Religions—Catholics and Hebrews as well as Protestants."[28]

The problems confronting white soldiers were compounded for those of color. If the food and equipment for white soldiers were bad, for

Negro troops they were worse. If white soldiers received harsh sentences from courts-martial, Negro soldiers were given more severe punishments for the same offenses. If life in the garrison was monotonous for white soldiers, colored troops found it intolerable. Where the civilian population scorned white troops, it despised the Negro soldier.[29] In June, 1890, Captain Edward T. Comegys, commenting on the attitude of civilians toward the colored troops in Texas, related how "a sick, colored soldier" returning from the Army General Hospital at Hot Springs, Arkansas, to his post at Fort Bayard, New Mexico, "had to go 48 hours without food because neither on the train or at a station could he buy even a cup of coffee."[30] And even though the colored troops had had more than their share of Indian fighting, they were confronted with greater obstacles in securing furloughs and in obtaining changes to garrisons near the cities. Some commanders felt that "centers of population at the South" should be avoided because of serious problems likely to arise between white civilians and colored troops. Eastern communities, constantly alert to any proposed changes of stations—which might bring colored units to their areas—were always ready with petitions to their congressmen and senators requesting that the orders be cancelled.[31] Chaplain T. G. Steward, the Negro chaplain of the Twenty-fifth Infantry Regiment, said: "When it has become known that a colored regiment was likely to be sent to some good post near an important city, the people of the place have usually made some sort of objection, and the matter has usually ended by the military authorities yielding, and the colored troops would find themselves in Arizona or somewhere else equally distant from the centers of life and population." And a colored soldier, whom the *Army and Navy Journal* characterized as an "educated and intelligent" man, complained sorrowfully that colored men always received nice notices "but never a good station."[32]

The Negro press joined in demanding that the colored soldiers be accorded the same treatment in assignments to stations as the white troops. In 1889, the New York *Age,* then the largest and most influential Negro newspaper, noted that the colored troops had done frontier service "for the past twenty-five years," and went on to say: "Is it not time to give these faithful soldiers a taste of garrison duty in the East? We think so."[33]

Up to the time of the outbreak of the war with Spain, only one company of colored soldiers served at a post east of the Mississippi River. In 1891, the New York *Times* observed: "Very many citizens have never seen a military organization of Negroes since the entire service of those troops has been on the Western frontiers." Many people in the United States realized for the first time that Negroes were actually serving in the regular army when they saw the black regiments on the way to Cuba.[34]

The white officer serving with Negro troops was also made to feel penalized by virtue of his association with these units. The attitude of the public frequently was that an officer assigned to a colored unit was not fully competent. To obtain a transfer to a white unit was virtually impossible since few officers would willingly exchange places with them.[35] In 1877, the New York *Times* published a dispatch from Washington which reported that the officers of the colored regiments were raising a clamor against this discrimination. They had been exiled for eleven years at the most disagreeable and unhealthy posts and could look forward to nothing "but perpetual banishment from the advantages of civilization and cooler climates for themselves and their families." As a result, many good officers had been compelled to resign. "Bright young officers keep away from the colored regiments if they can," wrote a colored soldier in 1892. "Many officers try their utmost to transfer because of what they have to take. . . . Of course, when they feel that way they do not feel any too good themselves to the men of the regiment in which it may be their lot to serve."[36]

Nor did the performance of the colored troops always bring them the recognition that was accorded to other regiments of the Army. An officer who had served many years with the Tenth Cavalry noted that although the colored soldiers did all the fighting at the Cheyenne Agency, I.T., and sustained nearly all the casualties, the white troops received all the commendations. The role of the Negro soldiers was tersely referred to as follows: "Two colored troops of the Tenth Cavalry were also engaged." The officer insisted that many similar cases had occurred.[37]

During the Ghost Dance troubles, the Ninth Cavalry "was the first in the field in November," wrote Lieutenant Grote Hutcheson, "and the last to leave in the following March, after spending the winter, the latter part of which was terrible in its severity, under canvas." That winter at Pine Ridge, Private W. H. Prather, Troop I, Ninth Cavalry, wrote "some lively rhymes on the Sioux War." After giving an account of the services of the various troops, he went on with the following verses, tinged with bitterness and resentment:

The rest have gone home to meet the blizzard's
    Wintry blast.
The Ninth, the willing Ninth, is camped here till
    the last.
We were the first to come; will be the last to leave.
    Why are we compelled to stay, why this reward receive?
In warm barracks our recent comrades take their ease
    While we poor devils, and the Sioux are left to freeze.[38]

For years the Army had difficulty in filling officer vacancies in the colored regiments. Upon learning of his assignment to a colored unit, a cadet felt he was being assigned to inferior service and sought at once to transfer to a white unit, even though this meant slower promotion. "In some instances," wrote Colonel Charles J. Crane, "the graduate requested assignment as 'additonal second lieutenant' in some white regiment in preference to accepting a vacancy existing in a colored regiment."[39] In a letter from West Point in 1875, Cadet Hugh L. Scott wrote to his mother:

> I am thinking seriously of the 10th Cav. as my stopping place. You know they are all moxies which creates a great prejudice against them here but there are four vacancies there now and soon to be another, and if I go into it as the ranking man I will start with five men below me instead of being foot myself which is a long step for promotion. . . . I would like much better to get into a white regiment but my class is crazy for the cavalry and there are very few vacancies. As to their being moxies I wont have near as much to do with them personally as you would with a black cook. . . . I have taken up all the this time to justify myself for such a proceeding for most of the men here will hoot me but I don't care so long as I see it is to my advantage.[40]

Another feature of the service viewed as discriminatory to the colored troops was their exclusion from numerous branches and positions. The initial postwar army bill SR 67, introduced on January 10, 1866, by Senator Henry Wilson of Massachusetts, had provided for a colored artillery regiment. General Grant, however, had objected to the employment of colored troops in the artillery since he felt that this branch was outside their competence. Grant's suggestion was followed by the Senate Military Committee. The colored artillery unit was eliminated from the bill and was never again mentioned in the postwar legislation setting up the four regiments of colored troops.[41] Recruiting officers thereafter assigned Negro enlisted men exclusively to the four infantry and cavalry units. The result was that all other branches of the service—artillery, ordnance, engineers and signal corps—were effectively closed to Negro soldiers, and for years they were also denied access to the positions of hospital steward, and ordnance, commissary or quartermaster sergeant.[42]

Critics of this exclusion policy pointed out that the regulations establishing the colored units did not actually prohibit Negroes from serving in other parts of the Army. The critics insisted that Negroes were competent to serve anywhere in the service, and they contended that it was clearly unfair to permit the Negro citizen to enlist and then to inform him that certain branches and positions were closed to him.[43] "Has not," wrote one correspondent to the *Army and Navy Journal,* "the colored soldier proved himself to be worthy of any honorable position that might be conferred upon him? Another correspondent asked: "Why is the colored man not represented in the artillery branch of the service . . . in which he proved himself during the war a capable soldier?" The service journal responded that there was "no good reason."[44]

In his annual report for 1889, General J. M. Schofield proposed that the existing five regiments of artillery be increased to seven regiments. Secretary of War Proctor endorsed this recommendation, stating that he deemed it important to consider whether one or both of the new regiments might be composed of colored enlisted personnel. He called attention to the excellent record made by the colored soldiers in the existing units and then went on to say: "They would seem to be especially well adapted for service at some of the sea coast fortifications and the discipline and instruction received would benefit them and be a public good."[45]

An officer of the Ninth Cavalry at Fort Robinson, Nebraska, hailed this recommendation and expressed the hope that Congress would heed it. "Now, by all means, let the two proposed artillery regiments be given and be made up of colored Americans. This is not asking too much. . . ." And a colored soldier wrote to the New York *Age* from the same post: "We need a colored artillery regiment badly, and I see no reason why we cannot have one."[46]

In December, 1889, a bill was introduced in the Senate to increase the artillery to seven regiments. The President was authorized to enlist colored men for one or more regiments at his discretion. Despite urgent pleadings from the Secretary of War, the bill failed to pass and the same fate befell a similar bill in the next Congress.[47] Chaplain Steward wrote regretfully:

> Had the changes sought in this proposition been secured, the field of the colored man in the army would have been considerably enlarged, and the number of colored men in the service thereby increased.[48]

In March, 1898, Congress authorized two new regiments of artillery, but despite the plea of Representative George A. White, the Negro Congressman from North Carolina, no provision was made for a colored regiment.[49] As a consequence, for years thereafter, infantry and cavalry regiments remained the only types of Negro combat units. The reason for this condition was not only the absence of a specific statute requiring colored artillery regiments, but the feeling that Negroes were only capable of serving in the infantry and cavalry. This point of view was graphically illustrated in May, 1898, when Captain Henry H. Wright, of the Ninth Cavalry, was asked by a correspondent why the colored soldier was not represented in the artillery. The Captain responded: "He lacks the brains. . . . He is brave enough and willing enough; but if we let him enlist in the artillery our shooting would very much resemble the fine marksmanship of the Spaniards."[50]

The commissioning of colored soldiers was another disputed issue both within and outside the service during these years. Thus when the New York *Freeman,* a Negro newspaper, published a letter in 1885 from an educated Negro complaining of the lack of opportunity in civil life for those like himself, the paper received two letters from Negro soldiers urging him to enlist in the Army. They assured him that color was not a barrier to the advancement of competent men. "Hence I advise all young men of the race who want to be independent, and yet rise, to join the army," concluded Sergeant Jacob O. Smith.[51]

But this advice was challenged by another serviceman who wrote bitterly:

> To our collegiate friends of high mental attainments and still higher expectations, of which plethoric salaries and perspective shoulder-straps form the principal component, I would most emphatically say, my colored brother, do not come, you will never get there. . . . Since the organization of the four colored regiments

now in the service, not a single colored soldier has been promoted from the ranks to the grade of an officer. . . . It is not that they do not possess the necessary qualifications for the office, but that the sentiment of the white men of the army is decidedly against it, and any ambitious aspirant for shoulder-straps in the ranks is promptly and effectually given to understand that "spades are not trumps" here.[52]

The dialogue was renewed seven years later when the New York *Age* published a communication from Chaplain T. G. Steward, in which he appealed to young colored men to enter the regular army and seek to secure a commission. He insisted there was no department of service where competent colored men could do more for themselves and their race, and he concluded with the words: "Covet the honor of a commission in the army of the country."[53]

The *Age* disputed this optimistic picture. In an editorial it said:

> . . . Until there shall be a very radical change in the law and the practice of promotion, the regular army of the United States is the very last place where Afro-Americans should seek to distinguish themselves; because, instead of distinguishing themselves they rather extinguish themselves,—gain neither glory nor wealth, while placing their lives at the service of a government which neither appreciates their patriotism nor rewards them as it does others for their sacrifices.[54]

Whatever the merits of this dispute, the fact is that not a single colored non-commissioned officer, before June, 1892, and not a single enlisted man after that date, rose from the ranks to a commission prior to the Spanish-American War.[55]

The policy of maintaining separate Negro units was also the subject of heated controversy. The arguments raised for and against the segregation of colored troops have a most contemporary ring. Defenders of this policy argued that it was necessary in order to avoid racial conflict and maintain morale and efficiency. Many of the proponents of segregated units contended that this policy served the best interests of the colored soldiers themselves, since it at least guaranteed that they would be permitted to serve in the Army. This argument was continually raised during the debates on two Congressional bills in 1876 and 1878 that would have eliminated the legal requirement that four regiments be composed of colored enlisted personnel. Critics of these measures contended that the inevitable consequence of their passage would be to eliminate almost all Negroes from the service or limit them to performing non-military duties of a menial character. Under the existing law, they noted, recruiting officers had no choice but to assign colored men to four units. But if there were no regiments set aside by law for Negro troops, recruiting officers might simply reject Negro enlistees as unfit and the result might very well be that in a short time the Army would be completely lily-white.[56] This point was made by Representative Edward W. Mackey of South Carolina, during the debate in 1876 on the Banning Bill. "The repeal of the law which now provides for these colored regiments," he insisted, "is only an indirect way, therefore, of getting rid of colored soldiers in the Army." It was made even more sharply by Senator James G. Blaine of Maine, during the debate in 1878 on the Burnside Bill, when he cautioned his colleagues:

> Do not let us deceive ourselves. Let us vote on this bill with the understanding that, whereas as a recognition of the services of the colored man in the Army of the Union during the war, we gave him a place and a recognition in the Army, we now declare an end to that, and that he shall not hereafter serve in the Army of the United States nor wear the uniform of the United States soldier.[57]

The Burnside Bill, like the Banning Bill of 1876, failed to pass the Senate. Nine years later a colored soldier protested vigorously against two new bills that had been introduced in Congress to establish mixed units. He wrote:

> While we want and should have representation in the Signal Corps, Artillery, and Ordnance, we do not want a measure adopted that will ultimately drive us from the service. Except the few who may elect to remain as cooks, teamsters, etc., such would be the result if the troops are mixed. . . . The equity of wiping out distinction in the service cannot be questioned. But when the facts are considered that the Negro as a soldier for over a quarter of a century has utterly failed (on account of prejudiced officers placed over him to administer justice) to rise above the grade of an enlisted man, a fact that has no parallel in the world's history, what can be accomplished by amalgamation? Nothing but absolute serfdom. . . .[58]

But the opponents of the system of segregated units were equally outspoken. Even in 1866, when the initial legislation was introduced, the anti-slavery publication the *Independent* viewed the creation of distinctive units of colored soldiers as retrogressive and editorialized:

> In addition to the old abuses of military service, it is now proposed to render the Army an instrument for degrading our colored population and keeping them a distinct caste. . . . They are not to be permitted to associate with their white compatriots. . . . The injustice and impolicy of such a measure are so patent that we do not see how anyone who advocates the political equality of all men, without respect of complexion or race, could give his support to such a measure.[59]

Thereafter, critics of the system insisted that it was neither legal nor necessary that this separation of the races be perpetuated in the service. They pointed out that Negro and white recruits lived, ate and slept together in the same quarters at the recruiting depots without protest or friction. They claimed that the experiment of a mixture of races had also been successfully tried at posts where white and colored companies served together. They called attention to the fact that only the Army practiced such separation; neither the Navy nor the Marine Corps made any distinction between personnel on the basis of color. And they emphatically denied that it was at all beneficial either to the colored enlisted men or the Negro population to maintain separate units in the Army.[60]

In 1874 a colored enlisted man insisted that it was "just as important for the prosperity of our race in the United States to have mixed soldiers as it is to have mixed public schools." His sentiments were shared by Senator Blanche K. Bruce, the Negro Senator from Mississippi who, in 1878, contended that there were hundreds of Negroes who would not enlist in the Army as long as "an opprobrious distinction" on account of color was retained.[61]

Support for desegregation was also voiced by General Sherman in 1880, when he expressed the conviction that all qualified men should be enlisted and assigned to regiments regardless of color. "Such has been the law and usage in the Navy for years," he went on, "and the Army would soon grow accustomed to it." "The people have made the colored man a citizen," an officer of colored troops wrote in 1882. "It is time the fact was accepted by the Army." And in April, 1883, General Samuel B. Holabird called upon Congress to abolish "the language of distinction between white and black troops in our statute books," and to at least permit Negroes and whites who wished to serve together to do so.[62]

These appeals were unavailing. There was no express repeal of the two sections of the revised statutes in any subsequent legislation concerning the Army, with the result that it remained a segregated institution until World War II. In 1906, Captain Matthew F. Steele, a Southerner, wrote an article entitled "The 'Color Line' in the Army," in which he complained bitterly over the failure of Congress to do away with the two controversial sections. The law, he said, was the only one on the statute books of the national government "which treats the negro citizen as a class apart—which sets up a 'Jim Crow car' for them, as it were, and requires them to ride in it or in none. No more exclusive law can be found in the codes of Alabama or Mississippi."[63]

During the 1880's some beginnings were made towards the elimination of racial discrimination in the Army—particularly in those branches of the service which had previously been closed to Negroes. In April, 1884, W. Hallett Greene, a Negro member of the graduating class of the College of the City of New York, applied for enlistment in the Signal Corps, which at that time was "lily white." Although the first response to his application was negative, there ensued a lengthy exchange of correspondence involving General Alexander S. Webb, President of the College, Brigadier General William B. Hazen, Commanding Officer of the Signal Corps and Secretary of War Robert T. Lincoln. In it General Hazen, who had rejected the first application, explained his position as being based not upon prejudice, but upon his understanding that Congress had decreed that Negro soldiers were to be confined to two regiments of infantry and two of cavalry. Nevertheless, this interpretation was overruled by Secretary Lincoln and on September 26, 1884, Greene was enlisted in the Signal Corps by direct order of the Secretary.[64]

The publication of this exchange of correspondence was greeted by *Frank Leslie's Illustrated Newspaper* as proof that Secretary Lincoln had again proved himself to be "his father's son." But not everyone acclaimed the Secretary's decision. The Jacksonville (Florida) *Times-Union* felt he had done "a very foolish thing" in forcing the enlistment of a Negro in the Signal Corps. It expressed the belief that, for the present, it was wiser to confine colored soldiers to the regiments allotted to them, since race prejudice was still too strong to allow for Negroes to be thrust into every place where an opening existed without provoking a hostile reaction. "It is a false philanthropy," it concluded, "that makes victims of its subjects." But the New York *Globe,* a Negro newspaper, rejected this concern and declared: "It should not be made compulsory for colored men to join colored regiments because they are colored. They should be bound by the limitations binding upon white men who offer themselves for enlistment."[65]

The enlistment of Greene in the Signal Corps was followed in 1885 by the acceptance of Negro enlisted men in the Hospital Corps, the Ordnance Corps and the Commissary and Quartermaster Departments.[66]

In August, 1885, Secretary of War William C. Endicott rejected the plea for a transfer submitted on behalf of a lieutenant who was reluctant to accept an assignment to one of the colored regiments, stating that the colored soldiers "hold the same status in the Army of the United States as any other troops of the line." The New York *Herald* congratulated the Secretary for treating the subject "with dignity and fairness." And the New York *Freeman* declared that the Secretary of War had shown himself "to be well up in the rights of man."[67]

Four years later an officer wrote to the *Army and Navy Journal* describing the excellent performance of the Ninth Cavalry during the autumn maneuvers held that year. He declared that "many an officer who came to the camp with false notions of our colored troops, left with the knowledge that they were the best of soldiers."[68]

Nor was this sentiment confined to the officers. Greater contact was also leading to greater respect and acceptance among the enlisted men. Writing to the *Army and Navy Register* in August, 1885, a colored enlisted man described the enthusiastic welcome extended by the white soldiers of the Seventh Infantry, to the colored men of Troop M, Ninth Cavalry, upon the latter's arrival at their new station, Fort Washakie, Wyoming, after a tedious march of over 800 miles. After noting that they were given a sumptuous banquet, the writer went on to say: "These and other little acts of kindness from one to another give the lie to the oft repeated assertion that white and colored troops wont affiliate together."[69]

Another example of such cooperation occurred several months later. Early in 1886, Sergeant John M. Harper, Twenty-fifth Infantry, stationed at Fort Meade, Dakota, read in the New York *Freeman* that Mrs. Prudence Crandall Philleo, now in her old age, was living in poverty and want. The paper recounted the story "of this truly heroic woman," the privations and suffering she endured in 1832 and thereafter because "she stood up for what was just and right" and persisted in her determination to maintain a free school for colored girls. Sergeant Harper was moved by the story to collect contributions from the enlisted men at his post in behalf of Mrs. Philleo. On April 3, he sent the *Freeman* $27.40, with a list of the contributors. Both white and Negro soldiers at the post had contributed to help "put this worthy lady above want."[70]

By the 1890's it appeared that racial antipathy among enlisted men was on the decline in the army. Indeed, it was possible for the *Army and Navy Journal* to declare in February, 1891, that "the prejudice against the colored troops which used to exist to some extent in the regular army has died out." It went on to note that during the recent troubles at and near Pine Ridge "the spirit of true comradeship between the white and black soldiers" had been strikingly exemplified.[71]

On January 26, 1891, Major Guy V. Henry wrote to General O. O. Howard, commanding the Division of the East, from Pine Ridge as follows:

> When a change of troops is made at Fort Meyer [Virginia], I believe you have it in your power to do a good service to the "colored troops" by asking for their detail there. . . . It would be a most gracious way of admitting their deserts.[72]

Three days later, General Howard responded: "I will do anything that is proper in the recognition and reward of your gallant command." On February 11, General J. M. Schofield sent a memorandum to Adjutant General J. C. Kelton suggesting that in the selection of troops of cavalry for station at Fort Meyer, "a representative troop be selected from Colonel Henry's battalion of the Ninth Cavalry" which had served in the Sioux campaign, as appreciation of gallant services in the field.[73] Early in March it was reported that General Schofield had directed Major Henry to choose a troop from the Ninth Cavalry for detail at Fort Meyer. The Washington correspondent of the New York *Herald* reported, however, that there was "some adverse criticism of the present proposition." "Some people here," he went on, ". . . consider it detrimental to the best interests of the service to bring white and colored troops together in the same garrison, especially at the nation's capital, where the color line is so frequently the cause of discussion." The New York *Herald* in an editorial entitled "Colored Troops," commented angrily on this opposition:

> We don't care whether a man is white, black or green; he should have the reward of his daring. Since the Ninth were exposed to the

rigors of frightful cold, and did their duty by the side of white troops, they should not be discriminated against when the prerequisites and pleasures of peaceful times are being distributed.[74]

General Schofield wrote to Secretary of War Redfield Proctor on March 6, that in accordance with the understanding they had reached that morning, he was recommending that "a troop of the Ninth Cavalry take station at Fort Meyer." On April 28, the annual spring transfer of troops was announced by Secretary Proctor. The order designated Troop K, Ninth Cavalry, and Troop A, First Cavalry, to relieve the units then stationed at Fort Meyer. A month later, Troop K left Fort Robinson, Nebraska, for its new station. Not long afterwards, the Washington *Post* reported: "Beautiful Fort Meyer, the most picturesque cavalry post in the country and the only one east of the Mississippi River, is now, for the first time in its history, garrisoned by colored cavalrymen."[75] And the *Army and Navy Journal* published a communication from a correspondent who wrote:

Let the good work go on. Let the authorities of the Government extend to the colored soldiers, as a just reward, and stimulus for future efforts, the same appreciative recognition as to details and stations, as that awarded to their more fortunate white comrades in arms. Let all stand by the record, and accord honor to whom honor is due, and then the sentinel, on the watch tower of freedom, can call, All is well!

On September 18, 1896, Secretary of War Daniel S. Lamont issued an order directing that the Twenty-fourth Infantry Regiment be transferred to Fort Douglas, Utah. General Wesley Merritt, commanding the Department of the Missouri, characterized the assignment as being "in the nature of a promotion" for what he called "a splendid regiment." "Fort Douglas is in Salt Lake City," he went on, "and a far pleasanter place for the soldiers than the posts in New Mexico and Arizona."[76]

Not everyone in Salt Lake City regarded the prospect with General Merritt's enthusiasm. The Salt Lake *Tribune,* the leading newspaper of the city, published an editorial entitled "An Unfortunate Change," in which it claimed that serious apprehension had been aroused among "the best people in the city," who, the newspaper said, feared that they might be forced into "direct contact with drunken colored soldiers on the way from the city to Fort Douglas." The *Tribune* expressed confidence that if these fears were drawn to the attention of the Secretary of

War, he could still be persuaded to change the order and transfer the colored men "to some other station where they would be just as comfortable, where they would have just as many privileges, and where they would not be a source of apprehension and discomfort to the people of a large city like this."[77]

A determined effort was made to have the order revoked. The War Department, however, refused to yield and Secretary Lamont informed all who visited him that the order could not be changed.[78] On October 11, Company F left Fort Bayard, New Mexico, as an advance contingent for Fort Douglas. On that day Private Thomas A. Ernest, of Company E, sent a communication to the *Tribune* which was published eleven days later with an introductory statment to the effect that it was written by a member of the Twenty-fourth Infantry, "which will be stationed here in a few days." Private Ernest wrote:

> . . . The enlisted men of the Twenty-fourth infantry, as probably the people of Salt Lake City know, are negroes, but there are some things about the Twenty-fourth that the people of Salt Lake City probably do not know. There are as many gentlemen in the Twenty-fourth infantry as there are in any other regiment of like arm of service. The Twenty-fourth ranks as one of the cleanest, best-drilled and best-disciplined regiments in the United States Army. . . . They are soldiers now, it is true, but they believe that they are engaged in an honorable calling. They have enlisted to uphold the honor and dignity of their country as their fathers enlisted to found and preserve it.
>
> The negro is known for his obedience to and respect for law and order, and we object to being classed as lawless barbarians. We were men before we were soldiers, we are men now, and will continue to be men after we are through soldiering. We ask the people of Salt Lake City to treat us as such. . . . Up to the 11th inst., when company F left for your city, there were stationed at this post five organizations of this regiment, with only one man in the guardhouse. Does that look like we do not know how to take care of ourselves, and is it not a very creditable showing? . . . It is true that we have been stationed on the frontier for the past twenty-two years, but none of us have become savages. We are proud of our regiment's reputation, and confident of our ability to maintain it, and the people of Salt Lake City have nothing to fear from the men of the Twenty-fourth infantry even though they are negroes.[79]

A Negro newspaper published in Salt Lake City, the *Broad Axe*, commended Private Ernest for his letter. It revealed, the paper said, "the intelligence and the high character of the writer, and speaks volumes for his regiment." A year later, on the occasion of the first anniversary of the regiment's arrival, the *Tribune* published an extensive apology which concluded with the complimentary words that "the regiment has lived down the apprehensions awakened when the announcement of their coming was made and they are now appreciated at their worth, as citizens and soldiers above reproach."[80]

On April 21, 1898, the Twenty-fourth regiment marched from Fort Douglas, through the streets of the city, to the Rio Grande depot, where its members boarded the trains and started on their journey to the Cuban front. "The citizens, school children, university students and the state officials turned out en masse to witness their departure and bid them bon voyage," wrote the *Broad Axe*, "and many flowers were showered upon them by the spectators."

But even as it was reporting this enthusiastic sendoff, the newspaper was realistic enough to understand that all was not sweetness and light in the relationship between the Negro soldiers and the white populace. It concluded its report with this sarcastic comment: "During their absence there is no danger of the members of the Anglo-Saxon race who detest riding in street cars with negroes of being frightened to death by coming in contact with Uncle Sam's black soldiers."[81]

The *Broad Axe's* cynicism turned out to be prophetic, for no sooner had the Negro troops left their stations in the West and entered the South, en route to Cuba, than their experiences changed markedly. While Negroes greeted them enthusiastically at the railroad stations of the cities they entered, white civilians pointedly absented themselves from such welcomes. "It mattered not if we were soldiers of the United States, and going to fight for the honor of our country," a Negro enlisted man commented bitterly. "We were 'niggers,' as they called us, and treated us with contempt."[82]

This attitude toward the Negro soldier became the predominant one following the war. Although all of the four colored regiments distinguished themselves by their conduct in the fighting and received a considerable amount of favorable publicity, and although many of them were accorded "a royal welcome and a well deserved praise" when they returned, it was not long before discouraging reports of hostile civilian attitudes toward them began to appear.[83] On October 22, the Cleveland

Gazette published a communication from Chaplain George Prioleau, the Negro Chaplain of the Ninth Cavalry, in which he described the journey of that regiment from Montauk Point to its new station at Fort Grant, Arizona. All along the line, he reported, the colored soldiers were received most enthusiastically until they reached Kansas City, Missouri, where the First Cavalry had arrived only a few minutes earlier. Chaplain Prioleau continued:

> The two regiments, regulars of the U.S.A. were there together. Both were in Cuba . . . both were under the same flag, both wore the blue. And yet these black boys . . . were not allowed to stand at the counters of restaurants and eat a sandwich and drink a cup of coffee, while the white soldiers were welcomed and invited to sit down at the tables and eat free of cost.[84]

So widespread were these incidents that Chaplain Steward characterized them as part of a calculated campaign to discredit the colored soldiers which, he noted regretfully, was singularly successful. By 1906, racial lines had hardened to the point where Captain Matthew F. Steele had to report:

> The prejudice against the negro and the negro regiment is national; it is as wide as our territory. There is, for instance, a cavalry post in Vermont, but no colored troop has ever been or is likely ever to be, stationed there. The people of Vermont do not want them.
> A few years ago, a fine troop of the Ninth Cavalry was stationed at Fort Meyers across the way from the National Capital, as a reward for specially good service in an Indian campaign. Never a word of complaint was made against the behavior of this troop; yet it is well known that never again will a colored troop be ordered to that post for station. The people of Washington do not want them. . . . Where then, are the colored regiments going to serve hereafter? . . .[85]

EPILOGUE

The need for harmonizing the requirements of military discipline, the welfare of the enlisted men, and the views of the American people has been a recurrent theme throughout the history of the United States Army.[1] It played a major role in the controversy that raged within the service for years on how to provide an effective deterrent to the "old evil" of desertion. Leading officers lined up on both sides of the argument. One group felt that only a policy of vigorously pursuing and punishing deserters was likely to discourage defections from the ranks. To this end they urged that a systematic effort be made by both the military and civilian authorities to apprehend deserters and bring them to trial. They also sought to insure that the most rigorous punishment would be imposed upon those who were captured and convicted. At the same time they felt that the Army had to change the public's view of the soldier. It was, they held, dangerous to the welfare of the country for the people to consider the contract of a soldier as being like any other agreement between employer and employee, the violation of which was no more culpable than the breach of a civil contract for service.[2]

But there was others who espoused a philosophy diametrically opposed to these views. These officers believed that in order to get to the root of the desertion problem, it was necessary to introduce such reforms as would render the military service at least tolerable to the men in the ranks. The adoption of such measures, they argued, would not only add to the efficiency of the Army, but would also serve to overcome much of the public prejudice against the enlisted men. It was their contention that if the conditions under which the men served were improved, the soldier would no longer be viewed with disdain and contempt, but rather would enjoy the respect due an individual who served his country.[3]

Probably the most eloquent exponent of this viewpoint in the Army during the period under consideration was Adjutant General John C. Kelton. A graduate of West Point, he had served on the frontier, had been an instructor at the Military Academy, and had held the post of Adjutant General of the Division of the Pacific before coming to Wash-

149

ington in 1885. In June, 1889, he was appointed Adjutant General of the Army.

General Kelton's term of office was marked by a number of improvements in the conditions of the enlisted men and reforms in the operation of the service. It was appropriate that his name is identified closely with the entire reform movement in the Army, and it was symbolic that when he died in 1893, while holding the position of Superintendent of the Army's Old Soldiers' Home, the epitaph placed on his grave by the residents of the institution read "The Soldiers' Friend."[4]

In his first annual report for 1889, General Kelton had written:

> It is unfortunate that the public do not regard desertion in time of peace a more serious offense than is now the case, but it will not sanction any more severe punishment than are now served at military prisons, for two reasons: First, the public believe that many men are compelled to desert as the only protest they can make to the treatment they receive; second, the soldier being a volunteer, the executive authority of the country can only permit such reasonable punishment to be inflicted for the offense as will not shock public opinion nor deter men from enlisting. All that can be done in the matter is to make military administration so perfect that the soldier will have no cause to desert his colors.[5]

As we have seen, in the years before the Spanish-American War a number of reforms were instituted in order to make the soldier's life more agreeable and attractive. They included reforms such as the addition of a pound of vegetables to the daily ration of the soldier, the creation of summary courts and a code of punishment, the purchase of discharge, the establishment of the canteen, changes in the recruiting system, as well as improvements in housing, clothing, recreation and in the method of promotion from the ranks.[6] However, the experiences of the Regular Army in the post-war years demonstrate that these measures did not eliminate the problem of desertion. From 1900 to 1905, the number of desertions increased steadily. In 1905 the strength of the Army was 63,022 men and the number of desertions was 6,533, for a rate of 10.3 percent.[7]

Beginning in 1905 and for several years thereafter, the Army, under Adjutant General Fred C. Ainsworth, reverted to the views advanced in the pre-war years by those who contended that only the certainty of apprehension and punishment was an effective deterrent. General Ainsworth was responsible for the adoption of several measures calculated to prevent desertion and to insure apprehension and effective punishment of defectors—an improved recruiting system, the fingerprint and photographic system of detection, and greater severity in the punishment of convicted deserters.[8]

In 1908, the number of desertions began to decline. Two years later, it had fallen to less than 3,500 and by the end of 1911, the rate reached the second lowest point in nearly a century.[9]

It is interesting to note, however, that even General Ainsworth, despite his strong support for severity in the treatment of deserters, still played a decisive role in obtaining from Congress the Act of May 1, 1908, that increased the pay of the Army enlisted men—the first increase in thirty-six years.[10]

And yet, even though the number of desertions decreased, the grievances of the enlisted men still remained, and were recognized. On the matter of military justice, for example, the ever-present need for revision of the Articles of War prompted Judge Advocate General Enoch H. Crowder to observe in 1912 that the administration of justice was still "seriously obstructed."[11]

It was not until the post-World War I period that remedial legislation was enacted to improve the court-martial system, and to provide some remedy for the injustices soldiers might suffer at the hands of their officers, both commissioned and non-commissioned.[12] It is important to recognize that these changes were among the objectives sought by the reformers of the post-Civil War years. And despite the fact that for the most part, their efforts were not crowned with lasting success, nevertheless, their philosophy that the Army's views must be in harmony with those of the people, and that it was the responsibility of the military authorities to see to it that the enlisted men were treated fairly, was the underlying key to these changes.[13]

The post-Civil War Army reformers share a quality with many others like them who came both before and after: their long-range influence was far greater than the immediate, tangible results of their efforts.

NOTES

ABBREVIATIONS USED IN FOOTNOTES

ANJ: Army and Navy Journal
ANR: Army and Navy Register
L.C.:   Library of Congress
MSIUS: Military Service Institute of the United States
N.A.:   National Archives

INTRODUCTION

[1]William Walton, *The Army and Navy of the United States* (Boston, 1889-95), I, 29; William A. Ganoe, *History of the United States Army* (New York, 1924), pp. 306-09, 324, 334; Oliver L. Spaulding, *United States Army in Peace and War* (New York, 1937), pp. 348-41; C. Joseph Bernardo and Eugene H. Bacon, *American Military Policy: Its Development Since 1775* (Harrisburg, 1955), pp. 237-41; Arthur A. Ekirch, Jr., *The Civilian and the Military* (New York, 1956), pp. 112-14; 44th Cong., 2d Sess., House Executive Document No. 1, Pt. 2, II, 80.

[2]45th Cong., 2d Sess., House Executive Document No. 1, Pt. 2, II, vii; 51st Cong., 1st Sess., House Executive Document No. 1, Pt. 2, II, 4; 52nd Cong., 1st Sess., House Executive Document No. 1, Pt. 2, II, 46-48; 53rd Cong., 3d Sess., House Executive Document No. 1, Pt. 2, 5, 59-60, 102; MSIUS *Journal*, V (1884), 237-71; New York *Times*, May 13, 1878, October 12, 1894; *ANJ*, October 13, 1894; John M. Schofield to Horace Porter, November 16, 1894, Schofield Papers, L. C.

[3]Bernardo and Bacon, *American Military Policy*, p. 239; Russell F. Weigley, *Quartermaster General of the Union Army: A Biography of M. C. Meigs* (New York, 1959), pp. 340, 348; Erna Risch, *Quartermaster Support of the Army: A History of the Corps, 1775-1939* (Washington, 1962), pp. 457-58, 491; *ANJ*, January 20, 1876; 42nd Cong., 2d Sess., House Executive Document No. 1, Pt. 2, II, 72.

[4]Robert M. Utley, *Frontiersman in Blue: The United States Army and the Indian, 1848-1865* (New York, 1967), pp. 13-17, 19; Donald N. Bigelow, *William Conant Church and the Army and Navy Journal* (New York, 1952), pp. 187-89; *Congressional Globe*, 35th Cong., 1st Sess., pp. 409, 518-21; *The United Service*, XII (June, 1885), 672; New York *Tribune*, May 8, 1865, January 20, February 8, 22, March 20, 1866; New York *Times*, May 3, 1865;

The Nation, II (March 8, 1866), 296; Russell F. Weigley, *Towards an American Army* (New York, 1962), pp. 127-36; *ANJ,* April 22, 1871, September 8, 1877.

⁵New York *Sun,* April 14, 1875, August 2, September 25, 1876, February 25, 1877, May 17, 1878; Brooklyn *Daily Eagle,* May 22, 1878, December 13, 1892; Philadelphia *Inquirer,* January 6, 1875; Cleveland *Plain Dealer,* May 30, 1874, November 16, 1876; *Ohio State Journal,* February 22, 1877; Hartford *Times,* November 13, 1877; *ANJ,* November 18, December 9, 16, 1876; Ekirch, *The Civilian and the Military,* pp. 109-18; Bernardo and Bacon, *American Military Policy,* pp. 236-43; Harry Barnard, *Rutherford B. Hayes and His America* (Indianapolis, 1954), pp. 303-04; MSIUS *Journal,* V (1884), 292-323; Russell F. Weigley, *History of the United States Army* (New York, 1967), pp. 266, 281-82; Cincinnati *Enquirer,* January 20, 1887; San Francisco *Examiner,* December 5, 1892; *Locomotive Fireman's Magazine,* X (August, 1886), 453-54; *American Federationist,* III (March 13, 1896), 13; *Scribner's,* XXXIII (1903), 668.

⁶Washington *Capital,* November 16, 1873; New York *Sun,* May 23, 1873, January 22, February 10, 16, 1874; New York *Times,* November 28, 1867; New York *Tribune,* December 11, 1869; New York *Evening Post,* June 13, 1870; New York *Herald,* June 23, 1870; *Congressional Record,* 43rd Cong., 1st Sess., pp. 116-17, 990-91; Bernardo and Bacon, *American Military Policy,* p. 236; Ekirch, *The Civilian and the Military,* pp. 114, 123.

⁷New York *Times,* March 5, 1877; Hartford *Times,* March 5, 1877; New York *Tribune,* March 13, 1877; New York *Sun,* November 16, 1877; *ANJ,* March 17, April 14, 28, May 19, September 8, 1877; *The Nation,* XXIV (March 22, 1877), 175; Hugh L. Scott, *Some Memories of a Soldier* (New York, 1928), pp. 174-75; S. E. Whitman, *The Troopers: An Informal History of the Plains Cavalry, 1865-1890* (New York, 1962), pp. 109-17; James T. King, *War Eagle: A Life of General Eugene A. Cox* (Lincoln, 1963), pp. 186, 293 n.11.

⁸*ANJ,* July 11, 1891; Allan Nevins, *Abram S. Hewitt, with Some Account of Peter Cooper* (New York, 1935), p. 407; George B. Davis (ed.), *Military Laws of the United States* (Washington, 1897), pp. 156-57; New York *Times,* August 20, October 30, 1887; Francis P. Prucha, *A Guide to the Military Posts of the United States, 1789-1895* (Madison, 1964), pp. 152-56. In 1891 the divisions were abolished and eight military departments were retained and their area extended. *ANJ,* July 11, 1891; Otto L. Nelson, *National Security and the General Staff* (Washington, 1946), pp. 13-14.

⁹Prucha, *Guide to the Military Posts,* pp. 24-34; Herbert M. Hart, *Old Forts of the Far West* (Seattle, 1964), pp. 5-6, 137, 146, 158, 166; Harold B. Simpson (ed.), *Frontier Forts of Texas* (Waco, 1966), vii-xx; San Antonio *Express,* April 18, 1876; Risch, *Quartermaster Support for the Army,* p. 487; James A. Huston, *The Sinews of War: Army Logistics, 1775-1953* (Washington, 1966), pp. 256-59; Edith M. Chappell, "Old Fort McKinney," *The Buffalo Bulletin,* Johnson County, Wyoming, April 25, 1929; George Forsyth, *The Story of the Soldier* (New York, 1900), pp. 104-05.

¹⁰Prucha, *Guide to the Military Posts,* pp. 34-36; Hart, *Old Forts of the Far West,* pp. 148-50; Risch, *Quartermaster Support of the Army,* p. 514; Bernardo and Bacon, *American Military Policy,* pp. 243-44; Huston, *Army Logistics,* p. 268.

[11]Davis, *Military Laws of the United States,* pp. 378-80; R. Williams, "Army Organization in the United States," *The Galaxy,* XXIV (November, 1877), 594-602; Loomis L. Langdon, "The Regular Army," *The Independent,* L (August 11, 1898), 388-89; *The United Service,* XI, N.S. (July, 1891), 4-5, 52-59; New York *Times,* August 1, 1890; *ANJ,* December 17, 1881; Weigley, *Towards an American Army,* pp. 137-38; Oswald Garrison Villard, "The New American Army," *The Atlantic Monthly,* LXXXIX (April, 1902), 437-51.

[12]R. Williams, "The Staff of the United States Army," *The Atlantic Monthly,* XLI (March, 1878), 379-80; Langdon, "The Regular Army," pp. 388, 391; Risch, *Quartermaster Support of the Army,* pp. 455, 476-77; Huston, *Army Logistics,* pp. 255-56, 268; Whitman, *The Troopers,* pp. 27-28; Weigley, *Towards an American Army,* pp. 166-67, 288, 300; Theo. Rodenbaugh and William L. Haskin (eds.), *The Army of the United States* (New York, 1896), pp. 1-149; Joseph M. Hawes, "The Signal Corps and its Weather Service," *Military Affairs,* XXX (Summer, 1966), 68-76.

[13]George B. Davis, *A Treatise on the Military Law of the United States* (Washington, 1898), p. 4; MSIUS *Journal,* I (1879), 385; Rollin A. Ives, *A Treatise on Military Law* (New York, 1879), pp. 16-17, 42-46; August V. Kautz, *Customs of the Service* (Philadelphia, 1864), p. 201; Anson Mills, *My Story* (Washington, 1917), pp. 366-67; W. Winthrop (ed.), *A Digest of Opinions of the Judge Advocate General of the Army* (Washington, 1880), pp. 67, 448-49; 51st Cong., 1st Sess., House Executive Document No. 1, Pt. 2, II, 85.

[14]Edgar S. Dudley, *Military Law and the Procedure of Courts-Martial* (New York, 1912), p. 11.

[15]James R. Jacobs, *Beginnings of the Army, 1783-1812* (Princeton, 1941), p. 272; George James Stanfield, "A History of the Judge Advocate General's Department," *Military Affairs,* IX (1945), 222; John F. Callan (ed.), *Military Laws of the United States* (Baltimore, 1958), pp. 136-62; Herbert Page, "Military Law—A Study in Comparative Law," *Harvard Law Review,* XXXII (1918-1919), 354-55, 364.

[16]*The United States Service Magazine,* V (March, 1866), 224; *ANJ,* August 31, 1867, April 10, 1869, March 22, 1873, January 10, 1874; 32nd Cong., 2d Sess., Senate Executive Document No. 1, p. 35; 33rd Cong., 1st Sess., Senate Executive Document No. 1, p. 96; 35th Cong., 1st Sess., Senate Executive Document No. 11, p. 48.

[17]*Hearing Before the Committee on Military Affairs, House of Representatives. 62nd Cong., 2d Sess., on H.R. 23628* (Washington, 1912), pp. 5, 17, 33; Dudley, *Military Law,* p. 6; *Journal of the United States Cavalry Association,* XX (1909), 482, 497; James A. Regan, *The Judge Advocate Recorder's Guide* (Washington, 1877), pp. 182-203; MSIUS *Journal,* I (1879), 57, XIII (1892), 103, XVII (1894), 19.

[18]47th Cong., 2d Sess., House Executive Document No. 1, Pt. 2, II, 110, 114-16; Winthrop, *Digest of Opinions* (1880), pp. 77-78.

[19]*ANJ,* September 27, 1884, December 13, 1884.

[20]Kansas City *Times,* April 26, 1886. Cf. MSIUS *Journal,* I (1879), 55-56, X (1889), 763; *ANJ,* August 3, 1867.

[21]MSIUS *Journal,* XVII (1895), 19. Cf. *ibid.,* I (1879), 55-56; *The United Service,* IX (August, 1883), 182; *ANJ,* September 14, October 12, November 16, 1889; W. Winthrop, *Military Law and Precedents* (Boston, 1896), I, 266, 291, II, 824-25, 855, 926-29, 940, 1016, 1020; A. W. Brown, "The Administration of Justice in the Army," *Cornell Law Quarterly,* III (1917-1918), 178.

[22]49th Cong., 1st Sess., House Executive Document No. 1, Pt. 2, II, 344-45; *ANJ,* January 1, 1889; J. C. Kelton to O. O. Howard, July 5, 1888, Howard Papers; Thomas F. Barr, Department Judge Advocate General, Department of Dakota, *General Orders and Circulars issued from Headquarters, Department of Dakota,* St. Paul, Minn., 1886.

[23]*The United Service,* VII (December, 1882), 597. Cf. VIII (March, 1883), 92-93, IX (April, 1884), 384; MSIUS *Journal,* XXXVII (1905), 17; Kansas City *Times,* February 17, 1890.

[24]Arthur Murray, *Instructions for Courts-Martial* (St. Paul, 1891), p. 92.

[25]*ANJ,* July 30, 1887; 47th Cong., 1st Sess., House Executive Document No. 1, Pt. 2, II, 203; Portland *Eastern Argus,* October 12, 1889. Cf. New York *Tribune,* March 6, 1872; D. B. Nichols, "The Devil's Article," *Military Law Review,* XXIII (October, 1963), 111-37.

[26]Winthrop, *Digest of Opinions* (1880), pp. 85-88; Mills, *My Story,* pp. 376-77; 46th Cong., 2d Sess., House Executive Document No. 1, Pt. 2, II, 193-94; 51st Cong., 1st Sess., House Executive Document No. 1, Pt. 2, II, 631.

[27]Dudley, *Military Law,* p. 6 n.1; 39 Statutes 619, 650, United States Statutes (1916), §2308a; Edmund M. Morgan, "The Existing Court-Martial System and the Ansell Articles," *Yale Law Journal,* XXIX (1919-1920), 52; Terry W. Brown, "The Crowder-Ansell Dispute: The Emergence of General Samuel T. Ansell," *Military Law Review,* XXV (January, 1967), 1-45.

[28]51st Cong., 1st Sess., House Executive Document No. 1, Pt. 2, II, 85. Cf. New York *Times,* March 13, 1892; Hearing Before the Committee on Military Affairs, 62nd Cong., 2d Sess., on H.R. 23628, p. 3.

[29]G. Norman Lieber, *Remarks on the Army Regulations and Executive Regulations in General* (Washington, 1898), pp. 6 n.1, 67; Davis, *Military Laws of the United States,* pp. 146-48; *ANJ,* August 4, 1866; *The United States Service Magazine,* V (March, 1866), 224.

[30]*ANJ,* December 28, 1867; cf. November 3, 1867, February 6, 1868.

[31]Lieber, *Remarks on the Army Regulations,* pp. 56-59, 67-73; 42nd Cong., 2d Sess., House Executive Document No. 1, Pt. 2, II, 23, 44; 42nd Cong., 3d Sess., House Report No. 85, pp. 1-2; J. D. Hittle, *The Military Staff, Its History and Development* (Harrisburg, 1944), pp. 167; *ANJ,* December 2, 1871.

[32]43rd Cong., 2d Sess., House Executive Document No. 1, Pt. 2, II, 89; General William T. Sherman to William C. Church, September 22, 1874, William C. Church Papers, L.C. Cf. *ANJ,* February 9, 1872, March 8, 1873.

[33]Lieber, *Remarks on the Army Regulations,* pp. 53, 73-82; *ANJ,* February 12, 1881; Davis, *Military Laws of the United States,* p. 148; Bernardo and Bacon, *American Military Policy,* pp. 256, 281-86; Weigley, *Towards an American Army,* pp. 166-67; Stephen E. Ambrose, *Upton and the Army* (Baton Rouge, 1964), pp. 154-56; *The United Service,* XI, N.S. (July, 1891), 52-59; Nelson,

National Security and the General Staff, pp. 14-22; Risch, *Quartermaster Support of the Army*, pp. 511-13; Marvin A. Kreidberg and Merton G. Henry, *History of Mobilization in the United States Army, 1775-1945* (Washington, 1955), pp. 144-45, 172-73; Philip C. Jessup, *Elihu Root* (New York, 1937), I, 226-27.

[34]James A. Parker, *The Old Army Memories, 1872-1918* (Philadelphia, 1929), pp. 121-22; 42nd Cong., 2d Sess., House Executive Document No. 1, Pt. 2, II, 22; 51st Cong., 2d Sess., House Executive Document, No. 1, Pt. 2, II, 64; New York *Herald*, April 4, 1882; Junction City (Kansas) *Republican*, March 16, 1889.

[35]Utley, *Frontiersmen in Blue*, pp. 40-41; Rodenbaugh and Haskin, *Army of the United States*, p. 532; Henry J. Coke, *A Ride Over the Rocky Mountains to Oregon and California* (London, 1852), pp. 151-57; Marvin E. Kroeker, "William B. Hazen, A Military Career in the Frontier West" (unpublished doctoral thesis, University of Oklahoma, 1967), p. 6; Pittsburgh *Dispatch*, December 16, 1848; *United Service Journal*, October 4, 1851; *The United Service*, VII (December, 1882), 82; 33rd Cong., 1st Sess., House Executive Document I, Pt. 2, pp. 7-8; 36th Cong., 2d Sess., Senate Executive Document II, p. 189.

[36]*ANJ*, August 16, 1866, November 2, 1867; Diary of Winfield S. Harvey, July 7, July 25, 1870, Edward C. Godfrey Papers, L.C.; see Appendix, Table 1.

[37]*ANJ*, August 2, 1870.

[38]45th Cong., 2d Sess., House Miscellaneous Document No. 56, p. 75.

[39]New York *Tribune*, January 27, 1872. Cf. *ANJ*, December 23, 1871.

[40]45th Cong., House Miscellaneous Document No. 56, p. 75; *The United Service*, VIII (January, 1883), 88, (May, 1883), 552; 51st Cong., 1st Sess., House Executive Document No. 1, Pt. 2, II, 7, 92; 51st Cong., 2d Sess., House Executive Document No. 1, Pt. 2, II, 44-45; MSIUS *Journal*, XVI (1895), 236; *Army and Navy Life*, X (February, 1907), 183; Bernardo and Bacon, *American Military Policy*, pp. 241-42; *International Quarterly*, XII (1906), 196. In 1891 Adjutant General Kelton reported that 88,475 or one-third of the men recruited between January, 1867 and 1891 had deserted. 51st Cong., 1st Sess., House Executive Document No. 1, Pt. 2, II, 64.

[41]MSIUS *Journal*, X (1889), 451; *The United Service*, VII (May, 1883), 552; 51st Cong., 1st Sess., House Executive Document No. 1, Pt. 2, II, 92.

[42]*ANJ*, November 2, 1867, February 17, 1872, May 31, 1873; New York *Times*, February 7, 1872, December 12, 1894.

[43]40th Cong., 3d Sess., House Executive Document No. 1, Pt. 2, II, 61-62; 51st Cong., 1st Sess., House Executive Document No. 1, Pt. 2, II, 7; 52nd Cong., 1st Sess., House Executive Document No. 1, Pt. 2, II, 62; *ANJ*, February 17, 1872, May 3, 1873, September 6, 1884.

[44]New York *Sun*, October 31, 1872; cf. May 18, 1872, October 11, 1874; New York *Herald*, August 22, 1870.

[45]Omaha *Republican*, August 18, 1889; 48th Cong., 1st Sess., House Executive Document No. 1, Pt. 2, II, 105, 396; New York *Herald*, December 16, 1883; Kansas City *Times*, December 28, 1884, October 18, December 18, 1892.

[46]*ANR*, December 6, 1884.

[47]New York *Sun*, March 20, 1874; New York *Times*, August 20, 1871; St. Louis *Globe-Democrat*, May 25, 1889; Chicago *Inter-Ocean*, February 22, 1890;

ANJ, March 3, 1873, April 22, 1876; D. H. Swaim to James A. Garfield, November 12, 1875, Garfield Papers, L.C.

⁴⁸William B. Hazen, *The School and the Army* (New York, 1872), p. 224; 48th Cong., 1st Sess., House Executive Document No. 1, Pt. 2, II, 396.

⁴⁹*ANJ,* April 20, September 7, 1867, January 14, 1871, September 14, 1872, May 24, 1873, September 7, 1876; Washington *Evening Star,* September 7, 1889; 42nd Cong., 3d Sess., House Executive Document No. 1, Pt. 2, II, 49; 45th Cong., 2d Sess., House Miscellaneous Document No. 56, pp. 62, 65, 249; Edward D. Townsend to John M. Schofield, August 13, 1874, Schofield Papers, L.C.; *The United Service, VIII* (January, 1883), 83, XII (June, 1885), 674-75; New York *Times,* April 30, 1882; Parker, *The Old Army,* pp. 121-22; Rodenbaugh and Haskin, *Army of the United States,* p. 283; Ernest Wallace, *Ranald S. Mackenzie on the Texas Frontier* (Lubbock, Texas, 1964), p. 61; Risch, *Quartermaster Support of the Army,* pp. 481-89, 505-06; Aubrey H. Wilson, "A Soldier on the Texas Frontier," *West Texas Historical Association Yearbook,* XXXIV (October, 1958), 89.

⁵⁰50th Cong., 2d Sess., House Executive Document No. 1, Pt. 2, II, 119.

⁵¹John M. Schofield to Commanding General, Department of Arizona, October 25, 1882, Schofield Papers.

⁵²48th Cong., 2d Sess., House Executive Document No. 1, Pt. 2, II, 103-04.

⁵³51st Cong., 1st Sess., House Executive Document No. 1, Pt. 2, II, 82-84.

⁵⁴*Ibid.,* p. 84; cf. *ibid.,* pp. 63-64, 85-86; *ANJ,* October 17, 1891.

⁵⁵MSIUS *Journal,* X (1889), 451; 33rd Cong., 1st Sess., House Executive Document I, Pt. 2, p. 8; 45th Cong., 2d Sess., House Executive Document No. 1, Pt. 2, II, p. vii; 53rd Cong., 3d Sess., House Executive Document No. 1, Pt. 2, II, 13; Don Rickey, Jr., *Forty Miles a Day on Beans and Hay* (Norman, 1963), pp. 17-18, 29, 178.

⁵⁶*ANJ,* February 9, 1895; *The United Service,* VIII (January, 1883), 88; J. W. Pope, "Desertion and the Military Prison," *The Cosmopolitan Magazine,* X (November, 1890), 111.

⁵⁷MSIUS *Journal,* XVI (1895), 238.

⁵⁸52nd Cong., 1st Sess., House Executive Document No. 1, Pt. 2, II, 63; MSIUS *Journal,* XVI (1895), 238; *ANJ,* October 26, 1876, June 5, 1886, December 22, 1888, October 17, 1891; Kansas City *Times,* December 17, 1886, September 13, 1889.

⁵⁹O. O. Howard to John M. Carson, January 7, 1885, Howard Papers, Bowdoin College. Cf. 42nd Cong., 2d Sess., House Executive Document No. 1, Pt. 2, II, 24.

⁶⁰William H. Leckie, *The Buffalo Soldiers: A Narrative of the Negro Cavalry in the West* (Norman, 1967), pp. 72, 99, 178 & n., 234-35, 239. From 1885 through 1889 there were 3,203 desertions from the eight white cavalry regiments and 283 desertions from the two colored regiments of cavalry. During the same period there were 5,585 desertions from the twenty-three regiments of infantry, and 67 desertions from the two colored infantry regiments. MSIUS *Journal,* X (1889), 465.

⁶¹51st Cong., 1st Sess., House Executive Document No. 1, Pt. 2, II, 9.

[62]42nd Cong., 2d Sess., House Executive Document No. 1, Pt. 2, II, 31, 45; 45th Cong., 2d Sess., House Miscellaneous Document No. 1, Pt. 2, II, 45.

[63]51st Cong., 1st Sess., House Executive Document No. 1, Pt. 2, II, 9. Cf. 48th Cong., 1st Sess., House Executive Document No. 1, Pt. 2, II, 152; 48th Cong., 2d Sess., House Executive Document No. 1, Pt. 2, II, 126; 51st Cong., 2d Sess., House Executive Document No. 1, Pt. 2, II, 10, 515; *ANJ*, March 24, October 20, 1877; Risch, *Quartermaster Support of the Army*, pp. 489-90, 506-07, 584-85; Lester D. Langley, "The Democratic Tradition and Military Reform, 1878-1885," *Southwestern Social Science Quarterly*, XLVII (September, 1967), 192-200.

[64]51st Cong., 2d Sess., House Executive Document No. 1, Pt. 2, II, 63; *Army and Navy Life*, X (February, 1907), 182-83, 187.

[65]Rickey, *Forty Miles a Day;* Leo E. Oliva, *Soldiers on the Sante Fe Trail* (Norman, Okla., 1967); Leckie, *The Buffalo Soldiers;* Whitman, *The Troopers;* J. Evetts Haley, *Fort Concho and the Texas Frontier* (San Angelo, Texas, 1952); Carl C. Rister, *Fort Griffin and the Texas Frontier* (Norman, 1956); Chris Emmett, *Fort Union and the Winning of the Southwest* (Norman, 1965); Lewis A. Holmes, *Fort McPherson* (Lincoln, 1963); James T. King, "The Military Frontier—What Was It," *Westerners Brand Book* (Chicago), XXI (February, 1965), 89-91, 95-96; James T. King, "The Sword and the Pen: The Poetry of the Military Frontier," *Nebraska History*, XLVII (September, 1966), 229-45; Roger T. Grange, Jr., "Fort Robinson Outpost on the Plains," *Nebraska History*, XXXIX (September, 1958), 191-240; Ray H. Mattison, "The Army Fort on the Northern Plains, 1865-1895," *Nebraska History*, XXXV (March, 1954), 17-34; Edward M. Coffin, "Army Life on the Frontier, 1865-1898," *Military Affairs*, XX (Fall, 1956), 192-201; Thomas F. Blades and John W. Wike, "Fort Missoula," *Military Affairs*, XII (Spring, 1949), 29-46; Edmund J. McClernard, "Service in Montana, 1870 and 1871," *Military Affairs*, XV (1951), 192-98; Daniel S. Day, "Fort Sedgwick," *The Colorado Magazine*, XLII (Winter, 1965), 17-35; Susan Miles, "Fort Concho in 1877," *West Texas Historical Association Year Book*, XXXV (October, 1959), 129-49; Aubrey H. Wilson, "A Soldier on the Texas Frontier, Brevet Major Robert Patterson Wilson, United States Army," *West Texas Historical Association Year Book*, XXXIV (1958), 82-96; Mildred Wertenberger (compiler), "Fort Totten, Dakota Territory, 1867," *North Dakota History*, XXXIV (Spring, 1967), 125-46; George H. Shirk, "Campaigning with Sheridan, A Farrier's Diary," *Chronicles of Oklahoma*, XXXVII (1959), 68-105; Frank D. Reeves (ed.), "Fredrick E. Phelps, A Soldier's Memoirs," *New Mexico Historical Review*, XXV (July, 1950), 37-38, (October, 1950), 305-27; Neil Baird Thompson, "Discipline and Morale of the U.S. Army Troops in the Division of the Missouri, 1866-1876" (unpublished Master's thesis, Kansas State College of Agriculture and Applied Science, Manhattan, Kansas, 1948); Patricia Louise Loge, "History of Fort Huachuca, 1877-1913" (unpublished Master's thesis, University of Arizona, 1949); James Weaver, "History of Fort Lowell" (unpublished Master's thesis, University of Arizona, 1947); Harvey J. Zabel, "History of Fort McPherson" (unpublished Master's thesis, Colorado State College, 1954); Richard Y. Murray, "The History of Fort Bowie" (unpublished Master's thesis, University of Arizona, 1951).

CHAPTER I: THE LIFE OF THE ENLISTED SOLDIER

[1]Robert M. Scott, *An Analytical Digest of the Military Laws of the United States* (Philadelphia, 1873), pp. 231-38; Geogre B. Davis (ed.), *The Military Laws of the United States* (Washington, 1897), p. 355; 42nd Cong., 2d Sess., House Executive Document No. 1, Pt. 2, II, 87; 51st Cong., 1st Sess., House Executive Document No. 1, Pt. 2, II, 91-93; New York *Times,* September 7, 10, 1870; Don Rickey, Jr., *Forty Miles a Day on Beans and Hay* (Norman, Oklahoma, 1963), pp. 31-32.

[2]46th Cong., 2d Sess., House Executive Document No. 1, Pt. 2, II, 32-33; New York *Herald,* August 22, 1870, February 28, 1876; *Harper's Weekly,* June 28, 1890, p. 512; Rickey, *Forty Miles a Day,* pp. 33-49; *ANJ,* August 10, 1872, March 20, 1880; Charles Alexander, *Battles and Victories of Allen Allensworth* (Boston, 1914), p. 325.

[3]*ANJ,* May 15, 1875. Cf. March 7, 1868, January 7, 1871, January 27, 1881; *ANR,* May 21, 1887; Diary of Private Wilmot P. Sanford, Co. D, 6th U.S. Infantry, Fort Buford, Dakota Territory, entries for December 9, 29, 30, 1874, January 3, 7, 8, 12, 1875, Yale University; Elizabeth J. Reynolds Burt, "An Army Wife's Forty Years in the Service (1862-1902)," pp. 213, 227, unpublished MSS, Burt Family Papers, L.C.

[4]New York *Herald,* March 23, 1891. Cf. *ANJ,* August 4, 1877; Kansas City *Times,* December 23, 1889; *ANJ,* September 17, 1870, May 1, 1880; Kansas City *Times,* April 3, 1894.

[5]Chicago *Herald,* November 7, 1893. Cf. Chicago *Times,* August 23, 1877; *ANJ,* July 22, 1882; Chicago *Herald,* September 19, October 17, 1896; *ANJ,* September 28, 1867, February 2, 1878, April 8, 1893; *ANR,* July 17, 1886; William H. Leckie, *The Conquest of the Southern Plains* (Norman, Oklahoma, 1963), pp. 3-7.

[6]*ANJ,* September 9, 1882; cf. September 28, 1867, March 21, June 6, 1868, November 5, 1870, May 1, 1880, July 22, 1882; MSIUS *Journal,* IV (1883), 389; Leo E. Oliva, *Soldiers on the Santa Fe Trail* (Norman, Oklahoma, 1967), p. 194.

[7]MSIUS *Journal,* V (1884), 194-95, VII (1886), 53; *ANJ,* December 28, 1867, December 22, 1871, May 25, 1872, April 10, 1880; Kansas City *Times,* January 13, 1890; New York *Sun,* May 23, 1880; 45th Cong., 2d Sess., House Miscellaneous Document No. 56, p. 159; Oliva, *Soldiers on the Santa Fe Trail,* p. 194.

[8]O. O. Howard to John M. Carson, January 7, 1885, Howard Papers, Bowdoin College. Cf. MSIUS *Journal,* VIII (1887), 289; Rickey, *Forty Miles a Day,* pp. 94-95, 97; *The United Service,* III (April, 1880), 184; New York *Times,* December 21, 1884; Frank Wheaton to O. O. Howard, May 12, 1880, J. S. Payne to Howard, May 5, 1883, Howard Papers.

[9]*ANJ,* February 23, 1867, January 15, March 16, 1878, May 24, 1883; New York *Times,* August 6, 1880, April 30, 1882; MSIUS *Journal,* IV (1883), 407; 49th Cong., 1st Sess., House Executive Document No. 1, Pt. 2, II, 113.

[10]48th Cong., 1st Sess., House Executive Document No. 1, Pt. 2, II, 100; New York *Herald,* December 19, 1878. Cf. New York *Herald,* July 19, 1879; New

York *Tribune*, September 1, 1879; *ANJ*, October 8, 1870, March 4, April 22, 1871, February 28, 1874, March 16, 1878; 45th Cong., 3d Sess., Senate Report 555, p. 487; MSIUS *Journal*, VIII (1887), 283.

[11]Scott, *Analytical Digest*, pp. 182-85; August V. Kautz, *Customs of the Service* (Philadelphia, 1864), p. 15; *The United Service Journal*, February 28, October 26, 1852; Rickey, *Forty Miles a Day*, p. 127; *Congressional Globe*, 41st Cong., 2d Sess., pp. 545, 3320, 5336, 5340; 45th Cong., 2d Sess., House Miscellaneous Document No. 56, p. 75.

[12]*ANJ*, August 22, 1870. Cf. New York *Sun*, August 8, 1870; Diary of Winfield S. Harvey, June 8, 1871, Edward L. Godfrey Papers, L.C.

[13]45th Cong., 2d Sess., House Miscellaneous Document No. 56, p. 75.

[14]*ANJ*, August 26, 1871. Cf. 42nd Cong., 2d Sess., House Executive Document No. 1, Pt. 2, II, 111.

[15]42nd Cong., 2d Sess., House Executive Document No. 1, Pt. 2, II, 73.

[16]*Congressional Globe*, 42nd Cong., 2d Sess., p. 2291.

[17]Scott, *Analytical Digest*, pp. 179-81, 189-92; 45th Cong., 2d Sess., House Miscellaneous Document No. 56, Appendix B, p. 358; *ANJ*, May 3, 1873; Edward Farrow, *Military Encyclopedia* (New York, 1885), II, 494.

[18]45th Cong., 2d Sess., House Miscellaneous Document No. 56, p. 75.

[19]*ANJ*, January 16, 1875; cf. May 3, 1873, March 4, 1876, November 11, 1882, November 19, 1883; New York *Herald*, August 27, 1883.

[20]Scott, *Analytical Digest*, p. 185; *ANJ*, December 28, 1867, September 7, December 7, 1876, August 15, 1868, February 8, 1873, January 20, 1883; St. Paul *Anti-Monopolist*, August 23, 1877; 40th Cong., 3d Sess., House Report No. 33, p. 121; 45th Cong., 3rd Sess., Senate Report No. 555, p. 87; 42nd Cong., 3d Sess., House Report No. 74, p. 159.

[21]*ANJ*, February 8, 1873.

[22]Scott, *Analytical Digest*, pp. 153-54; Davis, *The Military Laws of the United States*, p. 197; Rickey, *Forty Miles a Day*, p. 95; MSIUS *Journal*, IV (1883), 400.

[23]New York *Sun*, August 8, 1870; 51st Cong., 1st Sess., House Executive Document No. 1, Pt. 2, II, 90. Cf. *ANR*, December 6, 1884; *ANJ*, September 7, 1867, June 15, August 7, 1878, May 10, 1884, December 22, 1888.

[24]*ANJ*, May 24, 1873; cf. September 14, 1872; *Journal of the United States Cavalry Association*, II (1889), 5.

[25]*ANJ*, May 24, 1873.

[26]New York *Herald*, March 7, 1876, April 11, 1884; New York *Sun*, August 30, 1878; *ANJ*, April 4, 1868, July 13, 1878, April 14, November 11, 1883; MSIUS *Journal*, II (1882), 422; 48th Cong., 2d Sess., House Executive Document No. 1, Pt. 2, II, 86; Rickey, *Forty Miles a Day*, p. 89; MSIUS *Journal*, VI (1885), 51; Circular No. 4, War Department, Surgeon General's Office (Washington, 1870), pp. xxii-xxiii, 81-84, 129-30, 276-77, 387; Circular No. 8, Surgeon General's Office (Washington, 1875), pp. xvii, 140, 208, 213, 264, 346-52, 456, 475; *The United Service*, XII (April, 1885), 227-30, 437-40.

[27]*The United Service*, XII (April, 1885), 227-30, 437-40; 44th Cong., 1st Sess., House Report No. 351, p. 118; 50th Cong., 2d Sess., House Executive Document No. 1, Pt. 2, II, 133-37; 52nd Cong., 1st Sess., House Executive Document No.

1, Pt. 2, II, 603-09; *ANJ,* August 29, 1868, December 3, 1870, April 15, 1871, April 14, 1883; Kansas City *Times,* November 24, 1893.

[28]*ANJ,* May 9, 1868, December 18, 1880, January 6, September 27, 1884, September 5, 1885; 46th Cong., 3d Sess., House Executive Document No. 1, Pt. 2, II, 193; New York *Herald,* November 12, 1880.

[29]Kansas City *Times,* January 6, 1890; *ANJ,* December 18, 1880.

[30]*ANJ,* July 22, 1871; cf. October 5, 1867, August 29, 1869, April 15, July 2, 1871; MSIUS *Journal,* II (1882), 432, VII (1888), 43; Ernest Wallace, *Ranald S. Mackenzie on the Texas Frontier* (Lubbock, Texas, 1964), pp. 60-61; Theo. F. Rodenbaugh and William L. Haskin (eds.), *The Army of the United States* (New York, 1896), p. 283.

[31]42nd Cong., 2d Sess., House Executive Document No. 1, Pt. 2, II, 4, 127; *ANJ,* September 5, 1885.

[32]*Congressional Record,* 43rd Cong., 1st Sess., p. 990. Cf. *ANR,* August 21, 1886; *ANJ,* June 20, 1891; Columbus *Dispatch,* February 6, 1889; Omaha *Bee,* quoted in Kansas City *Times,* February 22, 1886.

[33]J. H. Taylor to O. O. Howard, August 12, 1883, Howard Papers; cf. C. G. Treat to O. O. Howard, December 20, 1891, Howard Papers; 52nd Cong., 1st Sess., House Executive Document No. 1, Pt. 2, II, 617-23.

[34]50th Cong., 1st Sess., House Executive Document No. 1, Pt. 2, II, 658. Cf. *The United Service,* XII (April, 1885), 488; MSIUS *Journal,* II (1881), 434; 50th Cong., 2d Sess., House Executive Document No. 1, Pt. 2, II, 736; New York *Herald,* April 11, 1884; Oliva, *Soldiers on the Santa Fe Trail,* pp. 174, 199.

[35]MSIUS *Journal* II (1881), 434. Cf. *The United Service,* XII (February, 1885), 438; 50th Cong., 2d Sess., House Executive Document No. 1, Pt. 2, II, 730; *ANJ,* April 15, 1871.

[36]*ANJ,* April 15, 1871, August 9, 1884, August 9, 1889, August 7, 1886; MSIUS *Journal,* IV (1883), 534, V (1884), 186, VI (1885), 53-54, 281; 51st Cong., 3d Sess., House Executive Document No. 1, Pt. 2, II, 100-01; New York *Herald,* April 1, 1884.

[37]MSIUS *Journal,* VI (1885), 53.

[38]51st Cong., 2d Sess., House Executive Document No. 1, Pt. 2, II, 104. Cf. Kansas City *Times,* October 20, 1891, June 21, 1892; New York *Times,* December 21, 1891.

[39]*ANJ,* August 10, 1867, November 6, 1869, August 12, 1871, August 17, 31, 1872; New York *Herald,* August 22, 1870.

[40]*ANJ,* August 10, 1867, September 7, October 5, 1867, July 22, December 23, 1871, January 6, March 16, August 17, 1872, July 19, 1873; S. F. Whitman, *The Troopers, An Informal History of the Plains Cavalry,* 1865-1900 (New York, 1962), pp. 191-94.

[41]General Order No. 73, July 10, 1873; *ANJ,* August 2, 1873; Whitman, *The Troopers,* pp. 194-98.

[42]*ANJ,* February 19, 1881. Cf. March 1, July 19, 1873, May 27, 1882, July 5, 1883; New York *Sun,* April 29, 1890; New York *Times,* January 23, 1894; New York *Graphic,* September 21, 1883; *The United Service,* XII (June, 1885), 674.

[43]*ANR,* May 10, 1884; *ANJ,* September 7, 1867, March 6, 1876, November 22,

1879, August 23, 1884; 44th Cong., 1st Sess., House Report No. 354, p. 200; 48th Cong., 2d Sess., House Executive Document No. 1, Pt. 2, II, 104; *The United Service*, IX (July, 1883), 48-50; XII (June, 1885), 628-29, 675; Portland *Eastern Argus*, October 12, 1881; William H. Leckie, *The Buffalo Soldiers, A Narrative of the Negro Cavalry in the West* (Norman, Oklahoma, 1967), p. 155; Donald Jackson, *Custer's Gold, The United States Cavalry Expedition of 1874* (New Haven, 1966), pp. 31-32.

⁴⁴Report of Assistant Surgeon Leonard Wood, Fort Bowie, A.P., September 8, 1886, p. 5, in *Annual Report of Brigadier General Nelson A. Miles, Commanding Department of Arizona*, 1886, Headquarters, Department of Arizona, Albuquerque, New Mexico, September 18, 1886.

⁴⁵43rd Cong., 2d Sess., House Executive Document No. 1, Pt. 2, II, 75; Rickey, *Forty Miles a Day*, pp. 123-24.

⁴⁶MSIUS *Journal*, VIII (1887), 272. Cf. *ibid.*, XIV (1893), 499; 44th Cong., 2d Sess., House Executive Document No. 1, Pt. 2, II, 75; New York *Herald*, July 20, 1893; Henry W. Lawton to Mamie Lawton, July 25, 1886, Henry W. Lawton Papers, L.C.

⁴⁷Davis, *Military Laws of the United States*, pp. 207-10; Scott, *Analytical Digest*, pp. 158-62; Rickey, *Forty Miles a Day*, pp. 116-17; 48th Cong., 2d Sess., House Executive Document No. 1, Pt. 2, II, 133; *ANJ*, May 24, 1873, January 15, 1881; St. Louis *Globe-Democrat*, January 30, 1890.

⁴⁸MSIUS *Journal*, XV (1894), 330, 333, 877; *ANR*, February 16, 1884; New York *Times*, August 24, 1895; 48th Cong., 2d Sess., House Executive Document No. 1, Pt. 2, II, 104; *ANJ*, May 15, 1869, March 13, 1875, December 25, 1886, December 29, 1889.

⁴⁹MSIUS *Journal*, XV (1894), 329; New York *Herald*, October 23, 1882; *ANJ*, April 20, September 28, 1867, April 11, 1868, September 7, 1871; *ANR*, February 16, 1884; 45th Cong., 3d Sess., Senate Report No. 555, p. 581; Rodenbaugh and Haskin, *Army of the United States*, pp. 283-84; Rickey, *Forty Miles a Day*, pp. 97-98.

⁵⁰*ANJ*, January 26, 1878; New York *Times*, January 23, 1878; 45th Cong., 2d Sess., House Miscellaneous Document No. 56, p. 113; Rickey, *Forty Miles a Day*, pp. 119-20.

⁵¹MSIUS *Journal*, X (1889), 768; *ANJ*, May 24, 1873, April 15, 1875; 48th Cong., 1st Sess., House Executive Document No. 1, Pt. 2, II, 104, 133; 48th Cong., 2d Sess., House Miscellaneous Document No. 1, Pt. 2, II, 155; 51st Cong., 1st Sess., House Executive Document No. 1, Pt. 2, II, 139; Oliva, *Soldiers on the Santa Fe Trail*, p. 198; J. Evetts Haley, *Fort Concho and the Texas Frontier* (San Angelo, Texas, 1952), pp. 293-94.

⁵²Scott, *Analytical Digest*, p. 383; MSIUS *Journal*, V (1884), 186, VI (1885), 274, VII (1886), 59, 186, VIII (1887), 275; *ANJ*, April 3, 1869, February 20, 1875, May 15, 1886; 50th Cong., 1st Sess., House Executive Document No. 1, Pt. 2, II, 82; 48th Cong., 2d Sess., House Executive Document No. 1, Pt. 2, II, 703-04; New York *Herald*, October 23, 1891.

⁵³Farrow, *Military Encyclopedia*, II, 568, III, 653; MSIUS *Journal*, VII (1887),

263; Chicago *Tribune,* July 30, 1887; *ANJ,* June 12, 1869; *Public Service Review,* March 24, 1888.

[54]*Regulations of the Army of the United States* (1881), pars. 524-27, 530, 537; Farrow, *Military Encyclopedia,* II, 568-69, 653. The post fund was also used for fruit and shade trees, fruit bearing vines and bushes, and for a printing press. *Ibid.,* pp. 568-69.

[55]*Regulations of the Army of the United States* (1881), pars. 194, 528-29.

[56]*ANJ,* April 20, 1867, November 1, 1873, November 16, 1889.

[57]*ANJ,* November 30, 1867, March 29, 1881. Cf. MSIUS *Journal,* V (1884), 186, IX (1888), 40; New York *Herald,* September 30, 1882; New York *Sun,* June 15, 1884.

[58]*Regulations of the Army of the United States* (1881), pars. 552-53; Farrow, *Military Encyclopedia,* I, 385; MSIUS *Journal,* VIII (1887), 147, IX (1889), 766-88.

[59]*ANJ,* April 3, May 24, July 24, September 25, 1869, November 12, 1870.

[60]44th Cong., 1st Sess., House Report No. 354, p. 197. Cf. 45th Cong., 2d Sess., House Miscellaneous Document No. 56, p. 65; 45th Cong., 3d Sess., Senate Report No. 555, p. 46; 51st Cong., 1st Sess., House Executive Document No. 1, Pt. 2, II, 11, 237; *ANJ,* July 2, 1871, February 20, 1875, July 5, 1879, September 9, 1881; St. Louis *Globe-Democrat,* May 16, 1889, January 30, 1890; New York *Herald,* March 7, 1876.

[61]Washington *Evening Star,* September 7, 1889; *ANJ,* August 29, 1868, April 3, 1869, November 1, 1873, July 5, 1879, August 29, 1881, May 15, 1886.

[62]*The United Service,* VIII (June, 1883), 637. Cf. *ANJ,* January 1, 1867, May 1, 15, 1869, June 25, November 12, 1870, December 29, 1888.

[63]*ANJ,* February 23, 1869. Cf. April 21, September 9, 1871, January 6, August 31, 1872; New York *Tribune,* February 6, 1869; Columbus *Capital,* quoted in Kansas City *Times,* May 11, 1885; New York *Sun,* June 15, 1884.

[64]*ANJ,* September 1, 1866, March 15, 1869, March 4, 1871.

[65]*ANJ,* November 12, 1870; cf. April 3, 1869; J. C. Kelton to O. O. Howard, July 5, 1888, Howard Papers; Washington *Evening Star,* September 7, 1889; G. Norman Lieber, *Remarks on the Army Regulations* (Washington, 1898), pp. 171-72.

[66]Percy M. Ashburn, *History of the Medical Department of the United States Army* (New York, 1929), pp. 116-17; *ANJ,* November 8, 1873, July 5, 1879, May 1, 1880, January 29, 1881; Mabel E. Deutrich, *Struggle for Supremacy, The Life of General Fred Ainsworth* (Washington, 1962), pp. 6-7, 140; Rickey, *Forty Miles a Day,* pp. 130-33; James A. Huston, *The Sinews of War: Army Logistics, 1775-1953* (Washington, 1966), p. 255; George E. Omer, Jr., "An Army Hospital from Dragoons to Rough Riders—Fort Riley 1853-1903," *Kansas Historical Quarterly,* XXIII (Winter, 1957), 337-67.

[67]51st Cong., 1st Sess., House Executive Document No. 1, Pt. 2, II, 1044. Cf. Edward A. Hummel, "The Story of Fort Sisseton," *South Dakota Historical Review,* II (April, 1937), 136.

[68]Deutrich, *Struggle for Supremacy,* p. 7; Ashburn, *History of Medical Department,* p. 117; *ANJ,* August 10, 1872, September 18, 1880; Fort Hays, Kansas,

Special Order Book, October 15, 1866—May 26, 1868, Post Order No. 15, dated July 27, 1867, Kansas State Historical Society, Topeka, Kansas.

[69]*ANJ*, September 6, 1884.

[70]*ANJ*, May 31, 1873; Ashburn, *History of Medical Department*, p. 108; Washington *Evening Star*, quoted in Brooklyn *Daily Eagle*, August 8, 1901.

[71]*ANJ*, May 31, 1873. Cf. *The Journal of the Association of Military Dental Surgeons of the United States*, I (September, 1917), 9; Brooklyn *Daily Eagle*, January 16, 20, 1899. In 1901 Congress authorized the Surgeon General to employ dental surgeons, not to exceed thirty in all. Ashburn, *History of Medical Department*, p. 209.

[72]*ANR*, February 16, 1884; cf. November 9, 1867, March 21, August 29, 1868, November 20, 1869, April 13, 1872, February 18, 1881; New York *Times*, February 16, 1890; St. Paul *Pioneer Press*, January 19, 1882; 45th Cong., 2d Sess., House Miscellaneous Document No. 56, pp. 118, 233; *Overland Monthly*, IV (December, 1870), 520; *Appleton's Journal*, XV (April, 1876), 564-65; Arthur Brigham Carpenter to his mother, April 9, 26, 1867, April 4, 1869, September 11, 1870, Arthur Brigham Carpenter Papers, Yale University; William T. Sherman to Philip Sheridan, October 7, 1872, Sherman Papers, L.C.; E. F. Townsend to O. O. Howard, July 9, 1888, Howard Papers.

[73]50th Cong., 2d Sess., House Executive Document No. 1, Pt. 2, II, 166; *ANJ*, May 2, 1868; MSIUS *Journal*, XII (1891), 1184; Reginald Hargreaves, "Idle Hours," *Military Review*, XLVI (December, 1966), 29-35; Douglas C. McCurtie, "The Fourth Infantry Press at Fort Bridger," *Annals of Wyoming*, XIII (October, 1941), 347-51; E. W. Ely, "A History of Fort Missoula, Montana," p. 22, unpublished MSS in possession of Montana Historical Society, Helena, Montana.

[74]*ANJ*, January 25, 1868, June 26, 1871; cf. May 21, August 27, October 22, November 12, 1870, April 15, 1871, April 13, 1878, February 18, 1882, November 4, 1884; *Arizona Citizen*, February 4, 1871; *Arizona Weekly Star*, January 31, 1884; Pembina, Dakota *Express*, October 19, 1883; W. F. Pride, *The History of Fort Riley* (Fort Riley, 1926), pp. 163, 167, 170, 183.

[75]Scott, *Analytical Digest*, pp. 216, 218; *ANJ*, September 24, 1866; MSIUS *Journal*, IX (1888), 440-41.

[76]*ANJ*, April 17, 1869, June 29, 1878; 46th Cong., 2d Sess., House Executive Document No. 1, Pt. 2, II, 123; 48th Cong., 2d Sess., House Executive Document No. 1, Pt. 2, II, 125-26.

[77]*ANJ*, January 16, 1869; cf. February 13, 1869.

[78]*ANJ*, April 17, 1869; *U.S. Military Post Library Association Annual Report 1852-73* (New York, 1873), p. 50. Cf. New York *Times*, October 14, 1878.

[79]*ANJ*, April 17, 1874. Cf. *The New National Era*, July 30, 1874, 42nd Cong., 3d Sess., House Report No. 74, p. 149; *The United Service*, II (April, 1880), 478; *ANJ*, March 21, 1868, September 17, 1870, September 28, 1872.

[80]MSIUS *Journal*, IX (1888), 441-42, XII (1891), 523, 1179; *ANJ*, June 29, 1878; 45th Cong., 3d Sess., House Executive Document No. 1, Pt. 2, II, ix, 441; Farrow, *Military Encyclopedia*, III, 568, 570, 596; Ira Reeves, *Military Education in the United States* (Burlington, Vermont, 1914), p. 315; *Regulations of the United States Army* (1881), pars. 558-65.

[81]48th Cong., 1st Sess., House Executive Document No. 1, Pt. 2, II, 45, 295, 715; Henry A. Morrow to O. O. Howard, July 3, 1880, Howard Papers; 47th Cong., 1st Sess., House Report No. 1425, pp. 1-2; Columbus *Dispatch,* November 21, 1888.

[82]*The United Service,* II (April, 1880), 478. Cf. Alexander, *Battles and Victories of Allen Allensworth,* pp. 344-47.

[83]*ANJ,* November 25, 1882. Cf. MSIUS *Journal,* VIII (1887), 277-78.

[84]*ANJ,* February 4, 1882, January 8, 1887; St. Paul *Pioneer Press,* October 2, 1880; 47th Cong., 2d Sess., House Executive Document No. 1, Pt. 2, II, 25, 83; 48th Cong., 1st Sess., House Executive Document No. 1, Pt. 2, II, 55.

[85]Frank Wheaton to O. O. Howard, May 12, 1880, Howard Papers; *ANJ,* May 28, December 3, 1881, October 21, 1882; Haley, Fort Concho, pp. 314-17; 48th Cong., 1st Sess., House Executive Document No. 1, Pt. 2, II, 716.

[86]MSIUS *Journal,* IX (1888), 443, XII (1891), 181; *ANJ,* December 20, 1879, October 25, November 25, 1882, June 14, 1884; New York *Times,* December 16, 1879.

[87]*ANJ,* October 21, 1882, October 8, 1881.

[88]Omaha *Bee,* quoted in *ANJ,* April 24, 1886; 48th Cong., 2d Sess., House Executive Document No. 1, Pt. 2, II, 716.

[89]47th Cong., 1st Sess., House Report No. 1425, p. 2. Cf. New York *Freeman,* February 27, 1886; *ANJ,* February 18, December 17, 1881, February 11, October 18, November 11, 1882; 50th Cong., 2d Sess., House Executive Document No. 1, Pt. 2, II, 150; *The United Service,* II (April, 1880), 484.

[90]51st Cong., 1st Sess., House Executive Document No. 162, Appendix C, pp. 12-14; *ANJ,* March 27. June 22, 1876, July 5, 1879, February 19, 1881; Farrow, *Military Encyclopedia,* III, 570; New York *Herald,* February 1, 1876; Haley, *Fort Concho,* pp. 301-05; Columbus *Dispatch,* November 14, 1888.

[91]Cheyenne *Daily Leader,* March 10, 1881. Cf. New York *Sun,* June 15, 1884; *ANJ,* April 22, 1871, January 20, August 2, 1872, April 29, May 28, 1881, August 9, 1884, May 8, 1886; Ami Frank Mulford, *Fighting Indians in the 7th United States Cavalry* (Corning, N.Y., 1879), pp. 59, 98; Marvin E. Kroeker, "William B. Hazen, A Military Career in the Frontier West, 1855-1880" (unpublished doctoral thesis, University of Oklahoma, 1967), pp. 188-89, 249-65, 293; New York *Tribune,* February 16, 1876.

[92]Kansas City *Times,* August 26, 1886, February 23, 1887, August 7, October 14, 1889; New York *World,* December 20, 1886; New York *Times,* July 18, 1889.

[93]Kansas City *Times,* July 22, 1889.

[94]*ANR,* June 26, 1926; Scott, *Analytical Digest,* pp. 216-18; *U.S. Military Post Library Association, Annual Report, 1874-75* (New York, 1875), p. 12; 51st Cong., 1st Sess., House Executive Document No. 1, Pt. 2, II, 12; Roy J. Honeywell, *Chaplains of the United States Army* (Washington, 1958), pp. 152-57; David A. Stratton, "The Army and the Gospel in the West," *Western Humanities Review,* VII (Spring, 1954), 247-62; W. F. Hubbard to O. O. Howard, July 22, 1890, Charles C. Pierce to Howard, December 13, 1891, Jan G. Kerr to Howard, July 21, 1891, Howard Papers.

[95]*U.S. Military Post Library Association, Annual Report, 1874-75,* p. 34; *ANJ,*

March 19, 1870; cf. December 7, 21, 1867, December 2, 1871, December 1, 1877, March 16, June 29, 1878, May 21, 1887; H. A. Morrow to O. O. Howard, September 17, 1885, Howard Papers; Rickey, *Forty Miles a Day,* p. 108.

[96]New York *Tribune,* February 10, 1877; 42nd Cong., 3d Sess., House Executive Document No. 1, Pt. 1, II, 49; *Military Affairs,* V (1941), 188; *U.S. Military Post Library Association Annual Report, 1874-75,* pp. 14, 24-25, 34; *1875-76,* p. 25. For a contrary view see Bruce White, "ABC's for the Enlisted Man," *History of Education Quarterly,* VIII (Winter, 1968), 490.

[97]*ANJ,* September, 4, 1870; *U.S. Military Post Library Association, Annual Report, 1872-73* (New York, 1873), p. 22; New York *Tribune,* March 22, 1876.

[98]New York *Herald,* July 28, 1891; General O. O. Howard to Colonel William Carlin, July 30, 1883, Howard Papers.

[99]*ANJ,* March 8, 1873, July 5, 1879, April 19, December 21, 1884.

[100]*ANJ,* September 7, 1867, June 17, 1876, March 10, 1877, February 19, 1881; Kansas City *Times,* September 28, 1894, March 20, 1895; 45th Cong., 2d Sess., House Miscellaneous Document No. 56, p. 139; MSIUS *Journal,* VIII (1887), 268, 316.

[101]*ANJ,* July 22, 1882; cf. July 23, 1870, December 27, 1890; 45th Cong., 2d Sess., House Miscellaneous Document No. 56, p. 124; New York *Times,* March 19, 1892; New York *Herald,* March 23, 1891; Kansas City *Times,* February 19, September 28, 1894, March 20, 1895; J. M. Green to O. O. Howard, November 19, 1890, Howard Papers.

CHAPTER II: THE ENLISTED SOLDIER AND THE ARMY'S LEGAL SYSTEM

[1]*ANJ,* December 13, 1884. Cf. St. Louis *Post Dispatch,* July 7, 1889; MSIUS *Journal,* XVII (1895), 19; *ANJ,* March 22, 1873, January 29, March 15, 1876, July 31, 1880; Kansas City *Times,* April 28, 1886, July 5, 1887. For Code of 1874, see *supra,* p. 10.

[2]New York *Tribune,* March 15, 1873.

[3]49th Cong., 1st Sess., House Executive Document No. 1, Pt. 2, II, 344-45.

[4]W. Winthrop, *A Digest of the Opinions of the Judge Advocate General of the Army* (Washington, 1880), pp. 450, n. 2, 53-54, 58, 63-65; Edgar S. Dudley, *Military Law and the Procedure of Courts-Martial* (New York, 1912), pp. 6n., 180. For Articles of War defining offenses for which enlisted men might be punished, see Arthur Murray, *Instructions for Courts-Martial* (St. Paul, 1891), pp. 81-92.

[5]Robert N. Scott, *An Analytical Digest of the Military Laws of the United States* (Philadelphia, 1873), pp. 283-90, 293; Winthrop, *Digest of Opinions* (1880), pp. 70, 202, 296-98; Murray, *Instructions for Courts-Martial,* pp. 12-14.

[6]*ANJ,* August 9, 1871; New York *Times,* March 20, 1891. Cf. Eugene F. Ware, *The Indian War of 1864* (New York, 1960), p. 150.

[7]Don Rickey, Jr., *Forty Miles a Day on Beans and Hay* (Norman, Oklahoma,

1963), p. 142; W. Winthrop, *Military Law* (Washington, 1886), I, 157, 164, 166; Arthur Murray, *A Manual for Courts-Martial* (Washington, 1895), p. 6; Don Rickey, Jr. says that since there was nothing to prevent a post commander from repeatedly issuing such an order, this provision was "easily circumvented." *Forty Miles a Day,* p. 142.

⁸47th Cong., 1st Sess., House Executive Document No. 1, Pt. 2, II, 203; Kansas City *Times,* January 21, 1894; *ANJ,* December 13, 1884.

⁹Winthrop, *Digest of Opinions* (1880), pp. 145-46; Murray, *Instructions for Courts-Martial,* pp. 17-23, 92-103; *ANJ,* February 23, May 25, 1867; 46th Cong., 3d Sess., House Executive Document No. 1, Pt. 2, II, 181-82; 47th Cong., 1st Sess., House Executive Document No. 1, Pt. 2, II, 204-05; M. L. Crimmins, "Colonel J. K. F. Mansfield's Report of the Inspection of the Department of Texas in 1856," *Southwestern Historical Quarterly,* XLII (January, 1939), 254; Herbert M. Hart, *Old Forts of the Far West* (Seattle, 1965), p. 126.

¹⁰General Orders No. 20, Headquarters, 5th Military District, New Orleans, La., April 25, 1868, pp. 9-10, N.A.

¹¹*ANJ,* May 16, 1868; cf. 47th Cong., 1st Sess., House Executive Document No. 1, Pt. 2, II, 204; New York *Tribune,* January 27, March 6, 1872; *ANJ,* February 20, 1891; Kansas City *Times,* December 13, 1891.

¹²47th Cong., 1st Sess., House Executive Document No. 1, Pt. 2, II, 204. Cf. New York *Times,* November 22, 1884; Washington *Evening Star,* September 7, 1889; 50th Cong., 2d Sess., House Executive Document No. 1, Pt. 2, II, 283; *ANJ,* November 18, 1884, June 26, 1886; Ray H. Mattison, "The Army Fort on the Northern Plains, 1865-1895," *Nebraska History,* XXXV (March, 1954), 35; *The United Service,* VIII (May, 1883), 552; *Annual Report of the Acting Judge Advocate, Department of the Missouri,* dated August 16, 1889, pp. 1-2, N.A.

¹³*ANJ,* November 15, 1882.

¹⁴New York *Times,* November 1, 1888, December 17, 1889. Cf. *Harper's Weekly,* March 2, 1889; New York *Tribune,* December 20, 1889.

¹⁵49th Cong., 1st Sess., House Executive Document No. 1, Pt. 2, II, 148-49. Cf. *ANR,* January 12, 1886; S. W. Groesbeck, Acting Judge Advocate, Department of Dakota, August 20, 1889, Document B, pp. 8-10, issued from Headquarters, Department of Dakota, St. Paul, Minn., 1889.

¹⁶D. G. Swaim to James A. Garfield, October 1, 1870, James A. Garfield Papers, L.C.; cf. *ANJ,* December 8, 1868.

¹⁷*The United Service,* VIII (July, 1883), 47; 43rd Cong., 3d Sess., House Executive Document No. 1, Pt. 2, II, 88; *ANJ,* May 9, 1868, March 25, 1871, February 10, 1872, January 20, 1883, March 22, 1884, April 17, 1886; New York *Tribune,* January 27, 1872, April 15, 1873.

¹⁸*ANJ,* November 30, 1867.

¹⁹51st Cong., 2d Sess., House Executive Document No. 1, Pt. 2, II, 515.

²⁰51st Cong., 1st Sess., House Executive Document No. 1, Pt. 2, II, 334.

²¹Scott, *Analytical Digest,* pp. 140-42; Davis, *Treatise on Military Law,* pp. 23-27; 45th Cong., 1st Sess., House Miscellaneous Document No. 56, p. 10; 44th Cong., 1st Sess., House Report No. 354, pp. 37, 136, 155.

[22]47th Cong., 1st Sess., House Executive Document No. 1, Pt. 2, II, 207; *The United States Service Magazine,* V (March, 1866), 218-19.

[23]44th Cong., 1st Sess., House Report No. 354, pp. 37-38. Cf. *The United States Service Magazine,* V (March, 1866), 218; New York *Tribune,* January 27, 1872; *Congressional Record,* 48th Cong., 2d Sess., p. 2118.

[24]Hugh L. Scott to Mary Merrill Scott, December 27, 1889, Scott Papers, L.C.; New York *World,* quoted in *ANJ,* June 25, 1892; *ANJ,* August 22, 1885. Cf. *ANJ,* August 24, 1877, July 10, 1886; Kansas City *Times,* March 13, 1891; H. H. McConnell, *Five Years a Cavalryman* (Jacksboro, Texas, 1889), pp. 196-99.

[25]48th Cong., 1st Sess., House Executive Document No. 1, Pt. 2, II, 6. Cf. 44th Cong., 1st Sess., House Report No. 354, p. 103; 50th Cong., 1st Sess., House Executive Document No. 1, Pt. 2, II, 15-16, 290-91; *ANJ,* August 24, 1877, December 24, 1881, January 20, 1883.

[26]Augustus V. Kautz, *Customs of the Service* (Philadelphia, 1864), pp. 205-06; Winthrop, *Digest of Opinions* (1880), pp. 481-82; Edward Farrow, *Military Encyclopedia* (New York, 1885), I, 419; Rollin A. Ives, *A Treatise on Military Law* (New York, 1879), pp. 124-39.

[27]Winthrop, *Digest of Opinions* (1880), pp. 199, 481-82; Davis, *Treatise,* p. 40; Stephen V. Benet, *A Treatise on Military Law and the Practice of Courts Martial* (New York, 1868), p. 75; Washington *Evening Star,* October 30, November 6, 1885; Washington *Post,* October 29, 30, 1885; D. G. Swaim to W. T. Sherman, September 23, 1876, RG94, File 1316, ACP 1877, N.A.

[28]44th Cong., 1st Sess., House Report No. 354, p. 140. Cf. Junction City *Republican,* May 3, 1889; *ANJ,* January 10, 1874, July 22, 1876; Kansas City *Times,* March 18, 1893.

[29]Winthrop, *Digest of Opinions* (1868), pp. 205-08, *Digest of Opinions* (1880), pp. 296, 299; Winthrop, *Military Law,* I, 240-78. "The judge advocate is not challengeable; but in case of personal interest in the trial, he should apply to the convening authority to be relieved." Murray, *Instructions for Courts-Martial,* p. 15.

[30]47th Cong., 1st Sess., House Executive Document No. 1, Pt. 2, II, 207.

[31]*The United Service,* IX (August, 1883), 184. Cf. 47th Cong., 2d Sess., House Executive Document No. 1, Pt. 2, II, 16; 48th Cong., 2d Sess., Senate Report No. 1337, pp. 1-2; Benet, *Treatise on Military Law,* pp. 240, 248; *ANJ,* December 7, 1867, December 20, 1873, March 6, 1890; Chicago *Times,* March 3, 1890; New York *Sun,* June 15, 1884; MSIUS *Journal,* V (1884), 380. For contrary view, see James Regan, *The Judge-Advocate and Recorder's Guide* (Washington, 1877), p. 33.

[32]*ANJ,* December 7, 1867; *Congressional Record,* 48th Cong., 2d Sess., pp. 2118-20.

[33]49th Cong., 1st Sess., House Executive Document No. 1, Pt. 2, II, 341; New York *Times,* March 13, 1892.

[34]Farrow, *Military Encyclopedia,* I, 656; 45th Cong., 2d Sess., House Miscellaneous Document No. 56, p. 11; Winthrop, *Military Law,* I, 529-48; Winthrop, *Digest of Opinions* (1880), pp. 434-35.

[35]New York *Tribune,* March 15, 1873. Cf. March 29, 1873; *United States Service Magazine,* V (March, 1866), 215; *ANJ,* September 9, 1871, January 10, 1874, January 29, 1876.

[36]*ANJ,* January 12, 1878; cf. New York *Graphic,* September 21, 1883; D. G. Swaim to W. T. Sherman, September 23, 1876, RG94, File 1316, ACP 1877, N.A.

[37]Portland *Eastern Argus,* October 12, 1889. Cf. New York *Sun,* June 15, 1884; Kansas City *Times,* January 22, 1887.

[38]New York *Times,* December 20, 1889; Rickey, *Forty Miles,* pp. 141-42.

[39]Washington *Capital,* August 11, 1872; New York *Herald,* November 28, 1886; *Harper's Weekly,* December 8, 1888; Kansas City *Times,* June 24, 1889; *ANJ,* May 22, 1886. Cf. Chicago *Tribune,* March 28, 1890; Cincinnati *Commercial,* September 1, 1890; Cleveland *Leader,* September 18, 1889; Chicago *Herald,* September 14, 1892; Philadelphia *Inquirer,* March 20, 1890; Kansas City *Times,* July 5, 1889; Washington *Post,* October 29, 1885.

[40]William Duane, *Handbook for Infantry* (Philadelphia, 1813), p. 13; Winthrop, *Digest of Opinions* (1868), p. 15; Edward A. Dolph, *Sound Off: Soldier's Songs* (New York, 1923), p. 394; Maurer Maurer, "Military Justice Under General Washington," *Military Affairs,* XVII (Spring, 1964), 10-11, 13; John S. Hare, "Military Punishments in the War of 1812," *Military Affairs,* IV (Summer, 1940), 115-239. For a contrary view, see James R. Jacobs, *The Beginning of the U.S. Army* (Princeton, 1947), pp. 137-38.

[41]MSIUS *Journal,* XIV (1893), 921-22; *ANJ,* October 26, 1867.

[42]MSIUS *Journal,* XIII (1892), 104, XIV (1893), 924, XV (1894), 640, XVI (1895), 40; XXXVII (1905), 147-67.

[43]MSIUS *Journal,* XIII (1892), 104, XIV (1893), 893, 1042; New York *Herald,* February 1, 1884; Chicago *Chronicle,* October 17, 1897; *Harper's Weekly,* July 6, 1895; Carolyn T. Foreman, "Military Discipline in Early Oklahoma," *Chronicles of Oklahoma,* VI (June, 1928), 140-44; *ANJ,* November 21, 1874; Robert M. Utley, *Frontiersmen in Blue: The United States Army and the Indian, 1848-1865* (New York, 1867), pp. 38-39.

[44]31st Cong., 2d Sess., Senate Rep. Com. No. 226, pp. 13-21. Five members of the Court recommended that in the case of one of the accused soldiers, Private William Hanniver, the part of his sentence relating to wearing a ball and chain and a collar around his neck be remitted. The reviewing officer, Major-General John E. Wool, accepted this recommendation and remitted that portion of the sentence. *Ibid.,* pp. 17-18.

[45]31st Cong., 2d Sess., Senate Rep. Com. No. 226, pp. 3-4; Portsmouth *Journal,* November 2, 1850.

[46]31st Cong., 2d Sess., Senate Rep. Com. No. 226, pp. 221-22. Cf. *ibid.,* pp. 1-2, 11-12; *Congressional Globe,* 31st Cong., 2d Sess., p. 8; Rockingham (New Hampshire) *Messenger,* October 23, 1850; Concord (New Hampshire) *Daily Patriot,* November 6, 19, 1850; Portsmouth *Journal,* October 23, November 9, 1850; Boston *Post,* November 4, 23, 1850.

[47]Scott, *Analytical Digest,* p. 292; MSIUS *Journal,* XIV (1893), 922; *Regulations of the Army of the United States* (Washington, 1881), pp. 97-98; Rickey, *Forty Miles,* p. 179; *ANJ,* July 6, October 26, 1867, May 9, 1868.

[48]Joseph M. Hanson, *Conquest of the Missouri* (Chicago, 1909), pp. 122-23; Diary of Winfield S. Harvey, Private, 7th U.S. Cavalry, July 27, 1870, Edward S. Godfrey Papers, L.C.; 42nd Cong., 2d Sess., House Executive Document No. 1, Pt. 2, II, 58; *ANJ*, May 11, October 26, 1867, June 25, September 24, 1870, December 17, 1881; MSIUS *Journal*, XIV (1893), 21.

[49]*ANJ*, January 13, 1872.

[50]*ANJ*, October 12, 1872. Cf. Scott, *Analytical Digest*, p. 294; *ANJ*, April 13, 20, 1872; New York *Herald*, November 8, 1875.

[51]*The United Service*, VIII (January, 1883), 88, (March, 1883), 315; MSIUS *Journal*, XXXVII (1905), 14-15; *General Orders 20, Headquarters, Fifth Military District*, New Orleans, La., April 25, 1868, N.A.

[52]*ANJ*, January 13, 1872.

[53]*ANJ*, July 18, 1874.

[54]42nd Cong., 2d Sess., House Executive Document No. 1, Pt. 2, II, 58; *ANJ*, December 7, 1867, December 21, 1872.

[55]*ANJ*, September 9, 1871; New York *Tribune*, January 27, 1872.

[56]42nd Cong., 3d Sess., House Executive Document No. 1, Pt. 2, II, 4. Cf. *ANJ*, December 21, 1872.

[57]*ANJ*, February 1, 1873; G. Norman Lieber, *Remarks on the Army Regulations and Executive Regulations* (Washington, 1898), p. 175.

[58]50th Cong., 2d Sess., House Executive Document No. 1, Pt. 2, II, 18; *The United Service*, VIII (1883), 75, 319; MSIUS *Journal*, XIII (1892), 105; Regan, *Judge Advocates Guide*, p. 74.

[59]50th Cong., 2d Sess., House Executive Document No. 1, Pt. 2, II, 280. Cf. Farrow, *Military Encyclopedia*, III, Supplement, 122; MSIUS *Journal*, VIII (1887), 324.

[60]*ANJ*, December 6, 1879; Headquarters Department of Texas, San Antonio, Texas, October 21, 1879, *General Court Martial Orders*, No. 67, 1, 3, 4, 6, 7, N.A. Cf. *ANJ*, December 6, 1879; Report of Trials by General and Garrison Courts Martial, *Annual Report, Headquarters Department of Texas*, San Antonio, October 1, 1880, 3-4.

[61]45th Cong., 2d Sess., House Miscellaneous Document No. 56, 11; Washington *Evening Star*, March 2, 1891; *The United Service*, VIII (March, 1883), 315-16; 51st Cong., 1st Sess., House Executive Document No. 1, Pt. 2, II, 25-26, 86, 320-21.

[62]*ANJ*, January 13, 1877; 45th Cong., 2d Sess., House Miscellaneous Document No. 56, 22; Kansas City *Times*, December 29, 1884. Cf. Cleveland *Leader*, September 17, 1889.

[63]Farrow, *Military Encyclopedia*, III, Supplement, 121; 46th Cong., 3d Sess., House Executive Document No. 1, Pt. 2, II, 307; New York *Herald*, November 25, December 4, 1887; Junction City *Republican*, May 3, 1889.

[64]Quoted in newspaper article written by E. D. Bogart, sent from Fort Leavenworth, February 27, 1890, and entitled "Soldiers in the Pen—Shockingly Excessive Sentences by Courts-Martial," no place or date of publication, Redfield Proctor Notebooks, 1889-1890, pp. 173-74, Proctor Collection, Vermont Historical Society.

[65]John L. Bradley to O. O. Howard, July 5, 1894, Howard Papers. Cf. W. W. Worthington to John L. Bradley, August 1, 1894, Howard Papers.

[66]New York *Tribune*, December 4, 1887; cf. Kansas City *Times*, November 30, 1887; *ANR*, December 3, 1887.

[67]52nd Cong., 2d Sess., House Executive Document No. 1, Pt. 2, II, 211-21. Among the offenses for which a court-martial might sentence to death was disobeying the order of or striking a superior officer. Regan, *Judge Advocate and Recorder's Guide*, p. 75; Dudley, *Military Law and the Procedure of Courts-Martial*, pp. 158-59.

[68]Troy (New York) *Daily Press*, December 21, 1892; MSIUS *Journal*, XII (1892), 105.

[69]New York *Tribune*, March 17, 1883. Cf. New York *Times*, March 17, 1883; *ANJ*, March 24, 1893.

[70]Charles Rose, Private, Company K, 4th Infantry to O. O. Howard, January 27, 1884, Howard Papers.

[71]Kansas City *Times*, December 29, 1884.

[72]Kansas City *Times*, June 24, 1889; 51st Cong., 1st Sess., House Report No. 1051, p. 2.

[73]51st Cong., 1st Sess., House Executive Document No. 1, Pt. 2, II, 85; cf. *ANJ*, February 28, 1891; Kansas City *Times*, December 7, 1886, February 17, 1890.

[74]Farrow, *Military Encyclopedia*, III, Supplement, 122; cf. 51st Cong., 1st Sess., House Executive Document No. 1, Pt. 2, II, 86.

[75]*ANJ*, June 26, 1886. Cf. November 22, 1874, November 28, 1886, June 2, 1889; Kansas City *Times*, January 22, 1887, September 30, 1889; Washington *Evening Star*, September 7, 1889; New York *Times*, December 20, 1889; Buffalo *Courier*, October 6, 1889.

[76]*ANJ*, June 26, 1886.

[77]47th Cong., 1st Sess., House Executive Document No. 1, Pt. 2, II, 204.

[78]50th Cong., 2d Sess., House Executive Document No. 1, Pt. 2, II, 283-84; cf. Winthrop, *Digest of Opinions* (1880), pp. 434-39; *ANJ*, July 10, 1886; *The United Service*, VIII (1883), 319, 354; 44th Cong., 1st Sess., House Report No. 358, p. 38. On dispute over interpretation of Section 1199, Revised Statutes 1878, see Edmund M. Morgan, "The Existing Court Martial System and the Ansell Articles," *Yale Law Journal*, XXIX (1919-20), 65-66; Terry W. Brown, "The Crowder-Ansell Dispute," *Military Law Review*, XXXV (January, 1967), 4-8.

[79]Ives, *Treatise on Military Law*, pp. 193-94; Winthrop, *Digest of Opinions* (1880), pp. 66, 120, 440, (1895), pp. 673-74; *ANJ*, May 9, 1868; Farrow, *Military Encyclopedia*, II, 661; General Order No. 20, Headquarters of the 5th Military District, New Orleans, La., April 25, 1868, N.A.

[80]*ANR*, April 11, 1896; cf. *United States Army Regulations*, 1881, par. 923, p. 126; *Congressional Record*, 42nd Cong., 2d Sess., p. 2125; S. T. Ansell, "Some Reforms in Our System of Military Justice," *Yale Law Journal*, XXXII (1922-23), 150.

[81]*The United States Service Magazine*, V (March, 1866), 218.

[82]*ANJ*, December 8, 1866.

[83]*ANJ*, May 25, December 21, 1867. Cf. October 5, December 21, 1867.

[84]*ANJ*, January 12, 1878. Cf. January 11, 1879; 46th Cong., 3d Sess., House Executive. Document No. 1, Pt. 2, II, 182; Boston *Commercial Bulletin*, March 15, 1890; Toronto *Globe*, December 14, 1883.

[85]Winthrop, *Digest of Opinions* (1880), 92-93; *The United States Service Magazine*, V, (1866), 218; *ANJ*, February 10, 1872, January 1, 1879.

[86]Mary Mangel to O. O. Howard, January 27, 1886, Howard Papers. Cf. Mrs. D. C. Petit to O. O. Howard, December 1, 1885, Mrs. H. S. Martin to O. O. Howard, August 24, 1886, Sarah M. Neely to O. O. Howard, March 15, 1890, Howard to Mrs. Hattie Watkins, June 14, 1886, O. O. Howard to Katie M. Burt, January 23, 1891, Howard Papers.

[87]Winthrop, *Digest of Opinions* (1880), pp. 105-06; Ives, *Treatise on Military Law*, p. 219; 47th Cong., 2d Sess., House Executive Document No. 1, Pt. 2, II, 232.

[88]44th Cong., 1st Sess., House Report No. 354, pp. 149-55; 47th Cong., 1st Sess., House Executive Document No. 1, Pt. 2, II, 199-202; *ANJ*, February 12, 1876; *ANR*, December 4, 11, 1886; D. G. Swaim to James A. Garfield, November 28, 1874, Garfield Papers, L.C.

[89]40th Cong., 3rd Sess., House Report No. 33, p. 106; New York *Tribune*, March 15, 1873. Cf. 44th Cong., 1st Sess., House Report No. 354, p. 155; New York *Herald*, February 22, 1876; *ANJ*, February 12, 1876.

[90]44th Cong., 1st Sess., House Report No. 354, pp. 1, 51, 104, 107, 112, 116; *ANJ*, May 6, 1876.

[91]44th Cong., 1st Sess., House Report No. 354, pp. 8, 122.

[92]44th Cong., 1st Sess., House Report No. 354, pp. 28, 37, 100, 102, 156. Cf. *A Sketch of the History and Duties of the Judge Advocate General's Department of the United States Army* (Washington, 1878), pp. 9-14.

[93]44th Cong., 1st Sess., House Report No. 354, pp. 140, 156; 45th Cong., 2d Sess., House Miscellaneous Document No. 56, p. 11; Major D. G. Swaim to John A. Logan, April 15, 1876, Swaim to W. T. Sherman, September 23, 1876, Record Group 94, File 1316-ACP 1877, N.A.

[94]49th Cong., 1st Sess., House Executive Document No. 1, Pt. 2, II, 149. Cf. *ANJ*, May 19, 1890.

[95]New York *Times*, July 23, 1892; cf. 52nd Cong., 1st Sess., House Report No. 1074, pp. 1-2.

[96]Scott, *Analytical Digest*, p. 302; Winthrop, *Digest of Opinions* (1868), p. 277; 40th Cong., 3d Sess., House Executive Document No. 1, Pt. 2, II, 727; *ANJ*, January 19, 1867.

[97]Scott, *Analytical Digest*, p. 303n; 42nd Cong., 3d Sess., House Executive Document No. 1, Pt. 2, II, 5. Cf. *ibid.*, p. 13; *ANJ*, August 12, 1871, February 10, 1872; *Congressional Globe*, 42nd Cong., 2d Sess., p. 3165.

[98]*ANJ*, November 8, 1873. Cf. January 5, 1870; *The United Service*, VIII (August, 1883), 316.

[99]40th Cong., 2d Sess., House Executive Document No. 1, Pt. 2, II, 416; 40th Cong., 3d Sess., House Executive Document No. 1, Pt. 2, II, 212; 42nd Cong., 2d Sess., House Report No. 70, pp. 10-13; New York *Sun*, February 9, 1871;

New York *Tribune,* January 12, 1872; New York *Herald,* August 22, 1870; *ANJ,* February 10, 1866, May 25, October 5, December 21, 1867, May 8, 1868, January 16, December 4, 1869, January 6, January 27, February 10, 1872.

[100]Report of Judge-Advocate Thomas F. Barr to Assistant Adjutant-General, Department of the East, January 30, 1871, N.A., Record Group 94.

[101]40th Cong., 2d Sess., House Executive Document No. 1, Pt. 2, II, 416-17; 40th Cong., 3d Sess., House Executive Document No. 1, Pt. 2, III, 729. Cf. George P. Meade to Adjutant-General E. P. Townsend, August 28, 1867, N.A., Military Prison Division, Entry 456, N.A.; New York *Times,* August 5, 1868; *The Independent,* August 20, 1868; New York *Herald,* August 26, 1868; *ANJ,* August 29, 1868; *The United Service,* VIII (1883), 314.

[102]New York *Times,* November 22, 1868.

[103]Henry Shindler, *History of the United States Military Prison* (Ft. Leavenworth, Kansas, 1911), pp. 1-13; Scott, *Analytical Digest,* pp. 465-67; *The United Service,* VIII (1883), 314, 317-18; *Congressional Globe,* 42nd Cong., 2d Sess., pp. 3163-66; Letter of instructions from the Commanding General of the Department of the East and Report of the Board Appointed by the Secretary of War to Examine into the System of Army Prisons and Prison Discipline in the British Service, 1871, (3127 [DC], 1871), N.A.; Irvin McDowell to James A. Garfield, January 15, 1873, Garfield Papers, L.C.

[104]*ANJ,* February 14, 1874. Cf. John C. Coburn to William C. Church, March 7, 1874, Church Papers, L. C.

[105]Captain J. W. Pope, "Crimes and Criminals of the American Army," American Prison Association, *Proceedings of the General Congress,* 1891, p. 126; *The United Service,* IX (1883), 158; 43rd Cong., 1st Sess., House Executive Document No. 1, Pt. 2, II, 2; House Executive Document No. 19, pp. 1-2, 5, 9-10; *ANJ,* March 11, 1874.

[106]Shindler, *History of Prison,* pp. 24-26; Pope, "Crimes and Criminals," p. 127; *The United Service,* IX (1883), 158-59; New York *Times,* January 23, 1882. All military offenders convicted of serious crimes were sent to the Leavenworth Military Prison if serving east of the Rocky Mountains, and to Alcatraz Island, if serving west of the Rockies. Alcatraz, however, was not a military prison established by law. Captain J. W. Pope, "Desertion and the Military Prison," *Cosmopolitan Magazine,* X (1890), 116-18, 123-24.

[107]Shindler, *History of Prison,* pp. 28, 29, 55, 123; Pope, "Crimes and Criminals," p. 130; *ANJ,* February 26, 1876, March 26, 1881, January 12, 1884; New York *Times,* January 23, 1882; April 22, 1894; Elvid Hunt, *History of Fort Leavenworth* (Fort Leavenworth, Kansas, 1926), p. 205.

[108]48th Cong., 1st Sess., House Executive Document No. 1, Pt. 2, II, 88-89; cf. 47th Cong., 1st Sess., House Executive Document No. 1, Pt. 2, II, 211; 50th Cong., 1st Sess., House Executive Document No. 1, Pt. 2, II, 111; 51st Cong., 1st Sess., House Executive Document No. 1, Pt. 2, II, 25-26; St. Louis *Post Dispatch,* March 30, 1890; *ANJ,* December 3, 1887, August 3, October 5, 1889.

[109]50th Cong., 1st Sess., House Executive Document No. 1, Pt. 2, II, 162; cf. 51st Cong., 2d Sess., House Executive Document No. 1, Pt. 2, II, 97; Shindler, *History of Prison,* pp. 47-49, 78-79.

[110]49th Cong., 2d Sess., House Executive Document No. 1, Pt. 2, II, 220; cf. *ANJ*, May 29, 1886.

[111]51st Cong., 1st Sess., House Executive Document No. 1, Pt. 2, II, 236-37. Cf. Shindler, *History of Prison*, p. 49.

CHAPTER III: THE ENLISTED SOLDIER, HIS OFFICERS AND THE COMMUNITY

[1]*Revised United States Army Regulations* (Washington, 1863), Article I, 1-3; *Regulations of the Army of the United States* (Washington, 1881), Article I, 1-5; *Regulations of the Army of the United States* (Washington, 1895), Article I, 1-5.

[2]*ANJ*, February 10, 1866. Cf. 31st Cong., 2d Sess., Senate Rep. Com. No. 226, 2-3.

[3]*ANJ*, August 10, October 5, 1867, July 19, 1873, February 10, December 1, 1883, January 12, 1884; 51st Cong., 1st Sess., House Executive Document No. 1, Pt. 2, II, 84, 118-19; 45th Cong., 2d Sess., House Miscellaneous Document No. 56, 84, 135; 44th Cong., 1st Sess., House Report No. 354, 76; Otto L. Hein, *Memories of Long Ago* (New York, 1925), pp. 100, 179-81; *The Field Diary of Lieutenant Edward Steele Godfrey*, edited by Edgar Stewart and Jane R. Stewart (Portland, Oregon, 1957), p. iv; Don Rickey, Jr., *Forty Miles a Day on Beans and Hay* (Norman, Oklahoma, 1963), pp. 139-40.

[4]*ANJ*, November 6, 1875.

[5]*ANJ*, February 2, 1878.

[6]*ANJ*, March 4, 1882.

[7]John Brait, *Trials of Yesterday* (Lincoln, 1921), p. 169; William Murphy, "The Forgotten Battalion," *Annals of Wyoming*, VII (October, 1930), 385; Chris Emmet, *Fort Union and the Winning of the Southwest* (Norman, Oklahoma, 1965), pp. 351-52; Rickey, *Forty Miles a Day*, pp. 179-84; James D. Lockwood, *Life and Adventures of a Drummer Boy* (Albany, 1893), pp. 135-36; *ANJ*, May 7, July 6, 1867, December 28, 1872, November 28, 1874, September 24, 1876; London *Times*, April 2, 4, 10, 1867; Joseph Hanson, *Conquest of the Missouri* (Chicago, 1909), pp. 121-27; August V. Kautz, *Customs of the Service* (Philadelphia, 1964), pp. 201-02; Anson Mills, *My Story* (Washington, 1918), p. 365; R. G. Carter, *The Old Sergeant's Story* (New York, 1926), p. 20; Ernest Wallace, *Ranald S. McKenzie on the Texas Frontier* (Lubbock, Texas, 1964), p. 61; William A. Ganoe, *The Army of the United States* (New York, 1924), p. 353; S. Whitman, *The Troopers* (New York, 1962), pp. 91-93; *Journal of the United States Cavalry Association*, II (March, 1889), 5, 15.

[8]*ANJ*, May 9, 1868. Cf. June 13, 1868, November 18, 1874, April 29, 1876; Mrs. Hal Russell, "Memories of Marian Russell," *The Colorado Magazine*, XXI (1944), 133.

[9]*ANJ*, August 12, 1871, January 6, 1872. Cf. *The United Service*, XIII (June, 1885), 678-79; New York *Sun*, February 9, 1871, June 15, 1884.

[10]*ANJ*, July 26, 1873. Cf. October 11, 25, 1872, November 15, 1873; London *Pall-Mall Gazette*, September 1, 1873.

[11]42nd Cong., 2d Sess., House Executive Document No. 1, Pt. 2, II, 22; *The United Service,* VIII (March, 1883), 89, XIII (June, 1885), 677; 44th Cong., 2d Sess., House Report No. 56, pp. 140-41; *ANJ,* April 22, December 2, 1871, September 28, October 26, 1872, October 1, 1873, June 21, 1879; New York *Sun,* January 2, 1890; (St. Louis) Missouri *Republican,* July 26, 1876; St. Louis *Post Dispatch,* October 24, 1889; Rickey, *Forty Miles a Day,* pp. 139-41.

[12]*ANJ,* November 1, 1873. Cf. New York *Graphic,* September 21, 1883.

[13]*ANJ,* November 24, 1866, October 26, 1867. Cf. July 27, 1867; *New National Era,* July 30, 1874; *General Orders No. 3, Headquarters, Military Division of the Pacific and Department of California,* June 23, 1879, p. 8, N.A.; 47th Cong., 1st Sess., House Executive Document No. 1, Pt. 2, II, 206; Washington *Chronicle,* August 27, 1874.

[14]42nd Cong., 3d Sess., House Report No. 74, p. 72; *The United Service,* XII (June, 1885), 677; cf. E. O. C. Ord to Assistant Adjutant General, December 7, 1875, Record Group 94, File 1316-ACP 1877; MSIUS *Journal,* VI (1884), 374, XIII (1892), 102; *ANJ,* July 1, 1879; 42nd Cong., 3d Sess., House Executive Document No. 1, Pt. 2, II, 59; 46th Cong., 2d Sess., House Executive Document No. 1, Pt. 2, II, 192; 47th Cong., 1st Sess., House Executive Document No. 1, Pt. 2, II, 206, 581; 48th Cong., 1st Sess., House Executive Document No. 1, Pt. 2, II, 53.

[15]*ANJ,* January 21, 1871, April 13, May 25, 1872, February 3, 1877, June 15. 1878; San Antonio *Express,* March 3, 1871; New York *Sun,* December 2, 1877; Donald Jackson, *Custer's Gold: The United States Cavalry Expedition of 1874* (New Haven, 1966), pp. 30, 36-37.

[16]New York *Sun,* May 23, 1880. Cf. New York *Herald,* August 18, May 23, 1882, April 9, 1883; New York *Sun,* June 15, 1884.

[17]Kautz, *Customs of Service,* p. 94; Robert N. Scott, *Digest of Military Laws of the United States* (Philadelphia, 1873), p. 314, n23; Missouri *Republican,* July 11, 1867; Cincinnati *Commercial,* May 8, 1870; New York *Herald,* February 1, 1884; *ANJ,* July 27, 1867.

[18]Scott, *Digest of Military Laws,* p. 314; *Congressional Record,* 41st Cong., 2d Sess., p. 3320; General Order No. 19, Adjutant General's Office, February 25, 1873, in *ANJ,* March 15, 1873; *ANJ,* January 29, 1876, September 10, 1881, August 1, 1883, February 20, 1886, December 21, 1889; Washington *Evening Star,* September 7, 1889; New York *Star,* December 1, 1879; New York *Times,* December 21, 1884; *ANR,* July 19, 1884; Francis M. Roe, *Army Letters from an Officer's Wife* (New York, 1909), pp. 54-55; George A. Armes, *Ups and Downs of an Army Officer* (Washington, 1900), p. 477; 43rd Cong., 2d Sess., House Executive Document No. 1, Pt. 2, II, 94-95; Merrill J. Mattes, *Indians, Infants and Infantry: Andrew and Elizabeth Burt on the Frontier* (Denver, 1960), pp. 197-98; Chicago *Inter-Ocean,* March 22, 1890; Pittsburgh *Post,* July 9, 1893; Rickey, *Forty Miles a Day,* pp. 111-12.

[19]*ANJ,* June 10, 1882.

[20]*ANJ,* September 25, 1869, April 22, 1871, November 1, 1873, May 10, 1879, September 14, 1889; MSIUS *Journal,* VIII (1887), 156; *The United Service,*

VIII (June, 1883), 632, 637; New York *Sun*, September 29, 1876, January 14, 1878.

[21]New York *Herald*, October 23, 1882. Cf. Columbus *Dispatch*, quoted in Kansas City *Times*, May 11, 1885.

[22]48th Cong., 2d Sess., House Executive Document No. 1, Pt. 2, II, 96; *ANR*, November 22, 1884; Chicago *Herald*, August 12, 1885; 45th Cong., 2d Sess., House Report No. 56, pp. 359-62; *ANJ*, June 28, November 1, 1873, December 29, 1880, May 4, 1881; William T. Sherman to Phillip H. Sheridan, January 23, 1881, Sheridan Papers, L.C.

[23]*Regulations of the Army of the United States* (1881), par. 167; 48th Cong., 1st Sess., House Executive Document No. 1, Pt. 2, II, 53. Cf. *ANJ*, July 26, 1890; New York *Times* December 21, 1884; 48th Cong., 2d Sess., House Executive Document No. 1, Pt. 2, II, 88-89; Kansas City *Times*, November 11, 1889; O. O. Howard to John M. Carson, January 7, 1885; Howard to Rufus Saxton, July 28, 1891, Howard Papers, Bowdoin College.

[24]46th Cong., 2d Sess., House Executive Document No. 1, Pt. 2, II, 12; *The United Service*, XII (June, 1885), 678-79; *ANJ*, April 29, 1871, February 13, 1872, November 28, 1874, March 24, June 23, 1875, April 7, 1877, May 22, 1880, August 22, 1882, April 2, 1887; *ANR*, May 2, 1885; Ami F. Mulford, *Fighting Indians in the Seventh United States Calvary* (Corning, 1879), pp. 25, 60, 66; Private Patrick Welsh to O. O. Howard, January 18, 1884, Howard Papers; Diary of Private Winfield S. Harvey, March 14, 16, 1871, Edward S. Godfrey Papers, L.C.; Frank W. Belz to O. O. Howard, February 19, 1890, Howard Papers; St. Louis *Globe-Democrat*, August 4, 1889.

[25]*ANJ*, September 7, 1867; New York *Herald*, August 22, 1870. Cf. New York *Herald*, February 9, 1871.

[26]*ANJ*, May 29, 1875.

[27]*The United Service*, VII (November, 1882), 512. Cf. *ibid.*, XII (June, 1885), 678-79; Rickey, *Forty Miles a Day*, p. 70.

[28]MSIUS *Journal*, VIII (1887), 296; Edward Farrow, *Military Encyclopedia* (New York, 1885), I, 480; F. Horton to O. O. Howard, October 30, 1882, Thomas Campbell to Howard, March 1, 1886, James D. Gordon to Howard, September 23, 1888, Howard Papers.

[29]MSIUS *Journal*, VIII (1887), 296.

[30]Scott, *Analytical Digest*, p. 300; W. Winthrop, *Digest of the Opinions of the Judge-Advocate General* (Washington, 1868), pp. 12, 166; Kautz, *Customs of Service*, pp. 202-03.

[31]*ANJ*, August 31, 1867, January 16, 1869; New York *Herald*, June 14, 1873. Cf. *ANJ*, December 21, 1871, August 31, 1872, January 31, February 14, 1874; Abraham Nemerow, "Complaints of Wrongs Under Article 138," *Military Law Review*, II (September, 1958), 57.

[32]W. Winthrop, *Digest of the Opinions of the Judge-Advocate General* (Washington, 1880), pp. 15-16; Farrow, *Military Encyclopedia*, II, 346; *ANJ*, February 4, 1882, April 21, 1883, May 18, 1889; 51st Cong., 1st Sess., House Executive Document No. 1, Pt. 2, II, 84; Nemerow, "Complaints of Wrongs Under Article

138," p. 58; T. T. Cabaniss to O. O. Howard, September 18, 1880, Howard Papers.

[33]50th Cong., 2d Sess., House Executive Document No. 1, Pt. 2, II, 283. Cf. 51st Cong., 1st Sess., House Executive Document No. 1, Pt. 2, II, 84; ANJ, December 1, 1900.

[34]Farrow, Military Encyclopedia, II, 107; The United Service, IX (August, 1883), 183; New York Sun, April 9, 1883; ANJ, August 31, 1872, March 13, 1875, December 8, 1888, October 24, 1891.

[35]New York Tribune, February 10, 1869; New York Sun, May 18, 1872. Cf. New York Sun, February 9, 1871, May 26, 1873; Cincinnati Commercial, December 15, 1869, March 8, 1870; Baltimore American, November 10, 1880, November 14, 25, 1889; (New York) Irish World, June 7, 14, 1879.

[36]Anson Mills, My Story (Washington, 1918), pp. 366, 375-76; The Independent, August 20, 1868; ANJ, April 29, 1871, January 13, 1877, February 17, 1894; New York Sun, May 23, 1880; New York Times, April 20, 1882; John Joseph Lenney, Caste System in the Army (New York, 1949), p. xiii; Rickey, Forty Miles a Day, pp. 62-65.

[37]ANJ, March 24, 1877.

[38]ANJ, November 30, 1867. Cf. September 7, 1867, December 21, 1889; Chicago Inter-Ocean, March 29, 1890.

[39]ANJ, November 24, 1877.

[40]Scott, Analytical Digest, pp. 300-31; 41st Cong., 1st Sess., House Executive Document No. 1, Pt. 2, II, 202-03; The United Service, VIII (January, 1883), 924; Winthrop, Digest of Opinions (1880), p. 50; Farrow, Military Encyclopedia, I, 465; ANJ, November 24, 1877, August 26, 1882, December 21, 1889; Kansas City Times, January 6, 1890.

[41]47th Cong., 1st Sess., House Executive Document No. 1, Pt. 2, II, 202-03. Cf. Winthrop, Digest of Opinions (1880), p. 52.

[42]ANJ, November 22, 1873; 45th Cong., 2d Sess., House Miscellaneous Document No. 56, p. 37. Cf. ANJ, January 10, 1874; 35th Cong., 1st Sess., Senate Executive Document No. 11, p. 48; New York Graphic, September 21, 1883.

[43]Minneapolis Tribune, February 25, 1890; Cf. Cleveland Leader, September 17, 1889.

[44]ANJ, December 21, 1867, September 9, 1871, July 26, 1873. Cf. ANJ, October 26, 1869, July 18, 1874; New York World, February 26, 1885; T. T. Cabaniss to O. O. Howard, September 18, 1880, Howard Papers.

[45]MSIUS Journal, X (1889), 763, XI (1890), 163, XVI (1895), 239; ANJ, March 25, 1876, November 2, 1884, January 24, 1885, February 15, March 2, 1890; Rodney Glisan, Journal of Army Life (San Francisco, 1874), p. 453; New York Herald, February 20, 1884; New York Times, April 30, 1882, August 5, 1889; J. G. Steward (ed.), Active Service or Religious Work Among United States Soldiers (New York, 189?), p. 82; Charles Alexander, Battles and Victories of Allen Allensworth (Boston, 1914), pp. 316, 322, 324; Rickey, Forty Miles a Day, p. 65.

[46]ANJ, February 15, 1890, June 21, 1890.

[47]*ANJ*, May 25, 1872, January 23, May 4, 1875, April 2, 1882, February 10, 1883, July 19, 1890; Kansas City *Times*, January 6, 26, 1890; New York *Times*, April 30, 1882, MSIUS *Journal*, X (1889), 761-63, XI (1890), 160-63, 165, XVII (1895), 19-20; Mills, *My Story*, pp. 166-67.

[48]*ANJ*, March 8, 1890; cf. *The Century*, XXXVI (October, 1888), 940-41; St. Louis *Post Dispatch*, July 7, 1889; Mulford, *Fighting Indians*, p. 57; *The Independent*, L (June 30, 1898), 846.

[49]New York *Herald*, June 21, 1884 Chicago *Tribune*, March 22, 1890; *Henry George Standard*, April 6, 1889; Cincinnati *Commercial Gazette*, September 1, 1890. Cf. Omaha *Tribune*, August 18, 1889; New York *Sun*, May 12, 1874; St. Paul *Globe*, March 2, 1890; *The Nation*, XXII (June 23, 1881), 444; *The Boston Pilot*, March 8, 1890; Washington *Capital*, October 20, 1878.

[50]Scott, *Analytical* Digest, pp. 248-49; Kautz, *Customs of Service*, pp. 186-90; John J. Lenney, *Rankers, The Odyssey of the Regular Enlisted Solder of America and Britain* (New York, 1950), pp. 104-05; New York *Herald*, May 12, 1876; Alexander Mackay, *The Western World or Travels in the United States in 1846-47* (London, 1849), II, 119, 220; *The Independent*, January 18, 1866.

[51]Lenney, *Rankers*, pp. 84, 134-35, 140, 163-64; New York *Herald*, May 12, 1876; New York *Times*, December 21, 1884.

[52]42nd Cong., 3d Sess., House Report No. 74, p. 72.

[53]*ANJ*, December 2, 1871. Cf. April 21, 1871, December 27, 1872, July 5, August 23, 1873, February 5, 1876, July 7, 1877; New York *Herald*, February 26, 1876.

[54]44th Cong., 1st Sess., House Report No. 354, p. 123; *ANJ*, December 2, 1871, August 23, 1873, July 7, 1877.

[55]*ANJ*, November 28, 1874, October 6, 1877. Cf. New York *Times*, May 28, 1876; New Orleans *Times*, February 2, 1871; *The Independent*, January 18, 1866, August 20, 1868; Cincinnati *Commercial*, December 15, 1869; New York *Tribune*, March 8, 1870; *Congressional Globe*, 43rd Cong., 1st Sess., p. 4363; *ANJ*, March 25, 1876, October 27, December 1, 1877; Lenney, *Rankers*, p. 104; New York *Herald*, March 25, 1876; *Congressional Record*, 44th Cong., 1st Sess., p. 1344; Missouri *Republican*, July 6, 1877; New York *Herald*, April 6, 1878.

[56]Lenney, *Rankers*, pp. 105-06, 111; New York *Herald*, August 21, 1878; *ANJ*, August 16, 1878.

[57]New York *Times*, July 5, 1879. Cf. New York *Herald*, February 20, 1884.

[58]46th Cong., 3d Sess., House Executive Document No. 1, Pt. 2, II, 36; *ANJ*, September 16, 1882; *ANR*, December 31, 1887. Cf. *ANR*, December 3, 1880; *ANJ*, June 23, 1886; *Tuscon Daily Star*, November 18, 1880; New York *Times*, March 27, 1887; New York *Herald*, February 13, 1888; Columbus *Dispatch*, October 3, 1888, February 20, 1889; O. O. Howard to John M. Carson, January 7, 1885, Howard Papers.

[59]Lenney, *Rankers*, pp. 121-24, 134-35, 140, 160-64; New York *Times*, December 21, 1884. For a contrary view, see *ANJ*, September 14, 1889; New York *Times*, December 21, 1884; Kansas City *Times*, March 11, 1889, August 6, 22, 1891.

[60]*ANJ*, April 23, 1883. Cf. New York *Times*, January 22, 1885; Omaha *Bee*,

March 18, 1883; New York *Herald,* January 17, 1891; *The Nation,* XL (January 8, 1885), 33.

[61]New York *Times,* July 29, 1879, March 27, 1886, February 12, 1888; Washington *Post,* June 20, 1891; Philadelphia *Inquirer,* February 1, 1890; *The Nation,* XXIX (August 7, 1879), 88; Chicago *Inter-Ocean,* February 1, 1890; New York *Herald,* April 4, 1882; New York *Sun,* April 29, 1890; St. Paul *Press,* September 7, 1889; *The New Nation,* January 31, 1891; St. Louis *Globe-Democrat,* November 4, 1889; *ANJ,* July 24, 1879.

[62]51st Cong., 2d Sess., House Executive Document No. 1, Pt. 2, II, 11.

[63]St. Louis *Post Dispatch,* July 7, 1889. Cf. New York *Freeman,* January 1, 1887.

[64]Scott, *Analytical Digest,* pp. 267-71; 31st Cong., 2d Sess., Sen. Rep. Com. 227, 1-2; *Congressional Globe,* 34th Cong., 3d Sess., p. 149; Sergeant Martin M. Beach to John P. Hale, December 19, 1856, Hale Papers, New Hampshire Historical Society; *ANJ,* August 26, 1882; MSIUS *Journal,* VIII (1887), 285.

[65]*The United Service,* IX (July, 1883), 47; Kansas City *Times,* September 12, 1889, November 29, 1892, December 12, 1894; *ANR,* December 1, 1888; *ANJ,* July 5, 1879, August 26, December 3, 1881, November 25, 1882, April 21, 1883; Washington *Capital,* September 21, 1879; Missouri *Republican,* July 6, 1877.

[66]45th Cong., 3d Sess., Senate Report 555, p. 488; New York *Herald,* December 19, 1878. Cf. *ANR,* October 29, 1887; 42nd Cong., 3d Sess., House Executive Document No. 1, Pt. 2, II, 49; 47th Cong., 1st Sess., House Executive Document No. 1, Pt. 2, II, 204, 2d Sess., House Executive Document No. 1, Pt. 2, II, 283; New York *Times,* January 21, 1884.

[67]*The United Service,* VIII (1883), 47, X (1884), 675; *ANJ,* February 5, 1871, November 2, 1878, November 9, 1889.

[68]*Regulations of the Army of the United States* (1881), par. 233; *The United Service,* XII N.S. (1893), 337; Farrow, *Military Encyclopedia,* I, 186; *ANJ,* April 13, 1878, February 17, 1894; M. L. Kezerter to Samuel L. Chapman, December 6, 1878, MSS 43, Nebraska State Historical Society; Joseph F. Mason to Alexander T. Stewart, February 8, 1873, Stewart Papers, New York Public Library; New York *Sun,* November 21, 1888.

[69]42nd Cong., 2d Sess., House Executive Document No. 1, Pt. 2, II, 6; *ANJ,* November 9, 1889. Cf. Kansas City *Times,* November 30, 1886; Chicago *Herald,* November 11, 1888; St. Paul *Press,* September 2, 1889.

[70]MSIUS *Journal,* VIII (1887), 263; New York *Times,* March 2, 1890.

[71]*Regulations of the Army of the United States* (1895), par. 85; Kansas City *Times,* August 6, 1894.

[72]Kansas City *Times,* August 6, 1894; Mills, *My Story,* p. 375; Hugh Lenox Scott, *Some Memories of a Soldier* (New York, 1928), p. 144.

[73]New York *Tribune,* November 18, 1883; St. Louis *Globe-Democrat,* May 11, 1889. Cf. New York *Tribune,* November 4, 1883; New York *Herald,* August 12, 1870.

[74]New York *Times,* December 25, 1883; cf. *ibid.,* July 7, 1883; Pembina (Dakota) *Northern Express,* December 20, 1883; New York *Herald,* December 31, 1883, November 21, 1887; Chicago *Inter-Ocean,* April 7, 1890; Brooklyn

Daily Eagle, March 16, 1895; 49th Cong., 1st Sess., House Executive Document No. 1, Pt. 2, II, 113; J. W. Pope, "Desertion and the Military Prison," *Cosmopolitan Magazine*, X (November, 1890), 110.

[75]*The United Service*, X (1884), 673; 42nd Cong., 2d Sess., House Executive Document No. 1, Pt. 2, II, 86; *ANJ*, December 18, 1886.

[76]John M. Schofield to Redfield Proctor, February 24, 1890, Schofield Papers, L.C.

[77]*The Independent*, August 20, 1868; New York *Sun*, September 18, 1877; New York *Herald*, November 21, 1887. Cf. St. Louis *Republic*, October 15, 1889; Chicago *Times*, February 1, 1890; Tuscon *Star*, November 10, 1880; *The New Nation*, August 15, 1891; *ANJ*, March 24, October 20, 1877, June 26, 1886.

[78]*ANJ*, September 1, 1877; New York *Herald*, April 6, 1878. Cf. *ANJ*, April 13, May 11, 1867, August 10, 1869, March 25, 1871, March 24, 1877, January 13, 1883; New York *Herald*, February 1, 1884, September 21, 1885; *Iron Moulders' Journal*, March 10, 1877; Marion (Kansas) *Record*, May 21, 1893; Billings *Post*, July 15, 1882.

[79]New York *Times*, August 5, 1889; New York *Herald*, August 22, 1868; *ANJ*, November 28, 1874, March 24, October 20, 1877, December 4, 1880; New York *Tribune*, November 4, 1883; New York *Graphic*, August 20, September 21, 1883; 45th Cong., 2d Sess., House Miscellaneous Document No. 56, p. 249.

CHAPTER IV: THE ARMY REFORM MOVEMENT, 1880-1886

[1]44th Cong., 1st Sess., House Executive Documents No. 1, Pt. 2, II, 103; 42nd Cong., 1st Sess., House Executive Documents No. 1, Pt. 2, II, 25, 173; 45th Cong., 2d Sess., House Miscellaneous Documents No. 56, 70, 249; New York *Herald*, August 27, 1876, February 25, May 10, October 25, 1878; New York *Tribune*, January 4, 1878; *Irish World*, August 2, 1878; *Iron Moulder's Journal*, March 10, 1877; *ANJ*, October 25, November 1, 1873; see Table 1, Appendix.

[2]*General Orders No. 3, Headquarters Military Division of the Pacific and Department of California*, June 23, 1879, p. 8, N.A. Cf. *ANJ*, July 5, 26, 1879, October 22, 1881; New York *Herald*, December 19, 1878.

[3]47th Cong., 2d Sess., House Executive Document No. 1, Pt. 2, II, 27; New York *Herald*, April 14, 1882; Providence *Morning Star*, January 23, 1884; New York *Times*, December 7, 1879; *Field Glass*, March, 1879, February, April, May, August, September, 1880; *ANJ*, June 18, September 25, 1880, August 12, 1882.

[4]*ANJ*, April 1, 1880; January 8, 15, 1881, April 11, 1882; New York *Times*, January 10, 1881.

[5]*ANJ*, April 1, 1882.

[6]46th Cong., 1st Sess., House Executive Document No. 1, Pt. 2, II, 70.

[7]*ANJ*, May 26, 1881; Cf. *ANJ*, January 1, 1881; Kansas City *Times*, January 6, 1890.

[8]New York *Herald*, quoted in *ANJ*, October 1, 1881; cf. *ANJ*, October 9, 1880, September 3, 1881; *Field Glass*, November, 1880; Cheyenne *Daily Leader*, September 23, 1880.

[9]51st Cong., 1st Sess., House Executive Document No. 162, 10-11, 21-22; *ANJ*, February 4, 1882, June 29, 1895; *Harper's Weekly*, April 9, 1892.

[10]*ANJ*, February 5, 1881; *Medical History of Fort Sully*, II, 285-87, N.A.

[11]*ANJ*, February 22, 1881; New York *Herald*, March 29, 1881.

[12]Cheyenne *Daily Leader*, quoted in *ANJ*, March 26, 1881. Cf. Bismark *Tribune*, March 8, 1881; *ANJ*, March 12, April 2, 1881.

[13]Edward A. Packard to Peter Fay, November 28, 1882, O. O. Howard Papers, Bowdoin College. Cf. New York *Herald*, March 29, 1881.

[14]*ANJ*, March 5, 26, April 2, 1881. Cf. George A. Forsyth, *The Story of the Soldier* (New York, 1900), p. 134.

[15]*The United Service*, X (April, 1884), 384, 387; 47th Cong., 2d Sess., House Executive Document No. 1, Pt. 2, III, 71; 48th Cong., 2d Sess., House Executive Document No. 1, Pt. 2, II, 83; *ANR*, October 29, 1887; *ANJ*, February 18, 1882.

[16]*ANR*, March 25, 1886. Cf. August 10, 1886.

[17]W. Winthrop, *Digest of Opinions of the Judge Advocate General* (Washington, 1880), pp. 296-97; New York *Herald*, December 17, 1881; *ANJ*, December 24, 1881; Arthur Murray, *Instructions for Courts-Martial* (St. Paul, 1891), pp. 11-12, 27-28; Edward Farrow, *Military Encyclopedia* (New York, 1895), III Supplement, 122.

[18]46th Cong., 3d Sess., House Executive Document No. 1, Pt. 2, II, 36, 111; New York *Herald*, April 4, 1882; Chicago *Inter-Ocean*, August 24, 1883.

[19]*ANJ*, December 9, 1882, August 25, 1883; Chicago *Inter-Ocean*, August 24, 1883.

[20]*ANJ*, August 19, 1882. Cf. *ANJ*, June 4, August 12, November 25, 1882; June 13, 1883; *The Council Fire and Arbitrator*, V (December, 1882), 344.

[21]New York *Sun*, May 23, 1882.

[22]New York *Telegram*, August 21, 1882.

[23]New York *Graphic*, August 29, 1882. Cf. New York *Herald*, September 30, 1882, August 27, October 22, 1883, February 1, 1884; New York *Tribune*, November 4, 18, 1883; New York *Sun*, June 15, 1884; New York *Freeman*, May 8, 1886; New York *Times*, December 21, 1884; Kansas City *Times*, June 25, 1884; Omaha *Bee*, December 13, 1883.

[24]48th Cong., 2d Sess., House Executive Document No. 1, Pt. 2, II, 50-51, 81-97, 299; 47th Cong., 2d Sess., House Executive Document No. 1, Pt. 2, II, 90; 49th Cong., 1st Sess., House Executive Document No. 1, Pt. 2, II, 113; 48th Cong., 1st Sess., House Executive Document No. 1, Pt. 2, II, 52, 105, 127; 50th Cong., 2d Sess., House Executive Document No. 1, Pt. 2, II, 12, 119-20, 167, 283; Omaha *Bee*, September 15, 1889; St. Louis *Globe-Democrat*, May 24, 1889; O. O. Howard to John M. Carson, January 7, 1885, Howard Papers.

[25]*The United Service*, IX (August, 1883), 102, 182; XII (June, 1885), 676, 680; *ANJ*, June 23, November 25, 1882, January 12, 1884, December 14, 1889; 48th Cong., 2d Sess., House Executive Document No. 1, Pt. 2, II, 127, 297; New York *Herald*, September 28, 1889; Major A. S. Burt to O. O. Howard, June 1, 1886, Howard Papers; MSIUS *Journal*, V (1884), 373-75, VI (1885), 274-75; New York *Times*, December 9, 1883; New York *World*, December 10, 1883; Omaha *Republican*, December 14, 1883.

[26]O. O. Howard to J. C. Kelton, June 25, 1888, Kelton to Howard, July 5, 1888, Howard Papers.

[27]*ANJ*, November 22, 1882.

[28]Ari Hoogenboom, *Outlawing the Spoils: A History of the Civil Service Reform Movement 1865-1883* (Urbana, Illinois, 1961), pp. 195-99, 213, 217, 237-38, 259-61; The *Nation*, XL (January 8, 1885); *ANJ*, November 15, 1884, March 11, 1885.

[29]*ANJ*, November 25, December 31, 1882; 48th Cong., 1st Sess., House Executive Document No. 1, Pt. 2, II, 92; New York *Times*, December 21, 1884.

[30]51st Cong., 1st Sess., House Executive Document No. 1, Pt. 2, II, 328; MSIUS *Journal*, X (1889), 28, 450; *ANR*, November 22, 1884.

[31]MSIUS *Journal*, X (1889), 28, XV (1894), 79-80; *ANJ*, August 10, 1889; *The United Service*, X (April, 1884), 384; Ellwood Bergey, *Why Soldiers Desert from the United States Army* (Philadelphia, 1903), p. 61. Assistant Adjutant General Kelton went even further, saying: "When steps are taken by Courts of Inquiry to find out the officers who by maladministration *compel* men to desert and to arraign them and punish them, desertions will be greatly reduced." J. C. Kelton to O. O. Howard, July 5, 1888, Howard Papers.

[32]*ANJ*, February 21, 1885; George B. Davis, *Military Laws of the United States* (Washington, 1897), p. 358.

[33]New York *Times*, April 7, 1885; *ANJ*, February 21, 1885; *ANR*, February 21, 1885. Cf. Kansas City *Times*, May 11, June 8, 1885.

[34]*ANR*, September 26, October 23, 1885, December 1, 1886, November 12, 1887; New York *Times*, April 15, 1888; Pembina (Dakota) *Northern Express*, May 23, 1884; 47th Cong., 2d Sess., House Executive Document No. 1, Pt. 2, II, 85.

[35]49th Cong., 1st Sess., House Executive Document No. 1, Pt. 2, II, 163, 167; 50th Cong., 2d Sess., House Executive Document No. 1, Pt. 2, II, 44; *ANJ*, March 19, 1887, March 18, June 29, 1889; George A. Forsyth, *The Story of the Soldier* (New York, 1900), pp. 106-107; Francis Paul Prucha, *A Guide to the Military Posts of the United States, 1789-1895* (Madison, 1964), p. 36; Redfield Proctor to O. O. Howard, September 15, 1890, Howard Papers.

[36]*ANJ*, June 23, 1888; *ANR*, December 3, 1887. Cf. *ANR*, May 21, 1887; Omaha *Bee*, April 6, 1886.

[37]Davis, *Military Laws of the United States*, pp. 242-45; P. M. Ashburn, *A History of the Medical Department of the United States Army* (Boston, 1925), p. 141; Edward Farrow, *Military Encyclopedia* (New York, 1895 ed.), III, Supplement, 97-98; Kansas City *Times*, March 14, 1893; Mabel E. Deuterich, *Struggle for Supremacy, The Career of General Fred C. Ainsworth* (Washington, 1962), p. 9.

[38]*ANJ*, September 20, 1884. Cf. New York *Herald*, February 23, 1884.

[39]50th Cong., 1st Sess., House Executive Document No. 1, Pt. 2, II, 696; *ANJ*, August 1, 1891; *ANR*, November 26, 1887.

[40]Leavenworth *Times*, quoted in *ANJ*, February 11, 1888. Cf. Kansas City *Times*, July 19, 1889; Omaha *Excelsior*, July 2, 1887.

[41]48th Cong., 2d Sess., House Executive Document No. 1, Pt. 2, II, 332-35, 609-13, 827; Kansas City *Times,* December 25, 1884, February 4, April 17, July 19, 1886; *ANJ,* April 2, 1887, September 14, 1889, January 25, June 14, November 29, 1890; *ANR,* February 2, 1884, July 17, 1886, December 31, 1887; *Regulations and Decisions Pertaining to the Uniform of the Army of the United States* (Washington, 1897), pp. 31-32, 36.

[42]*ANR,* October 15, 1887. Cf. *ANJ,* January 4, 1888.

[43]50th Cong., 1st Sess., House Executive Document No. 1, Pt. 2, II, 664; New York *Times,* February 7, 1886; *ANR,* May 22, 1887.

[44]New York *Times,* October 27, 1888. Cf. *ANJ,* August 3, 1889.

[45]Kansas City *Times,* April 24, 1885, April 17, 1886, August 14, 1891; *ANJ,* June 27, 1885, July 5, 1890, March 21, 1891; 50th Cong., 2d Sess., House Executive Document No. 1, Pt. 2, II, 737; MSIUS *Journal,* VIII (1887), 276, 285; Forsyth, *Story of the Soldier,* pp. 114-15; *Harper's Weekly,* June 28, 1890.

[46]Kansas City *Times,* June 16, 1890. Cf. *ANJ,* June 14, 1890.

[47]*ANR,* February 2, 9, 1889; 51st Cong., 1st Sess., House Executive Document No. 1, Pt. 2, II, 4, 8; Columbus *Dispatch,* February 20, 1889.

[48]49th Cong., 1st Sess., House Executive Document No. 1, Pt. 2, II, 74, 157; MSIUS *Journal,* VIII (1887), 266.

[49]Kansas City *Times,* December 28, 1884. Cf. May 11, 1885.

[50]*ANJ,* October 26, November 9, 23, 1889; New York *Times,* October 19, 1889, January 3, 1892; New York *Herald,* September 28, 1889.

[51]*ANJ,* August 25, 1883; 48th Cong., 2d Sess., Senate Report No. 1337, p. 1.

[52]50th Cong., 1st Sess., House Executive Document No. 1, Pt. 2, II, 289; Kansas City *Times,* December 7, 1886; Farrow, *Military Encyclopedia,* III, Supplement, 122; *ANJ,* April 25, 1885; W. W. Winthrop, *Military Law and Precedents* (Boston, 1896), p. 673.

[53]*ANJ,* September 13, 1884; New York *Times,* November 20, 1886; cf. 51st Cong., 1st Sess., House Executive Document No. 1, Pt. 2, II, 325.

[54]*ANJ,* November 27, 1886, April 2, May 7, 1887; *ANR,* July 3, 1886; New York *Times,* November 20, 1886; Murray, *Instructions for Courts-Martial,* pp. 52-53.

[55]*ANR,* July 3, 1886. Cf. 50th Cong., 1st Sess., House Executive Document No. 1, Pt. 2, II, 294.

[56]Murray, *Instructions for Courts-Martial,* p. 10; 50th Cong., 1st Sess., House Executive Document No. 1, Pt. 2, II, 14-15; Annual Report of the Judge Advocate General (Washington, 1887), pp. 14-15.

[57]*ANJ,* June 2, 1888; New York *Herald,* May 25, 1888; *ANJ,* July 13, 1889; cf. Cleveland *Leader,* September 17, 1889; Kansas City *Times,* September 27, 1885; *ANR,* July 30, October 15, 1887, January 29, 1886.

[58]W. Winthrop, *Military Law* (2nd ed.; Washington, 1886); *ANR,* August 28, 1886; Sidney (Nebraska) *Telegraph,* quoted in *ANR,* April 3, 1886; William C. Mott, John E. Hartnett, Jr., and Kenneth B. Morton, "A Survey of the Literature of Military Law," *Vanderbilt Law Review,* VI (1952-1953), 335.

[59]*ANR,* August 13, 1887; *ANJ,* July 27, 1888; Murray, *Instructions for Courts-Martial.*

[60]*ANJ,* June 29, 1889, March 29, January 4, 1890; New York *Herald,* April 8, 1889; Chicago *Tribune,* July 31, 1887; St. Louis *Post Dispatch,* July 7, 1889; Forsyth, *Story of the Soldier,* p. 99.

[61]*ANJ,* November 15, 17, December 9, 1889; Kansas City *Times,* November 15, 17, December 9, 1889.

[62]Kansas City *Times,* December 9, 1889. Cf. Junction City (Kansas) *Republican,* November 22, 1889; New York *Times,* February 2, 1890.

[63]49th Cong., 2d Sess., House Executive Document No. 1, Pt. 2, II, 138; cf. *ANR,* December 18, 1886; New York *Sun,* July 29, 1891; Kansas City *Times,* February 2, September 7, 1891; Pembina (Dakota) *Northern Express,* May 25, October 5, 1883; May 23, 1884.

[64]*ANR,* September 11, 1886; cf. *ANR,* July 17, 1886, October 21, 1887; New York *Freeman,* November 8, 1884.

[65]Vancouver *Independent,* June 26, 1884; cf. 48th Cong., 2d Sess., House Executive Document No. 1, Pt. 2, II, 136-37.

[66]*ANJ,* April 18, 1885; cf. *ANJ,* February 28, May 30, 1885; *Public Service Review,* June 30, September 15, 1887.

[67]Cheyenne *Daily Leader,* July 21, 1886; cf. *ANR,* August 21, October 9, 1886; New York *Tribune,* June 25, 1887.

[68]New York *Times,* April 15, 1888; cf. New York *Times,* March 11, 1890; *The United Service,* n.s. XII (July, 1894), p. 32.

[69]51st Cong., 1st Sess., House Executive Document No. 1, Pt. 2, II, 69; 2d Sess., House Executive Document No. 1, Pt. 2, II, 61, 263; Kansas City *Times,* December 19, 1889, January 12, 1890; Report on the Post School at Madison Barracks, New York, 1893-4; Wilson L. Gill to John M. Schofield, October 8, 1890, Schofield Papers, L.C.; Columbus *Dispatch,* February 20, May 27, 1889; Charles Alexander, *Battles and Victories of Allen Allensworth* (Boston, 1914), p. 277.

[70]*ANJ,* April 6, 1889; New York *Herald,* March 31, 1889; John M. Schofield to Redfield Proctor, March 26, 1889, Schofield Papers.

[71]New York *Times,* June 22, 1889; *ANJ,* July 27, 1889; New York *Tribune,* June 9, 1889; Columbus *Dispatch,* February 20, May 27, 1889.

[72]51st Cong., 1st Sess., House Report No. 162, Appendix C, 21-22; Kansas City *Times,* November 26, 1886; *Harper's Weekly,* April 9, 1892.

[73]Kansas City *Times,* November 26, December 14, 1886; *ANJ,* September 26, 1886, May 28, June 4, 1887; *ANR,* November 13, 1886.

[74]51st Cong., 1st Sess., House Report No. 162, Appendix C, 23; *ANJ,* December 15, 22, 1888.

[75]*ANJ,* December 22, 1888; New York *Times,* July 18, September 13, 1889.

[76]*ANJ,* December 22, 1888.

[77]51st Cong., 1st Sess., House Report No. 162, Appendix C, 16-20, 24-26; Kansas City *Times,* March 1, July 22, 1889; St. Louis *Globe-Democrat,* January 1, 1890; *ANJ,* March 29, 1890.

[78]*ANJ,* February 9, 1889; Kansas City *Times,* July 22, 1889.

[79]51st Cong., 1st Sess., House Report No. 162, Appendix C, 27; *ANJ,* July 13, October 12, November 30, December 28, 1889.

[80]*ANJ*, November 23, 9, 1889. Cf. April 27, May 25, August 10, September 28, 1889; New York *Times*, March 2, 1890; New York *Herald*, December 24, 1889.

[81]52nd Cong., 1st Sess., House Executive Document No. 1, Pt. 2, II, 17; Kansas City *Times*, December 9, 1889, February 17, 23, 1890; *ANJ*, December 28, 1889, January 4, 1890, June 29, 1895.

[82]New York *Times*, January 6, 1890; *ANJ*, November 9, 1889, February 8, 1890; New York *Herald*, June 30, August 6, 1890; St. Louis *Globe-Democrat*, January 1, 1890.

Under the Army Appropriations Act of June 30, 1890, the sale of beer and wine in any canteen or post trader's store was prohibited, in any state or territory in which the sale of alcoholic liquors, beer or wine was illegal. *Congressional Record*, 51st Cong., 2d Sess., pp. 4374, 4379-82; Davis, *Military Laws of the United States*, p. 442. In February, 1892, Secretary of War Elkins, convinced that to the public the term "canteen" conveyed a picture of unrestrained drinking, issued an order changing the name to "post exchange." 52nd Cong., 2d Sess., House Executive Document No. 1, Pt. 2, II, 57; Forsyth, *Story of the Soldier*, pp. 136-37.

[83]51st Cong., 1st ess., House Report No. 162, Appendix C, 32-34; *ANJ*, September 1, 1889, January 4, 1890.

[84]New York *Sun*, quoted in *ANR*, November 26, 1886; New York *Times*, November 20, 1886. Cf. Omaha *Bee*, May 12, 1889; Kansas City *Times*, July 20, September 14, 1889.

[85]50th Cong., 2d Sess., House Executive Document No. 1, Pt. 2, II, 738. Cf. *ANJ*, September 14, December 14, 1889; Report of Lieutenant Colonel Edwin C. Mason, Document F, St. Paul, Minn., September 6, 1886; *General Orders and Circulars, Headquarters of the Department of Dakota*, 1886.

[86]49th Cong., 2d Sess., House Executive Document No. 1, Pt. 2, II, 80; *ANJ*, August 15, 1885.

CHAPTER V: THE ARMY REFORM MOVEMENT, 1887-1892

[1]*ANJ*, September 14, 1889; *Harper's Weekly*, December 8, 1888; Columbus *Dispatch*, April 21, 1889.

[2]New York *Tribune*, September 1, 1889; Kansas City *Times*, November 18, 1889. Cf. Kansas City *Times*, June 20, September 9, November 18, 1889; New York *Herald*, August 17, 1887, November 26, 1889; New York *Times*, September 1, 1889; 51st Cong., 1st Sess., House Executive Document No. 1, Pt. 2, II, 335; *ANJ*, September 14, December 21, 1889; *ANR*, December 24, 1887.

[3]51st Cong., 1st Sess., House Executive Document No. 1, Pt. 2, II, 26, 82-89, 326, 331-34; New York *Tribune*, September 1, 1889; St. Louis *Globe-Democrat*, May 11, 15, 24, 25, August 4, November 7, 1889; John F. Finnerty, *Warpath and Bivouac* (Norman, Okla., 1961), p. 301; Columbus *Dispatch*, June 26, July 24, August 4, 21, 1889.

[4]St. Louis *Globe-Democrat*, November 4, 1889; cf. San Francisco *Call*, January 10, 1890; San Francisco *Chronicle*, August 13, 1889; New York *Commercial Advertiser*, September 7, 1889; Cleveland *Leader*, August 9, 1889; Chicago *Herald*, November 24, 1888.

[5]O. O. Howard to John M. Carson, January 7, 1885, Howard Papers, Bowdoin College. Cf. John M. Schofield to O. O. Howard, October 25, 1889, Howard Papers; John M. Schofield to Redfield Proctor, February 24, 1890; John M. Schofield to John C. Kelton, January 22, 1892, Schofield Papers, L.C.; 50th Cong., 2d Sess., House Executive Document No. 1, Pt. 2, II, 57, 157-58, 167-68; 51st Cong., 1st Sess., House Executive Document No. 1, Pt. 2, II, 314, 333; Omaha *Bee*, September 15, 1889; St. Louis *Globe-Democrat*, April 18, May 15, 24, 25, 1889.

[6]Private Mall Doyle to O. O. Howard, November 20, 1889, Howard Papers.

[7]MSIUS *Journal*, X (1889), 458, 461-65; *ANJ*, September 28, 1889, March 13, 1890; New York *World*, March 3, 1889; New York *Times*, July 19, 1891; St. Louis *Republic*, January 5, 1888, September 27, October 15, 1889; Philadelphia *Press*, February 1, 1890; Chicago *Inter-Ocean*, February 1, 1890; Kansas City *Times*, September 19, 1889, March 26, May 3, 1890; John E. Cox, *Five Years in the U. S. Army* (Owensville, Indiana, 1892), p. 159; Finnerty, *Warpath and Bivouac*, pp. 303-04; William Mitchell to O. O. Howard, July 24, 1889, Howard Papers.

[8]Kansas City *Times*, March 26, 1890. Cf. *ANJ*, April 5, 1890.

[9]St. Paul *Globe*, March 13, 1890. Cf. New York *Times*, March 13, 1890; O. O. Howard to William H. Courson, Jr., September 20, 1890, Howard Papers.

[10]MSIUS *Journal*, X (1889), 458. Cf. pp. 764-67; *ANJ*, April 5, September 11, 1889; Kansas City *Times*, September 15, 1889; Chicago *Inter-Ocean*, March 15, 1890.

[11]New York *Sun*, December 25, 1893. Cf. *ANJ*, October 28, 1893, April 16, 1895; *Seventh Regiment Gazette*, VIII (December, 1893), 8; *Frank Leslies' Illustrated Weekly*, May 31, 1894, p. 372.

[12]*ANJ*, July 19, 1890. Cf. MSIUS *Journal*, X (1889), 761-63, XI (1890), 160-63, 165; *ANJ*, September 28, December 21, 1889, February 1, 1890; Portland *Eastern Argus*, October 12, 1889; Chicago *Inter-Ocean*, February 1, 1890; St. Louis *Post-Dispatch*, December 1, 1889; Boston *Pilot*, March 8, 1890.

[13]St. Paul *Pioneer Press*, April 24, 1889. Cf. New York *Commercial Advertiser*, September 7, 1889; St. Louis *Globe-Democrat*, May 25, November 7, 1889; Annual Report of the Acting Judge Advocate, Department of the Missouri, August 16, 1889, p. 8, N.A.

[14]48th Cong., 1st Sess., House Executive Document No. 1, Pt. 2, II, 293; *ANJ*, January 22, 1890. Cf. New York *Times*, August 7, 8, 1889; Washington Evening *Star*, September 7, 1889; *ANJ*, August 3, November 9, 16, December 14, 1889; Portland *Eastern Argus*, October 12, 1889; MSIUS *Journal*, XII (1891), 79; Kansas City *Times*, July 14, October 15, 1889; John M. Schofield to R. C. Drum, September 12, 1887, Schofield Papers.

[15]Junction City *Republican*, February 15, 1889.

[16]*ANR*, May 21, 1887.

[17]Kansas City *Times,* November 11, 1889. Cf. *ANJ,* August 13, 1887, September 14, 1889; New York *Tribune,* September 1, 1889; New York *Freeman,* May 8, 1886, January 1, 1887; New York *Sun,* January 28, April 29, 1890; San Francisco *Chronicle,* August 13, 1889.

[18]See *supra,* pp. 23-24; Kansas City *Times,* November 14, 1889; *ANJ,* November 9, 1889; Chicago *Inter-Ocean,* February 22, 1890; Charles Morton to William C. Church, September 13, 1890, Church Papers, L.C.

[19]Portland *Eastern Argus,* October 12, 1889; Washington *Evening Star,* September 7, 1889; *ANJ,* January 8, April 2, July 27, 1887, September 4, October 26, 1889, July 18, September 26, 1891; Baltimore *American,* October 26, November 25, 1889; Kansas City *Times,* May 18, 1885, December 18, 1889; 51st Cong., 1st Sess., House Executive Document No. 1, Pt. 2, II, 64, 84, 85, 331-34; Col. J. S. Brisbin to O. O. Howard, January 29, 1886, Col. G. H. Smith to O. O. Howard, February 8, 1890, Howard Papers.

[20]*ANJ,* February 9, 1889. Cf. June 1, December 21, 1889, February 22, 1890; Kansas City *Times,* June 2, 1889, February 14, 1890; Boston *Commercial Bulletin,* March 15, 1890; Cleveland *Leader,* September 17, 1889; St. Louis *Post-Dispatch,* July 9, September 15, 1889; Portland *Eastern Argus,* October 12, 1889.

[21]Kansas City *Times,* November 21, December 18, 1889; *ANJ,* December 14, December 21, 1889; Hugh L. Scott to Mary M. Scott, November 4, 1889, Hugh L. Scott Papers, L.C.; San Francisco *Examiner,* June 11, 12, 1888.

[22]Kansas City *Times,* June 20, 1889.

[23]*Ibid.,* February 24, 1890.

[24]*Ibid.,* June 30, 1890. Cf. July 8, 1889, January 24, February 10, June 20, 1890; *ANJ,* September 7, 14, October 26, December 21, 1889; New York *Times,* November 3, 1889; Philadelphia *Press,* November 1, 1889; Baltimore *American,* November 25, 1889; J. C. Kelton to O. O. Howard, July 5, 1888, Howard Papers; 51st Cong., 1st Sess., House Executive Document No. 1, Pt. 2, II, 84-85.

[25]Boston *Advertiser,* July 15, 1887. Cf. William J. Arkell, *A Philosopher in Love and in Uniform* (New York, 1889), pp. 35-36; Detroit *Free Press,* September 19, 1889; *Henry George Standard,* January 27, 1887; Portland *Eastern Argus,* October 12, 1889; Russell (Kansas) *Record,* April 8, 1889; *ANR,* January 22, 1887; *ANJ,* June 4, 1887, January 28, 1888, September 14, 1889; Ellwood Bergey, *Why Soldiers Desert from the United States Army* (Philadelphia, 1903), pp. 27-31; New York *Herald,* August 4, 1892; (Topeka, Kansas) *Our State,* October 26, 1889.

[26]New York *Herald,* December 4, 14, 1887; cf. November 23, 25, 28, 1887, March 1, 1888; New York *Times,* March 3, 1888.

[27]Kansas City *Times,* September 24, 1888.

[28]St. Paul *Pioneer Press,* May 6, 1889; New York *Sun,* June 6, 1889.

[29]Kansas City *Times,* June 24, 1889. Cf. New York *News,* quoted in Bismarck *Daily Tribune,* July 5, 1889; St. Paul *Globe,* October 28, 1889; RG94, ACP File 34850, N.A., Personal file of Major Edmund G. Fechet.

[30]Bismarck *Daily Tribune,* July 6, 1889; *ANJ,* July 27, 1889; *ANR,* July 20, 1889. Cf. *ANJ,* July 20, 1889, March 8, April 12, June 14, 1890; *ANR,* August

31, 1889; New York *World*, February 26, 1890; Chicago *Herald*, February 27, 1890; St. Paul *Globe*, February 28, 1890.

[31]St. Louis *Post-Dispatch*, August 25-September 18, 1889. Cf. Frank R. Woodward, *The Dogs of War* (St. Louis, 1890); *United States Cavalry Journal*, I (1888), 179-83; Kansas City *Times*, April 8, 1889.

[32]St. Louis *Post-Dispatch*, August 27, 30, September 2, 1889; Washington *Evening Star*, September 7, 1889; San Francisco *Chronicle*, August 26, 27, 1889; Detroit *Free Press*, August 29, September 9, 15, 17, 1889; Denver *Times*, August 26, 1889; Seattle *Press*, September 7, 1889; Philadelphia *Press*, November 1, 1889; Baltimore *American*, November 25, 1889.

[33]Detroit *Free Press*, September 9, 1889. Cf. September 4, 17, 1889; St. Louis *Post-Dispatch*, September 3, 1889; *ANJ*, September 14, 1889; St. Louis *Republic*, October 4, 10, 15, 1889.

[34]St. Louis *Post-Dispatch*, September 26, October 2-18, 1889; Pittsburgh *Post-Gazette*, October 1, 1889; Woodward, *Dogs of War*, pp. 148-60, 172-73; *ANJ*, October 26, November 16, 1889; Washington *Post*, October 15, 1889; New York *Times*, October 22, December 13, 1889.

Three non-commissioned officers were also reduced to the ranks. St. Louis *Post-Dispatch*, October 25, 1889.

[35]New York *Times*, December 12, 1889; St. Louis *Post-Dispatch*, November 12, 1889.

[36]*ANJ*, December 28, 1889. Cf. Philadelphia *Press*, February 14, 1890; New York *Times*, February 16, 1890; Chicago *Inter-Ocean*, February 1, 1890; Pierre *Daily Free Press*, February 3, 1890; St. Paul *Globe*, February 13, 16, 1890.

[37]St. Paul *Globe*, February 18, 1890. Chicago *Tribune*, February 18, 1890. Cf. St. Paul *Globe*, February 15, 16, 1890; New York *Herald*, February 18, 1890; *ANJ*, February 22, 1890; *General Court Martial Orders*, No. 25, June 24, 1889, No. 62, December 31, 1889, Headquarters Department of Dakota, St. Paul, Minnesota; RG153, RR3845, N.A.

[38]Minneapolis *Tribune*, February 25, 1890; Chicago *Herald*, February 26, 1890; Chicago *Tribune*, February 19, 20, 1890; St. Paul *News*, February 28, 1890; New York *World*, February 22, 1890; New York *Times*, March 13, 1890; Helena *Independent*, February 27, 1890; San Francisco *Chronicle*, February 25, 27, 1890; Philadelphia *Press*, February 23, 1890; *Congressional Record*, 51st Cong., 1st Sess., pp. 1645, 1806; 51st Cong., 1st Sess., Senate Executive Document No. 74, pp. 1-2; *ANJ*, March 8, 1890; Frank Belz to O. O. Howard, February 19, 1890, Howard Papers.

[39]Chicago *Tribune*, February 22, 1890. Cf. Kansas City *Times*, February 27, 1890; New York *Sun*, February 24, 1890; New York *Herald*, February 22, 1890; St. Paul *Press*, February 26, 1890; RG153, RR3845, N.A.

[40]J. C. Kelton to the Commanding General, Division of the Missouri, February 26, 1890, RG153, RR3845, N.A.; Chicago *Tribune*, February 23, 1890; New York *Herald*, February 23, 1890; Boston *Pilot*, March 8, 1890.

[41]Washington *Evening Star*, February 24, 1890. Cf. New York *World*, February 26, 1890; St. Paul *Globe*, February 22, 1890; San Francisco *Bulletin*, February 22, 1890; St. Louis *Post-Dispatch*, February 24, 1890.

[42]*U.S. Army Visitor,* April, 1890, clipping in Scrapbook, Redfield Proctor Papers, Vermont Historical Society.

[43]San Francisco *Chronicle,* February 28, 1890. Cf. Chicago *Herald,* February 26, 27, 1890; Chicago *Tribune,* March 13, 23, 1890; New York *World,* February 26, March 14, 19, 1890; Philadelphia *Inquirer,* March 22, 1890; St. Paul *Globe,* February 20, 24, March 14, 1890; Kansas City *Times,* February 26, March 23, 1890.

[44]St. Paul *Pioneer Press,* March 14, 1890. Cf. March 8, 23, 1890; *ANJ,* March 1, 22, April 5, 1890; St. Paul *Globe,* February 18, 1890.

[45]*Ibid.,* March 14, 1890; New York *Times,* March 14, 1890; New York *World,* March 14, 16, 1890; *ANJ,* March 15, 22, April 5, 1890; Boston *Pilot,* March 22, 1890; Proceedings of a General Court-Martial appointed by Special Orders No. 8, Headquarters Department of Dakota, January 13, 1885, Case 25, Private Lewis Carter, Co. C, Twenty-fifth Infantry, RR 35-39-25, 1-26, N.A.

[46]Kansas City *Times,* March 19, 1890; cf. February 26, 1890.

[47]*ANJ,* March 29, 1890. Cf. March 15, 1890; New York *Herald,* March 10, 1890.

[48]Chicago *Tribune,* March 19, 1890; St. Paul *Globe,* March 19, 20, 1890; Headquarters Division of the Missouri, Chicago, Illinois, April 10, 1890, General Court Martial Orders No. 1, pp. 1-96, RG153, RR3978, N.A.

[49]Chicago *Tribune,* March 21, 1890.

[50]*ANJ,* March 29, 1890. Cf. St. Paul *Pioneer Press,* March 25, 1890.

[51]*ANJ,* April 12, 1890. Cf. Chicago *Tribune,* April 11, 1890.

[52]St. Paul *Globe,* April 11, 12, 1890; Chicago *Herald,* April 12, 1890; Louisville *Courier-Journal,* April 14, 1890; San Francisco *Chronicle,* April 12, 13, 1890.

[53]Minneapolis *Tribune,* April 11, 1890; cf. St. Louis *Globe-Democrat,* April 11, 1890; Kansas City *Times,* March 21, April 11, 1890; New York *Times,* April 11, 1890; *ANJ, April* 19, 1890.

On Dell P. Wild after the trial, see *ANJ,* February 6, 1892; New York *Times,* February 14, 1892.

Lieutenant M. F. Steele went on to make a brilliant record for himself in the service; MSIUS *Journal,* XVI (1895), 1-40; XXIX (1901), 14-23; Russell F. Weigley, *Towards an American Army* (New York, 1962), p. 159; *History of the United States Army* (New York, 1967), p. 336.

[54]*ANJ,* March 22, 1890; New York *Herald,* February 13, March 1, 13, 1890; George B. Davis, *A Treatise on the Military Law of the United States* (New York, 1898), p. 40; George B. Davis, *Military Laws of the United States* (Washington, 1897), p. 513; 52d Cong., 1st Sess., House Executive Document No. 1, Pt. 2, II, 4.

[55]Davis, *Military Laws,* pp. 511, 513; Arthur Murray, *Instructions for Courts Martial* (St. Paul, 1891), pp. 73-80, 133-34; New York *Tribune,* October 8, 1890; *ANJ,* November 22, 1890.

[56]*ANJ,* October 11, 1890; Omaha *Bee* quoted in *ANJ,* August 8, 1891.

[57]New York *Times,* March 1, 1891; Kansas City *Times,* March 13, 1891; Murray, *Instructions for Courts Martial,* pp. 55-63; W. Winthrop, *Military Law and Procedures* (Boston, 1896), II, 1544-51.

[58]*ANJ*, February 28, 1891; 52d Cong., 2d Sess., House Executive Document No. Kansas City *Times,* March 13, 1891; John M. Schofield to Stephen B. Elkins, June 14, 1892, Schofield Papers, L.C. 1, Pt. 2, II, 210. Cf. New York *Times,* March 10, 1893; *ANJ,* March 12, 1891; [59]Davis, *Military Laws,* p. 495.

[60]*Ibid.,* pp. 208, 362; *ANJ,* July 19, 26, August 2, 30, November 22, 1890; New York *Tribune,* October 8, 1890.

[61]*ANJ,* June 28, 1890; George Forsyth, *The Story of the Soldier* (New York, 1900), pp. 99-100.

[62]Kansas City *Times,* January 27, February 16, 1891, January 30, 1892; Junction City *Republican,* February 15, 1891.

[63]John Lenney, *Rankers: The Odyssey of the Enlisted Regular Soldier of America and Britain* (New York, 1950), pp. 107-08, 112, 161; Parker City (Oregon) *Democrat,* December 24, 1892, clipping in Stephen B. Elkins Collection, University of West Virginia; 52d Cong., 1st Sess., Senate Report No. 268, pp. 1-3.

[64]*ANJ,* April 5, December 6, 1890; New York *Times,* July 23, 1891; Boston *Herald,* August 3, 1891; *The New Nation,* August 3, 1891; 52d Cong., 1st Sess., House Executive Document No. 1, Pt. 2, II, 10.

[65]Kansas City *Times,* March 24, September 23, 1891. Cf. New York *Tribune,* September 1, 1891, April 26, 1892.

[66]Kansas City *Times,* September 24, 1891; F. C. Partridge, "Redfield Proctor," *Proceedings of the Vermont Historical Society* (1915), pp. 86-87.

[67]51st Cong., 2d Sess., House Executive Document No. 1, Pt. 2, II, 4, 9, 63, 99; 52d Cong., 1st Sess., House Executive Document No. 1, Pt. 2, II, 65, 69; New York *Times,* December 9, 1892.

[68]Philadelphia *Ledger,* December 9, 1892; New York *Times,* December 9, 1892. Cf. New York *Mail and Express,* July 31, 1891; Boston *Post,* November 8, 1890.

CHAPTER VI: THE ARMY ON THE EVE OF THE SPANISH-AMERICAN WAR

[1]*ANJ,* April 12, 1890. Cf. November 8, 1890, January 21, 28, February 6, 1892; *ANR,* September 12, 1891; Kansas City *Times,* October 21, December 20, 1891, January 28, February 22, July 23, 1892, February 17, 1894; *Army and Navy Life,* X (January-June, 1907), 187; New York *Times,* March 13, 1893.

[2]*ANJ,* November 8, 1890.

[3]*ANJ,* July 4, 1891.

[4]Kansas City *Times,* December 20, 1891. Cf. New York *Herald,* December 28, 1891; Buffalo *Express,* December 30, 1891.

[5]Portland *Oregonian,* April 25, 26, 28, June 19, 22, 1891; 51st Cong., 1st Sess., House Executive Document No. 1, Pt. 2, II, 261-62; *ANJ,* May 2, June 13, July 25, August 8, 1891; Tacoma *Daily Ledger,* April 25-30, 1891.

[6]Portland *Oregonian,* May 24, 1891. Cf. New York *Tribune,* May 25, 1891; Kansas City *Times,* April 29, June 27, September 30, 1891; *ANJ,* April 12,

1890, July 4, 1891; Lewiston (Idaho) *Teller,* May 7, 1891; Chicago *Mail,* April 27, 1891; Cleveland *Plain Dealer,* April 26, 1891; St. Louis *Republic,* April 28, 1891; Battle Creek *Journal,* April 27, 1891.

[7]Kansas City *Times,* November 23, 1892, April 13, 26, 1893; New York *Times.* September 15, 1890; *ANJ,* January 4, April 8, October 21, 1893; 52d Cong., 1st Sess., House Executive Document No. 1, Pt. 2, II, 63, 670.

[8]*ANJ,* October 11, 1890.

[9]Kansas City *Times,* September 2, 1890; *ANJ,* April 11, 1891, March 25, October 21, 1893; *The United Service,* n.s. XII (November, 1894), 421; New York *Times,* February 12, 1893.

[10]*Ibid.,* May 9, 1892, February 12, 1893; Kansas City *Times,* April 26, 1893; New York *Herald,* May 19, December 8, 1890.

[11]New York *Times,* May 9, 1892.

[12]*Ibid.,* May 23, 1892.

[13]New York *Herald,* February 8, 20, 1893; *Congressional Record,* 52d Cong., 2d Sess., pp. 675, 734, 846, 1049-50, 1609-11; Kansas City *Times,* February 6, 7, 20, 1893.

[14]*Ibid.,* February 7, 1893. Cf. New York *Herald,* February 8, 1893.

[15]Kansas City *Times,* February 13, 1893.

[16]*Ibid.,* February 16, 21, 1893; *ANJ,* February 18, April 8, 1893.

[17]Kansas City *Times,* February 20, 28, March 9, 20, 1893; *ANJ,* February 18, March 25, April 8, 1893; New York *Herald,* February 20, April 3, 1893; Boston *Transcript,* August 7, 1894.

[18]Kansas City *Times,* March 30, 1893.

[19]*Ibid.,* March 30, October 24, 1893.

[20]*Ibid.,* April 13, 28, May 14, August 17, October 3, 1893; New York *Tribune,* July 17, December 21, 28, 1893; New York *Herald,* April 3, December 31, 1893; Washington *Post,* August 13, 1893.

[21]*Annual Report of the Judge Advocate General of the Army* (Washington, 1893), p. 9; *ANJ,* October 21, 1893. Cf. Chicago *Herald,* April 3, 1894; New York *Tribune,* July 23, 1894.

[22]New York *Times,* September 22, 1893; General Nelson P. Miles to Daniel S. Lamont, March 1, 22, 1894, Lamont Papers, L.C.; Kansas City *Times,* April 28, May 7, 16, September 26, December 6, 1893; *ANJ,* March 25, April 8, September 2, October 21, 1893; 53d Cong., 2d Sess., House Executive Document, No. 1, Pt. 2, II, 64, 65, 70-71; 53rd Cong., 2d Sess., Senate Report No. 151, pp. 1-3.

[23]Waterbury *American,* October 20, 1893. Cf. New York *Evening Telegram,* June 1, 1893; *The People,* January 1, 1893; New York *Herald,* November 5, 1893; New York *Times,* October 4, 1894.

[24]*ANJ,* September 2, 1893.

[25]New York *Times,* July 31, August 18, 1894; Kansas City *Times,* August 3, 1894; *ANJ,* December 15, 1894.

[26]George B. Davis, *Military Laws of the United States* (Washington, 1897), p. 356; New York *Times,* October 4, 1894; Boston *Transcript,* August 7, 1894.

[27]New York *Times,* December 20, 27, 1890; *ANR,* July 4, 1891; 55th Cong., 2d Sess., House Executive Document No. 1, Pt. 2, II, 23; Henry Schindler, *History of the United States Military Prison* (Fort Leavenworth, Kansas, 1911), pp. 47, 50, 58.

[28]Chicago *Herald,* October 19, 1897. Cf. 53d Cong., Senate Executive Document No. 176, p. 2; Brooklyn *Daily Eagle,* December 1, 1894, July 28, 1895; *ANR,* September 5, 1896; *ANJ,* August 3, 1895.

[29]*ANJ,* February 16, 1895.

[30]55th Cong., 2d Sess., House Executive Document No. 1, Pt. 2, II, 99.

[31]Chicago *Tribune,* October 10, 1897. Cf. October 11, 1897; Chicago *Times-Herald,* October 11, 12, 13, 1897. This post had been the subject of much discussion in the press because of allegations of neglect and mistreatment of enlisted men. See Chicago *Herald,* April 15, 1892; Kansas City *Times,* April 5, 1892, February 2, 1894; New York *Times,* June 6, 1897; *ANJ,* October 16, 1897; "History of Fort Sheridan, Illinois," unpublished MSS prepared by the Public Information Office, Fort Sheridan, Illinois, January, 1944, pp. 9-12.

On October 26, 1897 Hammond was tried by a general court-martial and found guilty of absence without leave and disobedience of orders, and sentenced to be dishonorably discharged from the service, forfeiting all pay and allowances and to be confined at hard labor for one year. Major General John R. Brooke approved the sentence but remitted the dishonorable discharge and mitigated the remainder to confinement for six months at hard labor, and the forfeiture of ten dollars per month for the same period. Office of the Judge Advocate General (Army) Case 5256, court-martial proceedings in the case of Private Charles Hammond, 13 pp., Washington National Records Center, Sutland, Maryland.

[32]Chicago *Journal,* October 12, 1897; *ANR,* October 23, 1897. Cf. Chicago *Chronicle,* October 16, 17, 21, 1897; *Appeal to Reason,* December 4, 25, 1897; Minneapolis *Tribune,* October 13, 1897; Chicago *Inter-Ocean,* October 12, 13, 1897; *ANJ,* October 16, 1897; Highland Park (Illinois) *News,* October 15, November 12, 1897; Chicago *Record,* October 12, 1897.

[33]New York *Times,* October 13, 1897. Cf. October 12, 15, 20, 1897; Chicago *Tribune,* October 12, 15, 17, 20, 1897; Chicago *Chronicle,* October 20, 1897.

[34]Chicago *Times-Herald,* October 24, 1897. Cf. Chicago *Tribune,* October 24, 1897; New York *Times,* October 23, 24, 1897; New York *Tribune,* November 10, 1897; Office of the Judge Advocate General (Army), Case 5311, Court of Inquiry Proceedings in the case of Captain Leonard A. Lovering, 56 pp., Washington National Records Center, Sutland, Maryland.

[35]*ANR,* October 30, 1897; Philadelphia *Public Ledger,* October 25, 1897. Cf. Chicago *Tribune,* October 25, 1897.

[36]New York *Times,* November 2, 6, 9, 10, 11, 24, 29, 1897; Chicago *Times-Herald,* November 2, 23, 24, 25, December 8, 1897; *ANJ,* December 11, 1897; Office of the Judge Advocate General (Army), Case 5312, Court-Martial Proceedings in the case of Captain Leonard A. Lovering, 157 pp., Washington National Records Center, Sutland, Maryland.

[37]Chicago *Times-Herald,* November 25, 1897. Cf. New York *Times,* November

25, 26, 27, December 2, 1897; *Frank Leslie's Illustrated Weekly,* December 9, 1897; Chicago *Tribune,* November 30, 1897.

[38]New York *Times,* December 7, 1897; Chicago *Times-Herald,* December 7, 1897.

[39]Chicago *Tribune,* November 30, 1897. Cf. December 11, 1897; Chicago *Times-Herald,* December 10, 11, 1897; New York *Times,* December 3, 11, 22, 1897; Brooklyn *Daily Eagle,* December 7, 1897; *ANJ,* December 11, 1897.

[40]*ANJ,* December 11, 1897. Cf. New York *Times,* December 22, 1897; New York *Herald,* December 20, 1897.

On July 20, 1898, in an article captioned "Capt. Lovering Squares his Account," the Chicago *Times-Herald* referred to the heroic achievements of the previously reprimanded officer in the Spanish-American War. "In actual warfare he found a chance to regain his former standing as a soldier and improved it instantly. The black mark against him has been wiped out."

[41]Ellwood Bergey, *Why Soldiers Desert From the United States Army* (Philadelphia, 1903), pp. 3, 9, 56, 59, 154; John J. Lenney, *Rankers: The Odyssey of the Enlisted Soldier of America and Britain* (New York, 1950), p. 185; John J. Lenney, *Caste in the American Army* (New York, 1949), pp. 134-35; Anson Mills, *My Story* (Washington, 1918), pp. 361-81; New York *Telegram,* July 20, 1897; Brooklyn *Daily Eagle,* June 18, 1897, December 28, 1909; New York *Tribune,* July 22, 24, 1893, November 10, 1895, September 17, 1900; Albion W. Tourgee, "The Story of a Thousand," *Cosmopolitan Magazine,* XVIII (December, 1894), 225-26; *ANJ,* December 29, 1894; Minneapolis *Tribune,* August 20, 1894; New York *Globe and Advertiser,* May 26, 1916; *Harper's Weekly,* November 11, 1901, May 24, 1913; W. Winthrop, *Digest of Opinions of the Judge-Advocate General* (Washington, 1901), 332-33.

[42]E. Anderson, "The Pay of Our Soldiers Affecting Desertion and Re-enlistment," *The American Monthly Review of Reviews,* XXXIII (1906), 333; Mills, *My Story,* pp. 362, 366, 371-72; *The American Federationist,* V (February, 1899), 203; *Army and Navy Life,* XI (1907), 408; *International Quarterly,* XII (January, 1906), 194.

[43]New York *Times,* August 24, 1895. Cf. ibid., June 5, 1897; Bergey, *Why Soldiers Desert,* p. 83; New York *Tribune,* February 17, 1894, November 12, 1902; *The Verdict,* January 30, 1899, February 6, 13, 1899.

[44]*ANR,* August 14, 1897. Cf. New York *Times,* January 23, 1894, December 8, 23, 1895; *Harper's Weekly,* May 4, 1895; MSIUS *Journal,* XXXIV (1902), 278.

[45]*ANR,* August 22, 1896. Cf. Mills, *My Story,* p. 376; New York *Times,* March 30, 1894, January 4, February 14, 15, 20, 28, March 11, 26, 28, 1919; Kansas City *Times,* January 10, 1894; New York *Tribune,* April 5, 1901; San Francisco *Examiner,* November 4, 1899; New York *Evening Post,* April 17, 1899, May 28, 1902; *ANJ,* November 23, 1901; Samuel T. Ansell, "Military Justice," *Cornell Law Review,* V (November, 1919), 1-17; *Harper's Weekly,* February 21, 28, March 7, 14, 21, 1914; New York *World,* January 19, 1919.

CHAPTER VII: THE NEGRO IN THE POST-CIVIL WAR ARMY

[1]*Official Opinions of the Attorneys General of the United States,* J. Hubley Ashton, ed. (Washington, 1869), XI, 57-58; W. Winthrop, *Military Law* (Washington, 1886), I, 765; *Revised Regulations for the United States Army* (Washington, 1863), par. 929; L. D. Reddick, "The Negro Policy of the United States Army 1775-1945," *Journal of Negro History,* XXXIV (January, 1949), 12-15, 18-19; *Congressional Globe,* 27th Cong., 2d Sess., pp. 805-07; 27th Cong., 3d Sess., p. 175.

[2]Augustus V. Kautz, *Customs of the Army* (Philadelphia, 1864), p. 11: cf. Benjamin Quarles, *The Negro in the Civil War* (Boston, 1953), p. 199; Winthrop, *Military Law,* I, 765.

[3]Constance M. Green, *The Secret City, A History of Race Relations in the Nation's Capital* (Princeton, 1967), p. 77; *Congressional Globe,* 39th Cong., 1st Sess., pp. 225, 261, 265-66, 1379-80, 1385, 2005-06; Marvin Fletcher, "The Blacks in Blue," (unpublished Master's thesis, University of Wisconsin, 1965), pp. 62-83; New York *Tribune,* February 14, March 15, 24, 1866.

[4]*ANJ,* March 31, 1866. Cf. New York *Times,* March 26, 1866.

[5]*U.S. Statutes at Large,* XVIII, 179; Theo. F. Rodenbaugh and William L. Haskin (eds.), *The Army of the United States* (New York, 1896), pp. 280, 288-89, 695-97); *Regulations of the Army of the United States* (Washington, 1881), par. 757.

[6]*The United Service,* IX (April, 1883), 425.

[7]J. Everts Haley, *Fort Concho and the Texas Frontier* (San Angelo, 1952), pp. 263-64, 284; John Bigelow, Jr., "Historical Sketch of the United States Tenth Cavalry," II, 23-24, 56-57, 64-65, MSS, N. A.; Adjutant General's Office. "The Negro in the Military Service of the United States, 1639-1886," VIII, 4686-90, MSS, N. A.; William H. Leckie, *The Buffalo Soldiers* (Norman, 1967), pp. 10, 16, 25, 29, 72, 99, 128, 163, 234, 259; Don Rickey, Jr., "The Negro Regulars—A Combat Record, 1866-1891," pp. 1-5, unpublished MSS in possession of author; New York *Times,* March 4, 1876, November 29, 1889; Chicago *Inter-Ocean,* February 1, 1890; Kansas City *Times,* April 15, 1885; Yankton *Press and Dakotan,* December 30, 1880; Carleton W. Kenyon, "History of Fort Randall" (unpublished Master's thesis, University of South Dakota, 1950), p. 120; *ANJ,* September 3, 1881.

[8]*ANJ,* January 27, 1877.

[9]B. H. Grierson to O. O. Howard, March 4, 1881, Howard Papers, Bowdoin College; 51st Cong., House Executive Document, No. 1, Pt. 2, II, 5. Cf. *ANJ,* November 30, 1889; New York *Times,* November 25, 29, 1889; New York *Age,* December 21, 1889; Cleveland *Gazette,* March 14, 1891.

[10]New York *Times,* February 22, 1891. Cf. Guy V. Henry to O. O. Howard, January 26, 1891, Howard Papers; Leckie, *Buffalo Soldiers,* pp. 257-58; Rickey, "Negro Regulars," pp. 11-12; Washington *Evening Star,* February 5, 1891.

[11]*The Independent,* August 11, 1898, p. 389. Cf. New York *Tribune,* April 16, 1898; Indianapolis *News,* April 16, 1898; Leckie, *Buffalo Soldiers,* pp. 258-60.

[12]New York *Herald,* March 2, 1891; MSIUS *Journal,* XV (1894), 1190, **XL** (1910), 264; *ANJ,* February 14, 1891; Hugh L. Scott, *Some Memories of a Soldier* (New York, 1928), p. 168; Richard Henry Pratt, *Battlefield and Classroom* (New Haven, 1964), pp. 176-77; Sarah Kinney to John M. Schofield, January 30, 1891, Schofield Papers, L.C.; William Bruce White, "The Military and the Melting Pot", unpublished doctoral dissertation, University of Wisconsin, 1968, 28-55.

[13]*ANJ,* March 14, 1891.

[14]*Ibid.;* H. B. Wharfield, *Apache Indian Scouts* (El Cajon, Calif., 1964), pp. 65-67; MSIUS *Journal,* XV (1894), 1190; Winthrop, *Military Law,* I, 234.

[15]New York *Tribune,* May 31, 1891; O. O. Howard to Sarah Kinney, March 31, 1891, Howard Papers. Cf. San Francisco *Post,* March 28, 1981; St. Louis *Republic,* March 31, April 5, 1891.

[16]MSIUS *Journal,* XV (1894), 1191-92; Richard Carl Brown, "Social Attitudes of American Generals 1898-1940" (unpublished doctoral thesis, University of Wisconsin, 1951), pp. 193-94; Rodenbough and Haskin, *Army of the United States,* p. 267; H. L. Scott to Post Adjutant, Fort Sill, January 18, 1891, Arthur L. Wagner to H. L. Scott, December 1, 1897, Hugh L. Scott Papers, L.C.

[17]Boston *Traveller,* May 6, 1891; New York *Advertiser,* December 5, 1892. Cf. New York *Sun,* May 21, 1891; Boston *Journal,* May 30, 1891; *ANR,* July 18, 1891; MSIUS *Journal,* XV (1894), 1188-90; A. S. Daggett to H. L. Scott, June 2, 1893, Scott Papers.

[18]*ANJ,* May 16, 1891. Cf. *ibid.,* January 2, March 26, 1892, August 26, 1893; Kansas City *Times,* April 8, July 24, 1893;. St. Louis *Globe-Democrat,* May 17, 1891; Harper's *Weekly,* March 26, 1892.

[19]Kansas City *Times,* March 6, 1894; *ANJ,* March 4, 1893, June 15, 1895; New York *Herald,* July 23, 1893, May 30, 1897; Wharfield, *Apache Indian Scouts,* p. 68.

[20]*Battle Flag,* April, 1896.

[21]*Autobiography of General O. O. Howard* (New York, 1907), II, 55.

[22]H. L. Scott, *Some Memories of a Soldier,* pp. 169-70.

[23]Sturgis (Dakota) *Record,* quoted in *ANR,* January 15, 1887; New York *Sun,* December 25, 1893. Cf. *ANJ,* March 9, 1867; 44th Cong., 1st Sess., House Report No. 354, p. 228; 45th Cong., 2d Sess., House Miscellaneous Document No. 56, p. 249; MSIUS *Journal,* XXXVI (1905), 105-06.

[24]Washington *Evening Post,* June 6, 1891. Cf. *ANR,* June 13, 1891; Detroit *Plain Dealer,* June 26, 1891.

[25]*Irish World,* June 27, 1891. Cf. Kansas City *Times,* June 14, 1891; 45th Cong., 2d Sess., House Miscellaneous Document No. 64, pp. 20, 151.

[26]*ANJ,* August 25, 1877, June 21, 1879; Boston *Pilot,* June 1, 1878; New York *Freeman's Journal,* April 13, 1889, February 1, 1890; New York *Observer,* quoted in *ANJ,* February 14, 1880; O. A. Mack to Dr. Mason Gallagher, January 7, 1861, sent by Reverend Gallagher to O. O. Howard, December 18, 1891, Howard Papers.

[27]New York *Herald,* January 20, 1890. Cf. John M. Schofield to Stephen B. Elkins, February 5, 1892, Schofield Papers.

[28]New York *Freeman's Journal,* January 25, 1890; Edward B. Browne to John M. Schofield, January 31, 1890, Schofield Papers. Cf. John M. Schofield to Edward B. Browne, February 2, 1890, Schofield to William Campbell, April 3, 1890, Schofield Papers; O. O. Howard to B. M. Cutcheon, January 25, 1890, Howard Papers; *ANJ,* February 1, 1890, July 25, 1891, November 10, 1894; New York *Tribune,* August 25, 1895; New York *Times,* January 30, 1892; Theophilus G. Steward, ed., *Active Service* (New York, n.d.), p. 211.

[29]Leckie, *Buffalo Soldiers,* pp. viii, 4, 8, 13-15, 51, 71-73, 82-83, 98-99, 107, 163-64, 258-60; *The United States Service Magazine,* V (February, 1866), 222; Haley, *Fort Concho,* pp. 268, 270, 273-78, 283; *ANJ,* January 19, 1867, March 11, 26, May 13, 1876, April 5, 1890; New York *World,* December 14, 1886; B. H. Grierson to O. O. Howard, March 4, 1881, Howard Papers; Galveston *Daily News,* March 1, 1878, January 21, February 3, 1881; New York *Globe,* April 28, 1883; Cleveland *Gazette,* July 26, 1890; New York *Freeman,* September 12, 1885. For a contrary view see Thomas Dirk Phillips, "The Negro Regulars," unpublished Master of Science thesis, University of Wisconsin, 1966, 124-25, 132-40, 169-73. See also reviews of Leckie, *Buffalo Soldiers,* in *Nebraska History,* XIV (Sept., 1968), 86-87; *Civil War History,* XI (July, 1968), 261-62.

[30]Edward T. Comegys to O. B. Wilcox, January 14, 1890, Records of the Office of the Judge Advocate General, Record Group 153. Proceedings in the cases of Sergeants Charles Connor and William Rose, RR 2351, N.A. Cf. El Paso *Daily Times,* March 11, 1892; *ANJ,* March 26, 1892; Bigelow, "Tenth Cavalry Sketch," II, 7-9, 64-65, N.A.

[31]C. C. Augur to W. T. Sherman, March 17, 1879, "Negro in the Military Service of the United States," VII, 4707-08, N.A. Cf. *ibid.,* pp. 4709-11; Leckie, *Buffalo Soldiers,* pp. 17, 98; New York *Herald,* March 2, 1891; Stephen Bonsal, "The Negro Soldier in War and Peace," *North American Review,* CLXXXV (June, 1907), 321-22.

[32]New York *Evening Post,* June 4, 1898; *ANJ,* January 16, 1892. Cf. Theophilus G. Steward, *Forty Years in the Gospel Ministry* (Philadelphia, n.d.), pp. 267-78.

[33]New York *Age,* December 28, 1889. Cf. *ibid.,* December 21, 1889; Cleveland *Gazette,* February 14, 1890.

[34]New York *Times,* February 22, 1891. Cf. *Atlantic Monthly,* XCI (June, 1903), 729.

[35]44th Cong., 1st Sess., House Report No. 354, p. 46; *ANJ,* June 17, 1876, March 21, 1885; San Antonio *Express,* May 11, 1876.

[36]New York *Times,* August 20, 1877; *ANJ,* January 16, 1892.

[37]Bigelow, "Tenth Cavalry Sketch," p. 54, N.A. Cf. Leckie, *Buffalo Soldiers,* VIII, 14, 37, 259; Pratt, *Battlefield and Classroom,* pp. 28-29; *The United Service,* ns XI (April, 1894), 327; Cleveland *Gazette,* February 14, 1890; Boston *Commercial,* February 17, 24, 1890; Norwalk (Conn.) *Bulletin,* February 25, 1890.

[38]Rodenbough and Haskin, *Army of the United States,* p. 287; *ANJ,* March 7, 1891. Cf. Rickey, "Negro Regulars," p. 10; Fairfax Downey, *Indian Fighting*

Army (New York, 1941), pp. 304-05; Indianapolis *Freeman,* January 17, 1891; New York *Times,* March 9, 1891; New York *Sun,* January 19, 1891.

[39]MSIUS *Journal,* XLIV (1909), 124-25. Cf. Charles Alexander, *Battles and Victories of Allen Allensworth* (Boston, 1914), pp. 286, 368; *ANJ,* June 1, 1878, July 14, 1888, February 28, 1891; *Lippencott's Magazine,* XL (1887), 125; Leckie *Buffalo Soldiers,* p. 8; Elizabeth Reynolds Burt, "An Army Wife's Forty Years in the Service 1862-1902," p. 262, unpublished MSS, Burt Family Papers, L.C.

[40]H. L. Scott to Mary Elizabeth Scott, December 24, 1875, Scott Papers. Cf. Scott, *Some Memories of a Soldier,* pp. 25-26. This hostile view of service with colored troops did not go unchallenged. Captain D. B. Wilson of the Twenty-fifth Infantry, a colored unit, said he had no patience with the "military, aristocratic sentiment that fears to come into contact with the negro in the Army." *The United Service,* ns. XI (April, 1894), 325.

[41]*Congressional Globe,* 39th Cong., 1st Sess., pp. 265-66; U. S. Grant to Henry Wilson, January 12, 1866, "The Negro in the Military Service of the United States," VIII, 4672, N.A.; *ANJ,* January 27, February 17, 1866; Fletcher, "The Blacks in Blue," pp. 66-67.

[42]44th Cong., 1st Sess., House Report No. 354, p. 63; *ANJ,* August 12, 1882.

[43]45th Cong., 2d Sess., House Misc. Documents No. 56, p. 89; New York *Times,* April 9, 1862.

[44]*ANJ,* November 8, 1873, April 21, 1883.

[45]51st Cong., 1st Sess., House Executive Document No. 1, Pt. 2, II, 7. Cf. New York *Times,* November 29, 1889; Guy V. Henry to O. O. Howard, February 20, 1890, Howard Papers.

[46]Buffalo (Wyoming) *Echo,* n.d., post marked December 19, 1889, Fort Robinson, Nebraska, Redfield Proctor Notebooks, 1889-90, Proctor Papers, Vermont Historical Society; New York *Age,* December 21, 1889.

[47]*ANJ,* December 21, 1889, February 1, 1890; New York *Times,* April 8, August 1, 1890; New York *Tribune,* March 1, 1891.

[48]*The United Service,* ns. XI (April, 1894), 323.

[49]*Congressional Record,* 55th Cong., 2d Sess., p. 2556; *Afro American* (Omaha) *Sentinel,* April 12, 1898; William A. Ganoe, *The History of the United States Army* (New York, 1924), p. 371.

[50]*The Independent,* L (June 16, 1898), 782. Cf. Theophilus G. Steward, *The Colored Regulars in the United States Army* (Philadelphia, 1904), pp. 104-05; New York *Tribune,* August 28, 1898; Cleveland *Gazette,* September 3, 1898; *The Atlantic Monthly,* XCI (June, 1903), 722; James Parker, *The Old Army* (Philadelphia, 1929), pp. 390-91; Ulysses Lee, *The Employment of Negro Troops —The United States Army in World War II* (Washington, 1966), p. 23.

[51]New York *Freeman,* January 23, 1886; *ibid.,* December 5, 1885. Cf. *ANJ,* July 22, 1865; John Harper to Thaddeus Stevens, February 16, 1866, Stevens Papers, L.C.; New York *Herald,* February 13, 1888; Alexander, *Battles and Victories of Allen Allensworth,* p. 287.

[52]New York *Freeman,* April 28, 1886. Cf. *ibid.,* January 1, 1887; Cleveland

Gazette, July 6, 20, 1889, July 26, 1890, February 14, 1891; New York *Times,* November 29, 1889; Parker, *The Old Army,* p. 92.

⁵³New York *Age,* January 23, 1892. Cf. St. Paul *Appeal,* July 26, 1890.

⁵⁴New York *Age,* February 13, 1892. Cf. Cleveland *Gazette,* June 24, 1893.

⁵⁵*ANR,* March 21, 1896; *The Independent,* June 16, 1898; p. 782; New York *Tribune,* March 23, 1898; Cleveland *Gazette,* October 22, 1898; Indianapolis *World,* May 21, 1898; *The Colored American,* October 29, November 12, 1898.

⁵⁶"The Negro in the Military Service of the United States," VII, 4688-4704, N.A.; John M. Schofield to Adjutant General, October 5, November 11, 1880, Schofield Papers; *Congressional Record,* 44th Cong., 1st Sess., pp. 1235, 2042, 2593, 3357-62, 3458-59, 3762-63, 4138-39; 44th Cong., 2d Sess., Senate Executive Document, No. 26, pp. 1-5; *ANJ,* February 25, 1871, December 25, 1875, January 8, 29, March 4, April 1, 1876, August 12, 1882; New York *Herald,* December 17, 1875, March 14, 25, 1876; New York *Times,* January 21, 1876, August 20, November 19, 21, 1877; Cincinnati *Enquirer,* November 7, 1877; L. D. Reddick, "Negro Policy in the United States Army," *Journal of Negro History,* XXXIV (January, 1949), 18; W. H. Head, "Negro as an American Soldier," *World Today,* XII (March, 1907), 322-24.

⁵⁷*Congressional Record,* 44th Cong., 1st Sess., p. 3457; *ibid.,* 45th Cong., 2d Sess., p. 2692. Cf. 45th Cong., 2d Sess., pp. 2189-91, 2325-28, 2440-42; General E. O. C. Ord to Lieutenant Colonel W. R. Shafter, May 15, 1876, January 3, October 3, 1877, William R. Shafter Papers, Stanford University Library; Chicago *Inter-Ocean,* June 8, 1876.

⁵⁸New York *Freeman,* January 1, 1887. Cf. *Congressional Record,* 48th Cong., 2d Sess., pp. 2, 56.

⁵⁹*The Independent,* January 18, 1866. Cf. *National Anti-Slavery Standard,* February 17, 1866.

⁶⁰*ANJ,* December 17, 1881, August 12, 1882; Pratt, *Battlefield and Classroom,* XI, 7; *Congressional Record,* 42nd Cong., 3d Sess., p. 184; 43rd Cong., 1st Sess., p. 3567; *New National Era,* January 13, 1873, New York *Times,* August 20, 1877; *Harper's Weekly,* February 22, 1890, June 28, 1890; Chicago *Times,* August 23, 1877; Oswald Garrison Villard, "The Negro in the Regular Army," *Atlantic Monthly,* XLI (June, 1903), 728.

⁶¹*New National Era,* July 30, 1874; *Congressional Record,* 45th Cong., 2d Sess., p. 2441. Cf. New York *Times,* August 20, 1877; 44th Cong., 1st Sess., House Report No. 354, pp. 46, 117; 45th Cong., 2d Sess., House Misc. Document No. 64, pp. 69-70.

⁶²46th Cong., 3d Sess., House Executive Document No. 1, Pt. 2, II, 160; *ANJ,* August 14, 1882; *The United Service,* VIII (April, 1883), 425 Cf. *ANJ,* March 21, 1885.

⁶³Matthew F. Steele, "The 'Color Line' in the Army," *North American Review,* CLXXXIII (December, 1906), 1286. Cf. Alexander Gumby Collection, "The Negro as a Soldier," I, 41, Columbia University; John P. Davis, *The American Negro Reference Book* (Englewood Cliffs, 1966), pp. 627-29.

⁶⁴*ANJ,* June 21, 1884; *ANR,* October 4, 1884; New York *Age,* June 28, 1884;

Cleveland *Gazette,* June 21, 1884; New York *Times,* September 28, September 30, 1884; New York *Herald,* September 30, 1884.

[65]*Frank Leslie's Illustrated Newspaper,* October 11, 1884; Jacksonville *Times-Union,* October 10, 1884; New York *Globe,* October 25, 1884; on service career of W. H. Greene, see New York *Tribune,* June 9, 1887.

[66]*ANJ,* June 13, 1885; New York *Times,* September 30, 1884, July 1, 1885; New York *Herald,* August 16, 1885; Kansas City *Times,* July 19, 1897.

[67]*ANR,* August 15, 1885; New York *Herald,* August 16, 1885; New York *Freeman,* August 22, 1885.

[68]*ANJ,* October 12, 1889. Cf. *Southern Workman,* January 7, 1884; *ANJ,* January 26, 1884.

[69]*ANR,* August 29, 1885.

[70]New York *Freeman,* February 27, April 17, 1886; cf. January 23, August 26, October 16, 1886; Cleveland *Gazette,* January 9, 1886.

[71]*ANJ,* February 28, 1891. Cf. El Paso *Daily Times,* March 11, 1892; *ANJ,* March 26, 1892.

[72]Guy V. Henry to O. O. Howard, January 26, 1891, O. O. Howard to Guy V. Henry, January 29, 1891, Howard Papers. Cf. Washington *Evening Star,* February 5, 1891; New York *Times,* July 26, 1887; New York *Herald,* March 2, 1891.

[73]John M. Schofield to J. C. Kelton, February 11, 1891, Schofield Papers.

[74]New York *Herald,* March 2, March 11, 1891. Cf. *ANJ,* March 7, 1891; New York *Age,* March 21, 1891; Cleveland *Gazette,* March 14, 1891.

[75]John M. Schofield to Redfield Proctor, March 6, 1891, Schofield Papers; Washington *Evening Star,* April 29, 1891; New York *Herald,* June 17, 1891; Washington *Post,* June 6, 1891; *ANJ,* November 21, 1891.

[76]New York *Times,* September 19, 1896; Chicago *Times-Herald,* September 19, 1896. Cf. Alexander, *Battles and Victories of Allen Allensworth,* pp. 288-91; *ANJ,* September 4, 1894, March 14, 21, 1896; *ANR,* January 4, April 11, 1896; Washington *Post,* March 11, 1896; New York *Times,* March 25, 1896.

[77]Salt Lake *Tribune,* September 20, 1896. Cf. *ANJ,* October 3, 1896; *The Broad Axe,* September 26, 1896.

[78]Alexander, *Battles and Victories of Allen Allensworth,* pp. 291-92; *The Broad Axe,* October 30, 1897; Salt Lake *Tribune,* September 23, 1896.

[79]Salt Lake *Tribune,* October 22, 1896; cf. October 16, 1896.

[80]*The Broad Axe,* October 31, 1896; Salt Lake *Tribune,* October 23, 1897. Cf. Salt Lake *Tribune,* October 24, November 1, 3, 1896; *The Broad Axe,* October 30, 1897; Cleveland *Gazette,* May 7, 1898; Indianapolis *Freeman,* May 7, 1898; Alexander, *Battles and Victories of Allen Allensworth,* pp. 294-99.

[81]*The Broad Axe,* April 25, 1898. Cf. Salt Lake *Tribune,* April 19, 1898.

[82]Edward A. Johnson, *History of the Negro Soldiers in the Spanish-American War* (Raleigh, 1899), p. 23. Cf. Cleveland *Gazette,* May 21, 1898; The Coffeyville (Kansas) *American,* April 23, 1898; New York *Tribune,* April 27, 1898; Denver *Statesman,* quoted in *Broad Axe,* June 14, 1898; Hershel V. Cashin, *Under Fire with the Tenth U.S. Cavalry* (New York, 1899), pp. 61-62; *Public Opinion,* XXIV (May 5, 1898), 575, (May 19, 1898), 610; New York *Evening*

Post, June 4, 1898; *The Commercial Appeal* (Memphis, Tenn.), April 19, 1898; Richmond *Planet,* April 30, 1898; New York *Sun,* April 10, July 12, 1898.

[83]*The Broad Axe,* October 8, 1898. Cf. Steward, *The Colored Regulars,* pp. 252-53; Cleveland *Gazette,* October 15, 1898; Alexander, *Battles and Victories of Allen Allensworth,* pp. 368-69, 381-88; New York *World,* August 26, 1899; Robert Steven Simpson, "The Regular Negro Soldier in the Campaign for Santiago de Cuba, 1898" (Unpublished Master's thesis, University of Colorado, 1949), pp. 1-92; New York *Sun,* July 24, August 28, 1898.

[84]Cleveland *Gazette,* October 22, 1898. A soldier of the Tenth Cavalry complained angrily of the "horrible treatment" he and his comrades were experiencing in Huntsville, Alabama. He told of the murder of two members of his regiment—Private Brook and Corporal Garrett—by civilians of the town. "Will the President of this glorious union," he asked indignantly, "suffer us (United States soldiers who are sworn to protect the Stars and Stripes) to be shot down in cold blood like dogs by an organized mob of Negro Haters? God forbid!" Richmond *Planet,* December 3, 1898. Cf. *ibid.,* November 19, 1898; Philadelphia *Press,* October 26, 1898; New York *Sun,* April 2, 1899.

[85]Steele, "The 'Color Line' in the Army," p. 1287. Cf. Steward, *Colored Regulars,* p. 252; Steward, *Forty Years in the Gospel Ministry,* pp. 357-62; Simpson, "The Regular Negro Soldier," pp. 93, 252-54, 299-321; The Crawford (Nebraska) *Tribune,* May 18, 1906; Davis, *The American Negro Reference Book,* p. 615; *Congressional Record,* 59th Cong., 2d Sess., pp. 776-80; Green, *The Secret City,* pp. 155-57; Theodore Roosevelt, "The Rough Riders," *Scribners Magazine,* XXV (April, 1899), 435-36; Johnson, *Negro Soldiers in the Spanish-American War,* pp. 39-46; *ANJ,* July 20, 1907.

EPILOGUE

[1]Albion W. Tourgee, "The Story of a Thousand," *Cosmopolitan Magazine,* XVIII (December, 1894), 224-26; *ANJ,* December 29, 1894.

[2]*ANJ,* November 21, 1903. Cf. Don Rickey, Jr., *Forty Miles a Day on Beans and Hay* (Norman, 1963), pp. 151-54; Henry Shindler, *History of the United States Military Prison* (Fort Leavenworth, 1911), pp. 78-82; see *supra,* pp. 74, 82, 98-99.

[3]See *supra,* pp. 83, 100-01; *The United Service,* VII (December, 1882), 592; IX (August, 1883), 184-85; New York *Herald,* September 28, November 8, 1889.

[4]Charles Dudley Rhodes, "John Cunningham Kelton," *Dictionary of American Biography,* X (New York, 1933), 314. Cf. New York *Sun,* June 8, 1889; *Harper's Weekly,* June 22, 1889; *ANJ,* June 15, 22, 1889; July 22, 1893; Washington *Evening Star,* July 17, 1893; see *supra,* pp. 23-24.

[5]51st Cong., 1st Sess., House Executive Document No. 1, Pt. 2, II, 84-85.

[6]See *supra,* Chapters IV-VI.

[7]MSIUS *Journal,* XXXVII (1905), 13; XXXIX (1906), 199; Brooklyn *Daily Eagle,* December 28, 1901; Elwood Bergey, *Why Soldiers Desert from the United*

States Army (Philadelphia, 1903), pp. 3-4, 56, 85, 117, 154; Charles W. Larned, "The Regeneration of the Enlisted Soldier," *The International Quarterly*, XII (January, 1906), 189-207; H. C. Carbaugh, "The Contract of Enlistment and its Violation in the United States Army," *Army and Navy Life*, X (January-June, 1907), 177-95.

[8]Mabel E. Deutrich, *Struggle for Supremacy: The Career of General Fred C. Ainsworth* (Washington, 1962), pp. 102-04; Shindler, *History of United States Military Prison*, pp. 85-88.

[9]Deutrich, *Strugle for Supremacy*, p. 104; Shindler, *History of United States Military Prison*, pp. 82-87; New York *Sun*, September 23, 1910.

[10]Deutrich, *Struggle for Supremacy*, p. 103; *ANJ*, May 16, 1890; *ANR*, November 30, 1907.

[11]*Hearing Before the Committee on Military Affairs, House of Representatives*, 62nd Cong., 2d Sess., House Report 23628 (Washington, 1912), p. 5; *ANJ*, December 1, 1900; Syracuse *Post-Standard*, April 2, 1902; New York *World*, January 19, 1919; New York *Times*, September 22, 1907; Brooklyn *Daily Eagle*, October 19, 1899; New York *Evening Post*, May 28, 1902; see *supra*, pp. 000-00.

[12]Terry W. Brown, "The Crowder-Ansell Dispute," *Military Law Review*, XXXV (January, 1967), 1-45; Edmund M. Morgan, "The Existing Court-Martial System and the Ansell Articles," *Yale Law Journal*, XXIX (1919-20), 52-74; S. T. Ansell, "Some Reforms in Our System of Military Justice," *Yale Law Journal*, XXXII (1922-23), 146-55.

[13]*The United Service*, IX (August, 1883), 84-85; *ANJ*, August 8, September 16, 1891; July 28, 1900; MSIUS *Journal*, XIV (1892), 113, XVII (1895), 40.

BIBLIOGRAPHY

Manuscripts

Arthur Brigham Carpenter Papers, Yale University.

William C. Church Papers, Library of Congress.

Stephen B. Elkins Collection, University of West Virginia, Morgantown, West Virginia.

James A. Garfield Papers, Library of Congress.

Edward S. Godfrey Papers, Library of Congress.

Alexander Gumby Collection, Columbia University.

John P. Hale Papers, New Hampshire Historical Society, Concord.

Diary of Private Winfield Scott Harvey, Seventh Cavalry Regiment. Part I: September 1, 1868-November 11, 1870, in E. S. Godfrey Collection, Box II, AC 5128, Library of Congress. Part II: January 10, 1871-September 11, 1871, in possession of Mrs. Alfred Du Barr, Lock Four, Pennsylvania.

Oliver O. Howard Papers, Bowdoin College, Brunswick, Maine.

Richard Louis D. Hunter Letters, Yale University.

Daniel S. Lamont Papers, Library of Congress.

Henry W. Lawton Papers, Library of Congress.

Redfield Proctor Collection, Vermont Historical Society, Montpelier.

Diary of Private Wilmot P. Sanford, Company D, 6th U.S. Infantry, Fort Buford, Dakota Territory, 1874-75. Yale University.

John M. Schofield Papers, Library of Congress.

William R. Shafter Papers, Stanford University Library.

Philip H. Sheridan Papers, Library of Congress.

William T. Sherman Papers, Library of Congress.

Hugh L. Scott Papers, Library of Congress.

Alexander T. Stewart Papers, New York Public Library.

Thaddeus Stevens Papers, Library of Congress.

Diary Journal of Lieutenant Alvin H. Sydenham, New York Public Library.

National Archives, Washington, D.C.

E. J. Comegys to O. B. Wilcox, January 14, 1889, Records of the Office of the Judge Advocate General. Record Group 153. Proceedings in the cases of Sergeants Charles Connor and William Rose, Co. F, Twenty-fourth Infantry, Fort Elliot, Texas, February 15, 1887. RR2351.

J. C. Kelton to the Commanding General, Division of the Missouri, February 26, 1890, Record Group 153, RR3845.

General George P. Meade to Adjutant General E. D. Townsend, August 28, 1867. Military Prison Division, Entry 456.

General E. O. C. Ord to Assistant Adjutant General, December 7, 1875. Record Group 94, File 1316, ACP 1877.

Major D. G. Swaim to John A. Logan, April 11, 1876; D. G. Swaim to General William T. Sherman, September 23, 1876. Record Group 94, File 1316, ACP 877.

General Orders No. 3, Headquarters Military Division of the Pacific and Department of California, June 23, 1879.

General Orders No. 20, Headquarters, Fifth Military District, New Orleans, La., April 25, 1868.

Headquarters Department of Dakota, St. Paul, Minn., June 24, 1889, General Court Martial Orders No. 25; December 31, 1889, General Court Martial Orders No. 62. General Court Martial Orders Department of Dakota, St. Paul, Minn., 1889. Record Group 153, RR3845.

Headquarters Department of Texas, San Antonio, Texas, October 21, 1879, General Courts Martial Orders No. 67.

Headquarters Division of the Missouri, Chicago, Illinois, April 10, 1890, General Courts Martial Orders No. 1. Record Group 153, RR3978.

Proceedings of a General Court Martial appointed by Special Order No. 8, dated Headquarters Department of Dakota, January 23, 1885, Case 25, May 15, 1885. Private Lewis Carter, Company "C," Twenty-fifth Infantry.

Adjutant General's Office, "The Negro in the Military Service of the United States, 1639-1886." Vol. VII. Record Group 94.

————. "Medical History of Fort Sully." Vols. I and II. Record Group 94.

Annual Report of the Acting Judge Advocate, Department of the Missouri, dated August 16, 1889, Headquarters Department of the Missouri, Office of the Judge Advocate, Fort Leavenworth, Kansas, August 16, 1889.

Bigelow, John, Jr. "Historical Sketch of the U.S. Tenth Cavalry." I, 1-18; II, 1-66. AG1195 363.

Letter of instructions from the Commanding General of the Department of the East and Report of the Board Appointed by the Secretary of War to Examine into the System of Army Prisons and Prison Discipline in the British Service, 1871 (3127, 1871).

Personal file of Major Edmund G. Fechet. Record Group 94, ACP File 34850.

Washington National Records Center,
Sutland, Maryland

Office of the Judge Advocate General (Army). Case 5256. Courts Martial Proceedings in the case of Private Charles Hammond.

————. Case 5311. Court of Inquiry Proceedings in the case of Captain Leonard A. Lovering.

————. Case 5312. Courts Martial Proceedings in the case of Captain Leonard A. Lovering.

United States Government Documents

Annual Reports of the Judge Advocate General of the Army. Washington: Government Printing Office, 1880-1893.

Annual Reports of the Secretary of War. 1866-1899.

Regulations and Decisions Pertaining to the Uniform of the Army of the United States. Washington: Government Printing Office, 1897.

Regulations for the Army of the United States. Washington: Government Printing Office, 1895.

Regulations of the Army of the United States and General Orders in Force on the 17th of February, 1881. Washington: Government Printing Office, 1881.

Revised United States Army Regulations of 1861. Washington: Government Printing Office, 1863.

Uniforms of the Army of the United States, 1774 to 1889. Illustrated. Washington: Government Printing Office, 1889.

United States Statutes (1916), 2308a, 39 Statutes 619, 650.

United States Statutes at Large, XVIII, 179.

War Department, Circular No. 4, Surgeon General's Office. "A Report on Barracks and Hospitals with Descriptions of Military Posts." Washington: Government Printing Office, 1870.

War Department, Circular No. 8, Surgeon General's Office. "A Report on the Hygiene of the U.S. Army With Descriptions of Military Posts." Washington: Government Printing Office, 1875.

Military Documents

Document C, Headquarters, Department of Dakota, Judge Advocate office, Fort Snelling, Minn., August 31, 1886.

Document E, Headquarters, Department of Texas, September 15, 1880, San Antonio, Texas.

General Orders No. 87, Index of Generan Orders, Department of Dakota, St. Paul, Minn., 1871.

S. W. Groesbeck, Acting Judge Advocate, Department of Dakota, August 20, 1889, Document B. Issued from Headquarters, Department of Dakota, St. Paul, Minn., 1889.

Headquarters Department of Dakota, Report of Captain S. W. Groesbeck, Acting Judge Advocate, St. Paul, Minn., August 31, 1889.

Headquarters, Department of the Platte, General Courts Martial Orders, Omaha, Nebraska, 1871, 1872.

Report of Assistant Surgeon Leonard Wood, Fort Bowie, A.T. September 8, 1886, in Annual Report of Brigadier General Nelson A. Miles, Commanding Department of Arizona, 1886, Headquarters, Department of Arizona, Albuquerque, New Mexico, September 18, 1886.

Report of Lieutenant Colonel Edwin C. Mason, Document F, St. Paul, Minn., September 6, 1886; General Orders and Circulars, Headquarters of the Department of Dakota, 1886.

Report of Major C. M. Terrell, Document M, Chief Paymaster's Office, Headquarters, Department of Texas, San Antonio, Texas, September, 1880.

Report of Trials by General and Garrison Courts Martial, Annual Report, Headquarters, Department of Texas, San Antonio, Texas, October 1, 1880.

United States Congress

Congressional Globe.
Congressional Record.
33d Cong., 1st Sess., House Executive Document I, Pt. 2.
40th Cong., 3d Sess., House Report Nos. 33, 121.
42d Cong., 2d Sess., House Report No. 70.
42d Cong., 3 Sess., House Report No. 74.
43d Cong., 1st Sess., House Executive Document No. 19.
44th Cong., 1st Sess., House Report No. 354.
44th Cong., 2d Sess., House Report No. 56.
45th Cong., 2d Sess., House Miscellaneous Document Nos. 56, 64.
51st Cong., 1st Sess., House Executive Document No. 162.
51st Cong., 1st Sess., House Report No. 1051.
62d Cong., 2d Sess., Hearing Before the Committee on Military Affairs, House of Representatives, on H.R. 23628. Washington: Government Printing Office, 1912.
21st Cong., 1st Sess., Senate Report No. 62.
31st Cong., 2d Sess., Senate Report Committee No. 226.
32d Cong., 2d Sess., Senate Executive Document No. 1.
33d Cong., 1st Sess., Senate Executive Document No. 1.
35th Cong., 1st Sess., Senate Executive Document No. 11.
36th Cong., 2d Sess., Senate Executive Documents II.
40th Cong., 3d Sess., Senate Executive Document Nos. 7, 10.
45th Cong., 3d Sess., Senate Report 555.
48th Cong., 2d Sess., Senate Report No. 1337.
52d Cong., 1st Sess., Senate Report No. 268.
53d Cong., 2d Sess., Senate Report No. 151.
56th Cong., 1st Sess., Senate Document No. 221.

Periodicals and Journals

Appeal to Reason.
Army and Navy Journal.
Army and Navy Register.
The Chautauquan.
The Churchman.
The Council Fire and Arbitrator.
Field Glass.
Iron Moulders' Journal.
Journal of the Association of Military Dental Surgeons.
Journal of United States Cavalry Association.
Literary Digest.
Military Service Institution of the United States Journal.
National Anti-Slavery Standard.
The New Nation.
The New National Era (Washington, D.C.).

New York *Freeman's Journal.*
Outing Magazine.
The People.
Public Opinion.
Public Service Review.
St. Paul *Anti-Monopolist.*
Seventh Regiment Gazette.
Southern Workman.
The United Service.
United Service Journal.
United States Battle Flag.
The United States Service Magazine.
The Verdict.

Newspapers

Afro American Sentinel (Omaha).
Arizona Citizen (Tucson).
Arizona Weekly Star (Tucson).
Baltimore *American.*
Battle Creek *Journal.*
Billings (Montana) *Post.*
Bismarck *Daily Tribune.*
Boston *Advertiser.*
Boston *Commercial Bulletin.*
Boston *Herald.*
Boston *Journal.*
Boston *Pilot.*
Boston *Post.*
Boston *Transcript.*
Boston *Traveller.*
The Broad Axe (Salt Lake City, Utah).
Brooklyn *Daily Eagle.*
Buffalo *Courier.*
Buffalo *Express.*
Cheyenne *Daily Leader.*
Chicago *Chronicle.*
Chicago *Herald.*
Chicago *Inter-Ocean.*
Chicago *Mail.*
Chicago *Record.*
Chicago *Times.*
Chicago *Times-Herald.*
Chicago *Tribune.*
Cincinnati *Commercial.*
Cincinnati *Commercial Gazette.*
Cincinnati *Enquirer.*

Cincinnati *Gazette*.
Cleveland *Leader*.
Cleveland *Plain Dealer*.
The Colored American (Washington, D.C.).
Columbus *Capital*.
Columbus *Dispatch*.
Commercial Appeal (Memphis, Tenn.).
Concord (N.H.) *Daily Patriot*.
Crawford (Nebraska) *Tribune*.
Dayton *Journal*.
Denver *Times*.
Detroit *Free Press*.
Detroit *Plain Dealer*.
El Paso *Daily Times*.
Galveston *Daily News*.
Hartford *Times*.
Helena *Independent*.
Henry George Standard (New York).
Highland Part (Illinois) *News*.
Indianapolis *Freeman*.
Indianapolis *News*.
Indianapolis *World*.
Irish World (New York).
Jacksonville *Times-Union*.
Junction City (Kansas) *Republican*.
Kansas City *Times*.
Leavenworth (Kansas) *Times*.
Lewiston (Idaho) *Teller*.
London *Pall-Mall Gazette*.
London *Times*.
Louisville *Courier-Journal*.
Mandan (North Dakota) *Pioneer*.
Marion (Kansas) *Record*.
Minneapolis *Tribune*.
Missouri *Republican* (St. Louis).
New Orleans *Times*.
New York *Advertiser*.
New York *Age*.
New York *Commercial Advertiser*.
New York *Evening Post*.
New York *Evening Telegram*.
New York *Freeman*.
New York *Globe and Commercial Advertiser*.
New York *Graphic*.
New York *Herald*.
New York *Mail and Express*.

New York *News.*
New York *Star.*
New York *Sun.*
New York *Telegram.*
New York *Times.*
New York *Tribune.*
New York *World.*
Norwalk (Connecticut) *Bulletin.*
Ohio State *Journal* (Columbus).
Omaha *Bee.*
Omaha *Evening Dispatch.*
Omaha *Excelsior.*
Omaha *Herald.*
Omaha *Republican.*
Omaha *Tribune.*
Our State (Topeka, Kansas).
Pembina (Dakota) *Northern Express.*
Pembina (North Dakota) *Pioneer Express.*
Philadelphia *Evening Telegram.*
Philadelphia *Inquirer.*
Philadelphia *Press.*
Philadelphia *Public Ledger.*
Pierre (South Dakota) *Daily Free Press.*
Pittsburgh *Dispatch.*
Pittsburgh *Post.*
Pittsburgh *Post-Gazette.*
Portland (Maine) *Eastern Argus.*
Portland *Oregonian.*
Portsmouth (New Hampshire) *Journal.*
Providence *Morning Star.*
Richmond *Planet.*
Rochester (New York) *Chronicle.*
Rochester (New York) *Express.*
Rockingham (New Hampshire) *Messenger.*
Russell (Kansas) *Record.*
St. Louis *Globe-Democrat.*
St. Louis *Post Dispatch.*
St. Louis *Republic.*
St. Paul *Globe.*
St. Paul *News.*
St. Paul *Pioneer Press.*
St. Paul *Press.*
Salt Lake *Tribune.*
San Antonio *Express.*
San Francisco *Bulletin.*
San Francisco *Call.*

San Francisco *Chronicle.*

San Francisco *Examiner.*

San Francisco *Post.*

San Sabina (Texas) *News.*

Seattle *Press.*

Spokane *Review.*

Sturgis (Dakota) *Record.*

Syracuse *Post-Standard.*

Tacoma *Daily Ledger.*

Toronto *Globe.*

Tucson *Daily Star.*

Vancouver *Independent.*

Walla Walla (Washington) *Statesman.*

Washington *Capital.*

Washington *Evening Star.*

Washington *Post.*

Waterbury (Connecticut) *American.*

Yankton (South Dakota) *Press and Dakotan.*

Books

Alexander, Charles. *Battles and Victories of Allen Allensworth.* Boston: Sherman, French & Company, 1914.

Ambrose, Stephen E. *Upton and the Army.* Baton Rouge: Louisiana State University Press, 1964.

Arkell, William J. *A Philosopher in Love and in Uniform.* New York: The Judge Publishing Co., 1889.

Armes, George A. *Ups and Downs of an Army Officer.* Washington: n.n., 1900.

Ashburn, Percy M. *History of the Medical Department of the United States Army.* New York: Houghton, Mifflin Co., 1929.

Ashton, J. Hubley, ed., *Official Opinions of the Attorneys General of the United States.* Vol. X, 1868; Vol. XI, 1869. Washington: McGill and Witherow, printers.

Athearn, Robert G. *William Tecumseh Sherman and the Settlement of the West.* Norman: University of Oklahoma Press, 1956.

Barnard, Harry. *Rutherford B. Hayes and His America.* Indianapolis: The Bobbs-Merrill Company, Inc., 1954.

Benet, Stephen V. *A Treatise on Military Law and the Practice of Courts Martial.* New York: D. Van Nostrand, 1868.

Bergey, Ellwood. *Why Soldiers Desert From the United States Army.* Philadelphia: W. F. Fell & Co., 1903.

Bigelow, David Nevius. *William Conant Church and the Army and Navy Journal.* New York: Columbia University Press, 1952.

Brait, John. *Trails of Yesterday.* Lincoln, Nebraska: n.n., 1921.

Brimlow, George F. *Life of General William Carey Brown* Caldwell, Idaho: The Caxton Printers, Ltd., 1944.

Callan, John F. *Military Laws of the United States.* Baltimore: J. Murphy & Co., 1858.

Carter, R. G. *The Old Sergeant's Story.* New York: F. H. Hitchcock, 1926.

Carter, William Harding. *The American Army.* Indianapolis: The Bobbs-Merrill Company, 1915.

Cashin, Herschel V., et al. *Under Fire With the Tenth U.S. Cavalry.* New York: F. T. Neely, 1899.

Coke, Henry J. *A Ride Over the Rocky Mountains to Oregon and California.* London: R. Bentley, 1852.

Coolidge, Dane. *The Fighting Men of the West.* New York: E. P. Dutton & Co., Inc., 1932.

Cox, John E. *Five Years in the U.S. Army.* Owensville, Indiana: General Baptist Publishing House, 1892.

Davis, George B. *A Treatise on Military Law.* New York: J. Wiley and Sons, 1898.

————, ed. *The Military Laws of the United States.* Washington: Government Printing Office, 1897.

Davis, John P. *The American Negro Reference Book.* Englewood Cliffs, N.J.: Prentice-Hall, Inc., 1966.

Deuterich, Mabel E. *Struggle for Supremacy, The Career of General Fred C. Ainsworth.* Washington: Public Affairs Press, 1962.

Dolph, Edward A. *"Sound Off": Soldier's Songs.* New York: Cosmopolitan Book Corporation, 1929.

Downey, Fairfax. *Indian Fighting Army.* New York: Charles Scribner's Sons, 1943.

Duane, William. *A Handbook for Infantry.* Philadelphia: Printed for the author, 1813.

Dudley, Edgar S. *Military Law and the Procedure of Courts-Martial.* New York: John Wiley & Sons, 1912.

Ekirch, Arthur A., Jr. *The Civilian and the Military.* New York: Oxford University Press, 1956.

Emmett, Chris. *Fort Union and the Winning of the Southwest.* Norman, Oklahoma: University of Oklahoma Press, 1965.

Farrow, Edward S. *Military Encyclopedia.* 3 vols. New York: By the Author, 1885. Second edition, 3 vols. and supplement: New York: Military-Naval Publishing Company, 1895.

Finnerty, John F. *Warpath and Bivouac.* Reprint of the 1890 edition. Norman: University of Oklahoma Press, 1961.

Forsyth, George A. *The Story of the Soldier.* New York: D. Appleton and Company, 1900.

Ganoe, William A. *The History of the Army of the United States.* New York: D. Appleton and Company, 1924.

Germain, Arden Henry. *Catholic military and naval chaplains, 1776-1917,* Washington: Catholic University Press, 1929.

Glisan, Rodney. *Journal of Army Life.* San Francisco: A. L. Bancroft & Co., 1874.

Green, Constance McLaughlin. *The Secret City: A History of Race Relations in the Nation's Capital.* Princeton, N.J.: Princeton University Press, 1967.

Haley, J. Evetts. *Fort Concho and the Texas Frontier.* San Angelo, Texas: San Angelo Standard-Times, 1952.

Hanson, Joseph Mills. *The Conquest of the Missouri.* Chicago: A. C. McClurg & Co., 1909.

Hart, Herbert M. *Old Forts of the Southwest.* Seattle: Superior Publishing Company, 1964.

———. *Old Forts of the Far West.* Seattle: Superior Publishing Company, 1965.

Hazen, William B. *The School and the Army.* New York: Harper & Brothers, Publishers, 1872.

Hein, Otto Louis. *Memories of Long Ago.* New York: G. P. Putnam's Sons, 1925.

Heitman, Francis B. *Historical Register and Dictionary of the United States Army From Its Organization September 29, 1789 to March 2, 1903.* 2 vols. Reprint of the 1903 edition. Urbana: University of Illinois Press, 1965.

Herschler, N. *The Soldier's Handbook For Use In The Army of The United States.* Washington: Government Printing Office, 1900.

Hittle, J. D. *The Military Staff: Its History and Development.* Harrisburg: The Military Service Publishing Company, 1944.

Holmes, Louis A. *Fort McPherson.* Lincoln, Nebraska: Johnson Publishing Company, 1963.

Honeywell, Roy J. *Chaplains of the United States Army.* Washington: Office of the Chief of Chaplains, 1958.

Hoogenboom, Ari. *Outlawing the Spoils: A History of the Civil Service Reform Movement 1865-1883.* Urbana, Illinois: University of Illinois Press, 1961.

Howard, O. O. *Autobiography of General O. O. Howard.* 2 vols. New York: The Baker & Taylor Company, 1907.

Hunt, Elvid. *History of Fort Leavenworth.* Fort Leavenworth: General Services School Press, 1926.

Huston, James A. *The Sinews of War: Army Logistics 1775-1953.* Washington: Office of the Chief of Military History, 1966.

Ives, Rollin A. *A Treatise on Military Law.* New York: D. Van Nostrand, 1879.

Jackson, Donald. *Custer's Gold: The United States Cavalry Expedition of 1874.* New Haven: Yale University Press, 1966.

Jacobs, James Ripley. *The Beginning of the U.S. Army (1783-1812).* Princeton: Princeton University Press, 1947.

Jessup, Philip C. *Elihu Root.* 2 vols. New York: Dodd, Mead and Company, 1937.

Johnson, Edward A. *History of the Negro Soldiers in the Spanish-American War.* Raleigh: Capital Printing Co., 1899.

Johnson, Virginia W. *The Unregimented General: A Biography of Nelson P. Miles.* Boston: Houghton Mifflin Company, 1962.

Kautz, August V. *Customs of Service.* Philadelphia: J. B. Lippincott & Co., 1864.

King, James T. *War Eagle: A Life of General Eugene A. Carr.* Lincoln: University of Nebraska Press, 1963.

Kreidberg, Marvin A., and Henry, Merton G. *History of Military Mobilization in the United States Army 1775-1945*. Washington: Department of the Army, 1955.

Lane, Lydia Spencer. *Old Days in the Old Army*. Albuquerque: Horn & Wallace, Publishers, Inc., 1964.

Layton, Ruth. *The Story of Jefferson Barracks*. St. Louis: Layton, Layton and Associates, 1961.

Leckie, William H. *The Buffalo Soldiers: A Narrative of the Negro Cavalry in the West*. Norman: University of Oklahoma Press, 1967.

————. *The Military Conquest of the Southern Plains*. Norman: University of Oklahoma Press, 1963.

Lee, Ulysses. *The Employment of Negro Troops: The United States Army in World War II*. Washington: Office of Chief of Military History, 1966.

Lenney, John Joseph. *Caste System in the Army*. New York: Greenberg, 1949.

————. *Rankers, The Odyssey of the Regular Enlisted Soldier of America and Britain*. New York: Greenberg, 1950.

Lieber, G. Norman. *Remarks on the Army Regulations and Executive Regulations in General*. Washington: Government Printing Office, 1898.

Litwack, Leon F. *North of Slavery: The Negro in the Free States 1790-1860*. Chicago: University of Chicago Press, 1961.

Lockwood, James D. *Life and Adventures of a Drummer Boy*. Albany: J. Skinner, 1893.

McConnell, H. H. *Five Years a Cavalryman or Sketches of Regular Army Life on the Texas Frontier*. Jacksboro, Texas: J. N. Rogers & Co., Printers, 1889.

McKay, Robert H. *Little Pills: An Army Story*. Pittsburg, Kansas: Pittsburg Headlight, 1918.

Mackay, Alexander. *The Western World or Travels in the United States in 1846-47*. London: R. Bentley, 1850.

Macomb, Alexander. *The Practice of Courts-Martial*. New York: Harper Brothers, 1841.

Mattes, Merrill J. *Indians, Infants and Infantry: Andrew and Elizabeth Burt on the Frontier*. Denver, Colorado: The Old West Publishing Company, 1960.

Mills, Anson. *My Story*. Washington: By the Author. Press of Byron S. Adams, 1918.

Mulford, Ami Frank. *Fighting Indians in the 7th Unted States Cavalry*. Corning, N.Y.: P. L. Mulford, 1879.

Murray, Arthur. *Instructions for Courts-Martial*. St. Paul, Minn.: Headquarters Department of Dakota, 1891.

————. *Manual for Courts-Martial*. Washington: Government Printing Office, 1895.

Nadeau, Remi. *Fort Laramie and the Sioux Indians*. Englewood Cliffs, N.J.: Prentice-Hall, Inc., 1967.

Nelson, Otto L. *National Security and the General Staff*. Washington: Infantry Journal Press, 1946.

Nevins, Allan. *Abram S. Hewitt With Some Account of Peter Cooper*. New York: Harper and Brothers, 1935.

Nye, W. S. *Carbine and Lance: The History of Old Fort Sill.* Norman: University of Oklahoma Press, 1937.

Oliva, Leo E. *Soldiers of the Santa Fe Trail.* Norman: University of Oklahoma Press, 1967.

Parker, James. *The Old Army Memories 1872-1918.* Philadelphia: Dorrance & Company, 1929.

Pratt, Richard Henry. *Battlefield and Classroom: Four Decades with the American Indian 1867-1904.* New Haven & London: Yale University Press, 1964.

Pride, Woodbury F. *The History of Fort Riley.* Fort Riley: n.n., 1926.

Prucha, Francis Paul. *A Guide to the Military Posts of the U.S. 1789-1895.* Madison: State Historical Society of Wisconsin, 1964.

Quarles, Benjamin. *The Negro in the Civil War.* Boston: Little, Brown and Company, 1953.

Randall, Ruth Painter. *Lincoln's Sons.* Boston, Little, Brown and Company, 1955.

Regan, James. *The Judge Advocate and Recorder's Guide.* Washington: Beresford, 1877.

Reeves, Ira L. *Military Education in the United States.* Burlington, Vermont: Free Press Prtg. Co., 1914.

Rickey, Don, Jr. *Forty Miles a Day on Beans and Hay: The Enlisted Soldier Fighting the Indian Wars.* Norman: University of Oklahoma Press, 1963.

Risch, Erna. *Quartermaster Support of the Army, A History of the Corps 1775-1939.* Washington: Office of the Quartermaster General, 1962.

Rister, Carl Coke. *Fort Griffin on the Texas Frontier.* Norman: University of Oklahoma Press, 1956.

Rodenbough, Theo. F., and Haskin, William L., eds. *The Army of the United States.* New York: Maynard, Merrill & Co., 1896.

Roe, Frances M. *Army Letters From an Officer's Wife.* New York: D. Appleton and Co., 1909.

Schmitt, Martin F., ed. *General George Crook: His Autobiography.* Norman: University of Oklahoma Press, 1946.

Scott, Hugh Lenox. *Some Memories of a Soldier.* New York: The Century Company, 1928.

Scott, Robert M. *An Analytical Digest of the Military Laws of the United States.* Philadelphia: J. B. Lippincott & Co., 1873.

Shindler, Henry. *History of the United States Military Prison.* Ft. Leavenworth: The Army Service Schools Press, 1911.

Simpson, Arnold B., ed. *Frontier Forts of Texas.* Waco, Texas: Texian Press, 1966.

A Sketch of the History and Duties of the Judge Advocate General's Department of the United States. Washington: Government Printing Office, 1878.

Smith, Helen Huntington. *The War on the Powder River.* New York: McGraw-Hill Book Company, 1966.

Spaulding, Oliver Lynn. *The United States Army in War and Peace.* New York: G. P. Putnam Sons, 1937.

Steward, Theophilus Gould. *The Colored Regulars in the United States Army.* Philadelphia: A.M.E. Book Concern, 1904.

————. *Fifty Years in the Gospel Ministry.* Philadelphia: A.M.E. Book Concern, n.d.

————, ed. *Active Service or Religious Work Among United States Soldiers.* New York: United States Army Aid Association, 189[?].

Stewart, Edgar, and Stewart, Jane R., eds. *The Field Diary of Lieutenant Edward Steele Godfrey.* Portland, Oregon: Champoeg Press, 1957.

Thompson, Donald A. *American Army Chaplaincy: A Brief History.* Washington: Government Printing Office, 1946.

Utley, Robert M. *Frontiersmen in Blue: The United States Army and the Indian 1848-1865.* New York: The Macmillan Company, 1967.

————. *The Last Days of the Sioux Indians.* New Haven: Yale University Press, 1963.

Wallace, Ernest. *Ranald S. MacKenzie on the Texas Frontier.* Lubbock, Texas: West Texas Museum Association, 1964.

Walton, William. *The Army and Navy of the United States.* 2 vols. Boston: G. Barrie and Son, 1889-95.

Ware, Eugene F. *The Indian War of 1864.* New York: St. Martin's Press, 1960.

Weigley, Russell F. *History of the United States Army.* New York: The Macmillan Company, 1967.

————. *Quartermaster General of the Union Army: A Biography of M. C. Meigs.* New York: Columbia University Press, 1959.

————. *Towards An American Army, Military Thought from Washington to Marshall.* New York: Columbia University Press, 1962.

Wharfield, H. B., U.S.A.F., Ret. *Apache Indian Scouts.* El Cajon, California: Copyright in 1964 by H. B. Wharfield.

Winthrop, W. *Military Law.* 2 vols. Washington: W. H. Morrison, 1886.

————. *Military Law and Precedents.* 2 vols. Boston: Little, Brown and Company, 1896.

————, ed. *Digest of Opinions of the Judge Advocate General of the Army.* Washington: Government Printing Office, 1868.

————, ed. *A Digest of Opinions of the Judge Advocate General of the Army.* Washington: Government Printing Office, 1880.

Woodward, Frank R. *The Dogs of War.* St. Louis: n.n., 1890.

Articles

Anderson, E. "The Pay of Our Soldiers Affecting Desertion and Re-enlistment." *The American Review of Reviews,* XXXIII (1906), 333-40.

Ansell, S. T. "Military Justice." *Cornell Law Quarterly,* V (November, 1919), 1-17.

Arnold, Paul T. "Negro Soldiers in the United States Army." *The Magazine of History,* X (August, 1909), 61-70, 185-87, (October, 1909), 187-93; XI (January, 1910), 1-12.

Bateman, Cephas C. "Old Fort Clark, A Frontier Post." *Frontier Times,* VII (October, 1933), 13-14.

Blades, Thomas F., and Wike, John W. "Fort Missoula." *Military Affairs,* XII (Spring, 1949), 29-36.

Bloom, Lansing B. "Bourke on the Southwest." *New Mexico Historical Review,* VIII (January, 1933), 1-30.

Bonsal, Stephen, "The Negro Soldier in War and Peace." *North American Review, CLXXXV* (June, 1907), 321-27.

Brown, A. W. "The Administration of Justice in the Army." *Cornell Law Quarterly,* III (1917-1918), 178-210.

Brown, Terry W. "The Crowder-Ansell Dispute." *Military Law Review,* XXXV (January, 1967), 1-45.

Browne, Mark D. "The Negro in the Indian Wars." *Negro History Bulletin,* XIV (March, 1951), 142, 144.

Bryan, Marilyn T. "The Economic, Political and Social Status of the Negro in El Paso," *Password,* XII (Fall, 1968), 74-86.

Bullard, R. L. "The American Negro as a Soldier." *The Literary Digest,* LXXV (April 27, 1925), 14-15.

Carbaugh, H. C. "The Contract of Enlistment and its Violation in the United States Army." *Army and Navy Life,* X (February, 1907), 176-95.

Carter, William H. "The War Department Military Administration." *Scribner's,* XXXIII (1903), 661-73.

Chappell, Edith M. "Old Fort McKinney." *The Buffalo Bulletin* (Johnson County, Wyoming), April 25, 1929.

Coffin, Edward M. "Army Life on the Frontier, 1865-1898." *Military Affairs,* XX (Fall, 1956), 192-201.

Cox, John E. "Soldiering in Dakota Territory in the Seventies. A Communication." *North Dakota Historical Quarterly,* VI (October, 1931), 62-81.

Cranston, Earl M. "The Existing Court-Martial System." *North American Review,* CLXVIII (February, 1899), 248-51.

Crimmins, M. L., ed. "Colonel J. K. F. Mansfield; Report of Texas in 1856." *Southwestern Historical Quarterly,* XLII (January, 1939), 215-57.

Day, Daniel S. "Fort Sedgwick." *The Colorado Magazine,* XLII (Winter, 1965), 16-35.

De Morgan, John. "Barbaric Military Punishments." *The Green Bag,* X (1898), 34-36.

Foreman, Carolyn Thomas. "Military Discipline in Early Oklahoma." *Chronicles of Oklahoma,* VI (June, 1928), 140-44.

———. "General Benjamin Henry Grierson." *Chronicles of Oklahoma,* XXIV (1946), 195-217.

Gleason, George. "Courts-Martial: Criticisms and Proposed Reforms." *Cornell Law Quarterly,* V (November, 1919), 18-47.

Grange, Roger T., Jr. "Fort Robinson Outpost on the Plains." *Nebraska History,* XXXIX (September, 1958), 191-233.

Greene, Lorenzo J. "The Negro in the Armed Forces of the United States, 1619-1783." *Negro History Bulletin,* XIV (March, 1951), 123-27, 138.

Hare, John S. "Military Punishments in the War of 1812." *Military Affairs,* IV (1940), 115-239.

Hargreaves, Reginald. "The Idle Hours." *Military Review,* XLVI (December, 1966), 29-35.

Hawes, Joseph H. M. "The Signal Corps and the Weather Service." *Military Affairs,* XXX (Summer, 1966), 68-76.

Head, W. H. "The Negro as an American Soldier." *World Today,* March, 1907, pp. 322-24.

Hoekman, Steven. "The History of Fort Sully." *South Dakota Historical Collections,* XXVI (1952), 222-74.

Hummel, Edward A. "The Story of Fort Sisseton." *South Dakota Historical Review,* XVI (April, 1937), 126-44.

King, James T. "The Military Frontier—What Was It." *Westerners Brand Book* (Chicago), XXI (February, 1965), 89-91, 95-96.

———. "The Sword and the Pen: The Poetry of the Military Frontier." *Nebraska History,* XLVII (September, 1966), 229-45.

Langdon, Loomis L. "The Regular Army." *The Independent,* L (August 11, 1898), 338-91.

Langley, Lester D. "The Democratic Tradition and Military Reform, 1878-1885." *Southwestern Social Science Quarterly,* XLVIII (September, 1967), 192-200.

Larned, Charles W. "The Regeneration of the Enlisted Soldier." *The International Quarterly,* XII (January, 1906), 189-207.

Larremore, Wilbur. "American Courts-Martial." *North American Review,* CLXXVII (October, 1903), 607-14.

"Lawlessness in the Army." *Frank Leslie's Illustrated Weekly,* LXXXV (December 9, 1897), 370.

"Letters About the End of Fort Belknap and the Beginning of Fort Griffin." *West Texas Historical Year Book,* XXXIV (October, 1958), 141-48.

McClernand, Edmund J. "Service in Montana 1870 and 1871." *Military Affairs,* XV (1951), 192-98.

McMurtie, Douglas C. "The Fourth Infantry Press at Fort Bridger." *Annals of Wyoming,* XIII (October, 1941), 347-51.

Mattison, Ray H. "The Army Fort on the Northern Plains, 1865-1895." *Nebraska History,* XXXV (March, 1954), 17-34.

Maurer, Maurer. "Military Justice Under General Washington." *Military Affairs,* XVII (Spring. 1964), 8-16.

Merrill, Dana T. "The Soldier's Pay." *Army and Navy Life,* XI (October, 1907), 408-10.

Miles, Susan. "Fort Concho in 1877." *West Texas Historical Association Year Book,* XXXV (October, 1959), 29-49.

"More Soldiers." *Locomotive Fireman's Magazine,* X (August, 1886), 453-54.

Morgan, Edmund M. "The Existing Court-Martial System and the Ansell Articles." *Yale Law Journal,* XXIX (1919), 152-74.

Morgan, Thomas J. "Epaulets or Chevrons." *The Independent,* L (June 30, 1898), 846.

Mott, William C.; Hartnett, John E., Jr.; Morton, Kenneth B. "A Survey of the

Literature of Military Law. A Selected Bibliography." *Vanderbilt Law Review,* VI (1952-53), 333-69.

Munson, Edward L. "Some Results of the Army Canteen." *Journal of the American Public Health Association,* XXVII (1901), 315-16.

Murphy, William. "The Forgotten Battalion." *Annals of Wyoming,* VII (October, 1930), 383-401; (January, 1931), 441-42.

Nelson, Henry N. "David's Island." *Harper's Weekly,* June 28, 1890, pp. 508-12.

Nemerow, Abraham. "Complaints of Wrongs under Article 138." *Military Law Review,* II, Department of the Army Pamphlet 27-100-2 (September, 1958), 43-96.

Nichols, D. B. "The Devil's Article." *Military Law Review,* XXII, Department of the Army Pamphlet 27-100-22 (October, 1963), 113-17.

Omer, George E., Jr. "An Army Hospital, from Dragoons to Rough Riders—Fort Riley, 1853-1903." *Kansas Historical Quarterly,* XXIII (Winter, 1957), 337-67.

Page, William Herbert. "Military Law, A Study in Comparative Law." *Harvard Law Review,* XXXII (1918-1919), 349-73.

Parker, W. Thornton. "The Evolution of the Colored Soldier." *North American Review,* CLXVIII (February, 1899), 223-28.

Partridge, Frank C. "Redfield Proctor, His Public Life and Services," *Proceedings of the Vermont Historical Society,* 1915, pp. 57-104.

"The Plain Truth." *Frank Leslie's Weekly,* LXXXVII (August 18, 1898), 122.

"Poetry of an Army Private." *Frank Leslie's Illustrated Weekly,* LXXVIII (May 31, 1894), 372.

Pope, J. W. "Desertion and the Military Prison." *Cosmopolitan Magazine,* X (November, 1890), 112-20.

Post, Charles Johnson. "The Honor of the Army." *Harper's Weekly,* LVIII (February 21, 1914), 14-19; (February 28, 1914), 10-13; (March 7, 1914), 21-24; (March 14, 1914), 18-21.

Powers, Fred Perry. "West Point, The Army and the Militia." *Lippincott's Magazine,* XL (1887), 111-26.

Reddick, L.D. "The Negro Policy of the United States Army 1775-1945." *Journal of Negro History,* XXXIV (January, 1949), 12-19.

Reeves, Frank D., ed. "Fredrick E. Phelps, A Soldier's Memoirs." *New Mexico Historical Review,* XXV (July, 1950), 37-58; (October, 1950), 305-27.

Rhodes, Charles Dudley. "John Cunningham Kelton." *Dictionary of American Biography,* X. New York, 1933.

Rice, James M. "Military Education and the Volunteer Militia." *Century Magazine,* XXXV (October, 1888), 939-43.

Riding, William H. "Life at a Frontier Post." *Appleton's Journal,* XV (April 29, 1876), 564-65.

Roberts, Theodore. "Negro Cavalry and Cow-Punchers." *The Independent,* L (June 16, 1898), 782.

Roosevelt, Theodore. "The Rough Riders." *Scribner's,* XXV (April, 1899), 420-40.

Russell, Hal, Mrs. "Memories of Marion Russell." *The Colorado Magazine,* XXI (January, 1944), 29-39.

"Secretary Lincoln and the Color Line." *Frank Leslie's Illustrated Magazine,* LIX (October 11, 1884), 114.

Shirk, George H. "Campaigning with Sheridan; A Farrier's Diary." *Chronicles of Oklahoma,* XXXVII (1959), 68-105.

Sibbald, John R. "Camp Followers All." *The American West,* III (Spring, 1966), 56-58.

"Standing Armies." *The American Federationist,* III (March 13, 1896), 13.

Stansfield, George James. "A History of the Judge Advocate General's Department." *Military Affairs,* IX (1945), 219-37.

Steele, Matthew F. "The Color Line in the Army." *North American Review,* CLXXXIII (December, 1906), 285-88.

Stratton, David H. "The Army and the Gospel in the West." *Western Humanities Review,* VIII (Spring, 1954), 247-62.

Steward, T. G. "The New Colored Soldier." *The Independent,* L (June 16, 1898), 781-82.

Thompson, Edwin N. "The Negro Soldiers on the Frontier: A Fort Davis Case Study." *Journal of the West,* XVII (April, 1968), 217-35.

Tourgee, Albion W. "The Story of a Thousand." *Cosmopolitan Magazine,* XVIII (December, 1894), 223-24.

Villard, Oswald Garrison. "The Negro as a Soldier and an Officer." *The Nation,* LXXIII (August, 1901), 85.

———. "The Negro in the Regular Army." *The Atlantic Monthly,* XCI (June, 1903), 721-29.

———. "The New Army." *The Atlantic Monthly,* LXXXIX (April, 1902), 437-51.

Welty, Raymond L. "The Army Post on the Frontier." *North Dakota Historical Quarterly,* II (January, 1928), 85-99; (April, 1928), 155-67.

———. "The Daily Life of the Frontier Soldier." *Cavalry Journal,* XXXVI (1927), 367-81, 584-94.

Wertenberger, Mildred, compiler. "Fort Totten, Dakota Territory, 1867." *North Dakota History,* XXXIV (Spring, 1967), 125-46.

"Western Frontier Life." *Overland Monthly,* IV (December, 1870), 520-25.

Williams, R. "Army Organization in the United States." *The Galaxy,* XXIV (November, 1877), 594-602.

———. "The Staff of the United States Army." *The Atlantic Monthly,* XLI (March, 1878), 376-80.

Wilson, Aubrey H. "A Soldier in the Texas Frontier, Brevet Major Robert Patterson Wilson, United States Army." *West Texas Historical Association Year Book,* XXXIV (1958), 82-96.

Unpublished Materials

Bliss, Zenas R. "Reminiscences," I-V. Unpublished MSS Yale University.

Brown, Richard Carl. "Social Attitudes of American Generals, 1898-1900." Unpublished doctoral thesis, University of Wisconsin, 1951.

Burt, Elizabeth Reynolds. "An Army Wife's Forty Years in the Service, 1862-1902." Unpublished MSS. Burt Family Papers, Library of Congress.

Ely, E. W. "History of Fort Missoula, Montana." Unpublished MSS in possession of Montana Historical Society, Helena, Montana.

Fletcher, Marvin. "The Blacks in Blue, Negro Volunteers in Reconstruction." Unpublished Master's thesis, University of Wisconsin, 1965.

"History of Fort Sheridan, Illinois." Unpublished MSS prepared by the Public Information office, Fort Sheridan, Illinois, January, 1944.

Kenyon, Carlton W. "History of Fort Randall." Unpublished Master's thesis, University of South Dakota, 1950.

Kroeker, Marvin E. "William B. Hazen, A Military Career in the Frontier West, 1855-1880." Unpublished doctoral thesis, University of Oklahoma, 1967.

Loge, Patricia Louise. "The History of Fort Huachuca 1877-1913." Unpublished Master's thesis, University of Arizona, 1949.

Mitten, Hamilton F. "Army Life on the Plains During the Indian Wars." Unpublished Master's thesis, University of Nebraska, 1930.

Thomas Dirk Phillips, "The Negro Regulars." Unpublished Master of Science thesis, University of Wisconsin, 1966.

Rickey, Don, Jr. "The Negro Regulars: A Combat Record, 1866-1891." Unpublished paper delivered at the Western History Association meeting at Helena, Montana, October, 1965, in possession of author.

"The Seventh Regiment of U.S. Cavalry." Unpublished MSS, in Edward Steele Godfrey Papers, Library of Congress.

Simpson, Robert Steven. "The Regular Negro Soldier in the Campaign for Santiago de Cuba, 1898." Unpublished Master's thesis, University of Colorado, 1949.

Stone, Jerome. "The History of Fort Grant." Unpublished Master's thesis, University of Arizona, 1941.

Thompson, Neil Baird. "Discipline and Morale of the U.S. Army Troops in the Division of the Missouri, 1866-1876." Unpublished Master's thesis, Kansas State College of Agriculture and Applied Science, Manhattan, Kansas, 1948.

Weaver, John. "The History of Fort Lowell." Unpublished Master's thesis, University of Arizona, 1947.

William Bruce White, "The Military and the Melting Pot." Unpublished doctoral dissertation, University of Wisconsin, 1968.

Zabel, Harvey J. "The History of Fort McPherson." Unpublished Master's thesis, Colorado State College, 1954.

Other Sources

American Prison Association. *Proceedings of the General Congress, 1891.*

Annual Reports of the U.S. Military Post Library Association. New York: Headquarters of the Association, 1870-71, 1871-72, 1872-73, 1873-74, 1874-75, 1875-76.

Fort Hays, Kansas, Special Order Book, October 15, 1866-May 26, 1868, Post Order No. 15, dated July 27, 1867, Kansas State Historical Society, Topeka, Kansas.

Fort Randall, Dakota Territory, Military Post Returns and Reports, June 1856-December 1892, University of South Dakota, Vermillion, South Dakota.

Private M. L. Kezerter, Camp Brown, Wyoming, to Hon. Samuel L. Chapman, December 6, 1878, MSS 43, Nebraska State Historical Society, Lincoln.

William A. Kimball, A Collection of Official Military Orders, 1878, November 8-1881, September 13. Yale University.

William P. Tomlinson to John G. Spence, February 5, 1848, Yale University.

CHART I. RATE OF DESERTION OF ENLISTED PERSONNEL, 1867-95

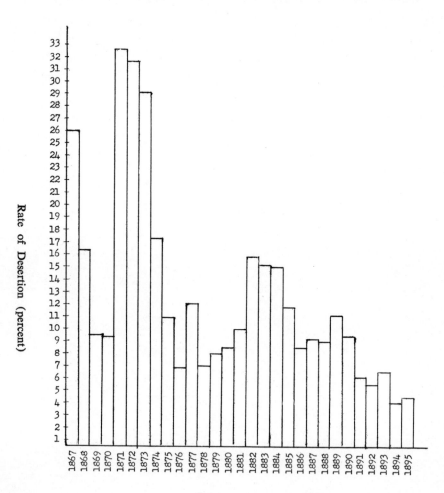

TABLE 1
Desertions in Relation to Aggregate
Strength of Army, 1867-1895

Fiscal Year	Enlisted Strength of Army	Desertions	Percent
1867	54,138	14,068	26.0
1868	48,231	7,893	16.4
1869	34,253	3,239	9.5
1870	34,699	3,253	9.4
1871	27,010	8,800	32.6
1872	26,218	8,313	31.7
1873	26,736	7,813	29.2
1874	26,559	4,606	17.3
1875	23,445	2,521	10.8
1876	26,414	1,832	6.9
1877	21,963	2,516	11.5
1878	23,870	1,678	7.0
1879	24,474	1,925	7.9
1880	24,442	2,043	8.4
1881	23,661	2,361	10.0
1882	23,649	3,741	15.8
1883	23,509	3,578	15.2
1884	24,519	3,672	15.0
1885	25,003	2,927	11.7
1886	24,625	2,090	8.5
1887	24,519	2,240	9.1
1888	24,830	2,244	9.0
1889	25,582	2,835	11.1
1890	25,205	2,344	9.3
1891	24,411	1,503	6.2
1892	25,050	1,382	5.5
1893	25,672	1,682	6.6
1894	26,119	1,073	4.1
1895	25,341	1,165	4.6

Sources:

Enlisted Strength: Russell F. Weigley, *History of the United States Army* (New York: 1967), pp. 567-68; Francis B. Heitman, *Historical Register and Dictionary of the United States Army* (2 vols: Washington, 1903), II, 604, 608, 610-13, 626.

Desertions:

1867-1870: 44th Cong., 1st Sess., House Report No. 354, p. 228.

1871-1876: 45th Cong., 2d Sess., House Miscellaneous Document No. 56, p. 75.

1877-1879: *United States Army and Navy Life*, X (1906), 181.

1880-1889: 51st Cong., 1st Sess., House Executive Document No. 1, Pt. 2, II, 92.

1890-1895: *International Review*, XII (1906), 194.

TABLE 2

Desertions in Relation to Enlistments, 1880-1889

Fiscal Year	Enlistments	Desertions	Percent
1880	5,006	2,043	40.81
1881	5,637	2,361	41.88
1882	7,734	3,741	48.37
1883	7,931	3,578	45.11
1884	8,775	3,672	41.84
1885	7,164	2,927	40.87
1886	5,327	2,090	39.23
1887	6,168	2,240	36.31
1888	6,693	2,244	36.39
1889	8,133	2,835	34.89

Source: 51st Cong., 1st Sess., House Executive Document No. 1, Pt. 2, II, 92.

INDEX